The Scottish Peaks

Plate 1 Liathach in Snowy Raiment

W. A. Poucher, Hon. F.R.P.S.

The Scottish Peaks

A Pictorial Guide to walking in this region
and to the safe ascent of its most spectacular mountains

with 250 photographs by the author
32 Maps and 76 Routes

Fifth Edition

Constable London

First published in Great Britain 1965
by Constable and Company Ltd
10 Orange Street London WC2H 7EG
Copyright © 1965 by William Arthur Poucher
Second edition 1968
Third edition 1971
Fourth edition 1974
Fifth edition 1979

ISBN 0 09 462680 4

Set in Monophoto Times New Roman 9pt
Filmset and printed in Great Britain by
BAS Printers Limited, Over Wallop, Hampshire

The author is a member of
The Climbers' Club
The Fell and Rock Climbing Club

British Library CIP data

Poucher, William Arthur
    The Scottish peaks. – 5th ed.
    1. Scotland – Description and travel – 1951– –
    Guide-books   2. Walking – Scotland   3. Mountains
    – Scotland
    I. Title
    796.5′22   DA867

    ISBN 0-09-462680-4

Preface to the fifth edition

In the last edition I drew attention to the problem of access to Ben Lui and I had hoped in this one to include details of the completed plan for direct access from Glen Lochy. But it is evident that things move slowly in Scotland like they do elsewhere in Britain, because although the promised car park between the A85 and the River Lochy opposite the exit of Eas Diamh has been completed, nothing has been done about the footbridge across the River Lochy because permission to cross the railway is still awaited from British Rail. Immediately this question has been settled the Forestry Commission will build the footbridge and I hope to include photographs of the completed scheme in the next edition.

Readers have asked me to illustrate some of my Routes in greater detail and I have therefore included additional prints of the Arran Hills, Ben Cruachan, Bidean nam Bian, the Torridon Peaks, Suilven, Quinag, Lochnagar and Skye. But the selection has not been easy as I have progressive shots of almost every step in all the ascents I have made, and I hope those I have chosen will prove useful and facilitate easy progress on these climbs.

A question that is frequently posed to me is "What cameras do you use?" Well, there is no reason why I should not divulge this seeming secret in print, so I will say that since the availability of 35 mm film I have always used Leicas, and replaced them as new models appeared. I have now two M2s (one of them in case of accident) with 35 mm wide angle, 50 mm normal, and 90 mm long focus lenses. These I use for monochrome and my favourite film is Kodak Plus X. I also have a Leicaflex, with 28 mm wide angle, 50 mm normal, 90 mm long focus and 135 mm telephoto lenses. I use them exclusively for colour and my favourite film is Kodachrome 25.

The best season in which to visit the Scottish Hills is spring, not only because the weather is then most favourable, but also as many of the hills are situated in strictly guarded deer forests where intruders are looked upon with little favour after the end of June. In view of the number of accidents that occur every year, I would remind readers that mountaineering is a risky sport, but that all the Routes in this book are within the powers of any fit and experienced climber, whereas some of them may well be dangerous to the ordinary walker.

In these circumstances I would urge Leaders of school and youth parties not to venture on these hills unless the weather is settled and favourable, and moreover, they should always insist upon everyone wearing boots and proper clothing. For, by doing so they will not only reduce the risk of accidents but also avoid the often needless call for Mountain Rescue.

A ROUTE CARD will be found at the end of this book and copies are available almost everywhere in the Scottish Hills. This should be completed by all climbers and walkers as it would be invaluable in the event of an accident by facilitating Mountain Rescue.

In view of the vast scope of this book it is obviously impossible to check frequently every one of the descriptions of the routes. Time, usage, rock falls and local weather may be responsible for slight variations, and should any reader encounter any inaccuracy I would appreciate a note of it for inclusion in future editions of this work.

Finally, it should be noted that the Routes described and illustrated herein have been frequented over the years without objection, but they do not necessarily constitute a right of way. Should a reader have any doubts, and especially so during the stalking season, he would be well advised to consult the owner of the land and ask permission to enter it before commencing his walk or climb.

The thirty-two maps are reproduced with the permission of John Bartholomew & Son Limited.

W. A. POUCHER
4 Heathfield
Reigate Heath Surrey

Contents

Contents

Introductory notes

For many decades Scotland has been the treasured venue of the angler, who, often coming from distant places to engage in this fascinating sport, has delighted in fishing for salmon on its famous rivers, and on occasion also for trout on the innumerable lochs and lochans that grace this wild and beautiful country. Before the Second World War its mountains were the special preserve of the connoisseur, largely because of their remote situation from the Midlands and the South of England, although Scotsmen themselves, living on the doorstep so to speak, have climbed them and revelled in their beauty with pride and gusto for many years. However, during the last two decades there has been an increased interest in mountain walking, ridge wandering and rock climbing, but it has been concentrated mainly in the regions between Arran and Lochaber, doubtless owing to their ready accessibility. But in recent years the remote and magnificent peaks of the North Western Highlands have attracted greater attention and due to the almost universal use of the motor car they are now more easily reached and explored. This approach has been facilitated by the improved road conditions; for while it was an adventure to drive over them thirty years ago almost all of them have now been resurfaced, and although they are mostly single-track, with ample passing places, they give fair access to a large number of the peaks cited in this work.

At the present time most of our young people have ample funds available for holidays, and since youth hostelling and camping are an inexpensive form of travel there is no valid reason why the Highlands, the Cairngorms and Skye should not become as cherished centres as others in Britain. Energetic young men and women who have a special predilection for hill country may well choose Lochaber for their first visit, and on arrival they will raise their eyes to the peaks and imagine themselves standing by one of the summit cairns, inhaling the invigorating mountain air and scanning the glens far below, the chain of engirdling hills and the distant glimmering seas. Come what may, they lose no time in setting out to climb one of them, and on reaching their objective gain that satisfaction that comes only after the ardours of the ascent. It is highly probable that Ben Nevis will be their first conquest, not only because it is the monarch of all our British hills, but also because they believe it will disclose the finest and most comprehensive panorama on account of its dominating altitude. On achieving this ambition they quite naturally speculate upon the merits of the views from the other high peaks in this region, and after talking over the question with their friends they will in all probability continue their exploration by climbing Bidean nam Bian, or walking over the ridges of the Mamores, or perhaps even traversing the exciting crest of Aonach Eagach.

And it is here that I must draw attention to the differences between the Scottish Peaks and those of English Lakeland and Snowdonia. Climbing experience in these two regions can be invaluable, but it must be borne in mind that not only are the summits of lesser altitude than those of the Highlands, but they are all fairly close together and easily reached from the network of roads that pattern both districts. In many parts of Scotland, and particularly so in the Cairngorms, the peaks are usually a very great distance from the starting point and may necessitate walking over vast stretches of moorland that is often dappled with bog. Moreover, when they are reached the climbs are longer and frequently more arduous, so that good planning, an early start and at least two companions are essential for safety. For in the event of an accident one can stay with the victim while the other goes for help, and in some places long tramps are involved to reach a spot where assistance can be obtained. To make sure of rapid location, please wear red stockings.

On returning home our young friends will often ponder over this advice and their own experiences, and especially so if they have been captivated by the spirit and mystery of the hills. The map will doubtless be unfolded at frequent intervals, and by tracing the routes thereon they will re-live these happy times. If they climbed Bidean nam Bian by way of Ossian's Cave and Aonach Dubh their thoughts will follow that pleasant route from Glencoe and Loch Achtriochtan with the first summit soaring overhead, their surprise at the spectacular view of Aonach Eagach on the other side of the glen on attaining the cairn, the tramp along the broad ridge to Stob Coire nan Lochan whose superb situation opens up magnificent scenes in all directions with a first view of Ben Nevis to the north above Aonach Eagach, the scramble across the narrow ridge that rises to the dominating peak of the group, with splendid prospects of the two buttresses on the right, followed by the exhilaration of standing by the highest cairn in Argyll with a whole kingdom spread out at their feet.

A close inspection of the map will suggest to our friends several other routes to this lofty peak, and curiosity will induce them to speculate upon their respective merits. Would the easier route by way of An t-Sron have been as interesting? Perhaps it would have been more thrilling to have made the ascent from Loch Achtriochtan by the Dinner Time Buttress, or what of the more circuitous route by the Allt Coire Gabhail? Then another line of thought may develop: for they had seen a grand array of peaks engirdling the horizon from Bidean and they will speculate again upon the merits of the panoramas from their summits, to realise with surprise that a lifetime is scarcely too long in which to become acquainted with them all.

The cogitations of our young friends will follow a normal course and they will do exactly the same as the rest of us did in our novitiate; for they will formulate the plans for their next holiday long before it is due. Next time they may decide to stay perhaps in Glen Torridon and explore its enclosing hills; but which ones? To solve this problem they will often get out the map, and while scanning it with happy anticipation compare it with the various guide-books which describe this marvellous countryside. There they will *read* what their authors have so lucidly written, but much will inevitably be left to their imagination.

It is here that my long experience of the Scottish Peaks will help to solve their problems; for by consulting this volume in conjunction with my other works devoted to the Highlands, the Cairngorms and Skye they will not only be able to choose their centre with certainty, their routes to the peaks in the vicinity in accordance with their powers as climbers, and the subjects for their cameras if they happen to be photographers, but they will also be able to *see* beforehand through the medium of my camera studies precisely the type of country that will satisfy every one of their needs.

Equipment

Anyone who ventures on the hills without proper equipment is asking for trouble, and since the weather is one of our greatest hazards it is wise, and indeed imperative, to be prepared for sudden and unexpected changes, as for instance from warm sunshine to rain or blizzard, by wearing proper boots and clothing, as well as other useful incidentals which I shall enumerate in these pages.

Boots are of course the most important item, and in the course of over thirty years climbing in Scotland I have seldom seen anyone wearing unsuitable footwear. Boots of stout construction are almost universally worn, with the one exception of light rubber-soled shoes which on the black gabbro of the Coolins, in Skye, afford a safe grip even on inclined slabs—elsewhere they would be useless and a liability.

Good climbing boots are expensive, but those who can afford the best will be amply repaid by their comfort and service through years of tough wear. There are several patterns of which I have already described and illustrated the best type of English *nailed* boots in my *Lakeland Peaks*, and hand-made Swiss *vibrams* in my *Welsh Peaks*, to which I respectfully refer readers who are interested. For Scotland I recommend the best quality English Vibrams which are hand-made and in consequence more expensive than the others. The main difference is that in the latter the leather is in one piece with the joint at the heel and no stitching at the toe. They are padded round the ankles only where most friction occurs, whereas the lacing and other features are almost identical. There are other models which afford additional security for Alpine climbing and they have No. 6 tricouni round soles and heels, or heel plates if preferred. There are advantages and disadvantages in vibrams without these trimmings: they are silent and easier on the feet on *dry* rock, but on *wet* rock or moss-covered slabs they can be a handicap to rapid progress because the utmost care becomes imperative to avoid a slip which in an exposed situation might result in a twisted or broken ankle. In order to prepare for any eventuality it might be advisable to possess two pairs of climbing boots; one with nails and the other with vibrams. Strong laces are vital and there is a wide choice between nylon, waxed fabric, leather and porpoise; my preference is for the latter because they stand up to all weathers admirably.

Stockings and socks are worthy of some attention and one of each worn together ensure comfort and warmth and reduce undue friction. The *colour* of these items may be important and for the last twenty years I have worn *red* ones because in case of accident this colour can be seen at a great distance, and in consequence would facilitate location and subsequent rescue.

Clothes are perhaps a matter of personal taste, and there are still a few climbers who delight in wearing their oldest cast-off suits, often intentionally with brilliant patches as a decoration! But there is more protection when wearing a properly made *Alpine Jacket*, of which there are a variety of patterns and colours. They are usually made from closely woven cotton of double texture at the main points of friction. They are windproof and reasonably waterproof and perfectly so if treated with silicone or polyurethane. The better models have four pockets, of which two are large enough to accommodate maps which are then kept dry. A skirt is now made to all types, and in heavy rain keeps moisture from percolating on to the small of the back. The collar could be lined with wool to keep the neck warm in the absence of a scarf. In some of the more expensive models there is a small zip opening below the back of the neck to accommodate the hood when not in use. Outside belts are no longer worn because they may put a rock climber off balance by inadvertently catching on a tiny excrescence of crag. They are now universally replaced by a draw cord which runs in a groove at the waist between the double-texture cloth. This type of Alpine Jacket has a zip fastener down the front and goes well up into the neck, whereas *Anoraks* are made in one piece, with a large kangaroo pocket at breast height and a short zip only at the neck. The most useful of these models have a lower pocket on each side. Nylon is now replacing cotton in some types and one of mine is of double texture, interspersed with nylon wool; it is very light and warm in very severe weather. In view of the very rapid changes of temperature encountered in hill country, it is always advisable to carry spare *Pullovers*. Those made of light Shetland wool are much better than a heavy one, because the layers of warm air between them maintain the body temperature, and the number worn can be easily adjusted to varying conditions. *String Vests* worn next to the skin have reduced the risks of cold, and by their use the number of pullovers can be cut down considerably. *Leg Gear* is a matter of personal taste; some climbers swear by trousers while others prefer plus twos. I have found the latter more comfortable and in addition they allow more freedom about the feet. The *material* from which they are made is another consideration. Many have a preference for corduroy, but I do not care for it because it is made of cotton and therefore cold to the skin, and when it gets very wet the material acts like a sponge and retains an excess of moisture. The weight about the legs then increases and is attended by much discomfort. Alternatively, hardwearing and close-woven tweed is warm and light in weight and altogether more amenable in all mountain weather. *Headgear* has changed considerably in recent years, and the feathered, velour Austrian hat is seldom seen nowadays. The more practical and useful protection is at present confined to two types; the woollen brightly coloured *Bob-Cap* and the old-fashioned *Balaclava Helmet*. In fair weather the former functions admirably and will not blow off in a strong wind, whereas the latter is indispensable in Alpine conditions. Most of the Scottish wool shops stock the former in attractive tartan colours and for years I have worn nothing else.

Rucksacks are a necessity and may be obtained in a variety of shapes, colours, sizes and weights. If the climber is moving from place to place and wishes to carry spare clothing, incidentals and photographic gadgets, then it must be a large one such as a Bergan or Karrimor, otherwise a small light model should give satisfactory service. Some prefer those having a light metal frame which keeps the sack off the back and so allows plenty of ventilation. In addition I have one with a leather base to both sack and side-pockets which increases its durability and prolongs its life.

Maps of this extensive region should be the guide and friend of all who climb the Scottish Peaks. There are two series of outstanding merit, and if dissected and mounted on linen they are more easily handled out of doors, but the present cost is so prohibitive that their general use is declining. The one-inch series issued by the Ordnance Survey have the contours at intervals of fifty feet, and Tourist Maps of Ben Nevis and Glencoe, and of Loch Lomond and the Trossachs, are outstanding pieces of cartography in which the shading of the mountain slopes reveals a clear indication of the ridges: the former includes all the peaks from Ben Cruachan to Ben Nevis and the latter includes the Cobbler, Ben More and Ben Lui. The new series of O.S. 1:50000 maps have now been issued, and since many of my readers may not possess them I give below the map numbers of each series applicable to this book, as follows:

	old series 1:63360	new series 1:50000
Arran Hills	66	69
Cobbler, Ben More and Ben Lui	Tourist	no change
Ben Cruachan to Ben Nevis	Tourist	no change
Creag Meaghaidh	36	34
Saddle and Five Sisters of Kintail	35	33

	old series	new series
Applecross and Torridon Peaks	26	24
Slioch, An Teallach and Ben More Coigach	20	19
Stac Polly to Quinag	13	15
Foinaven and Ben Hope	9	no change
Ben Loyal	10	no change
Lochnagar	41	44
Ben Macdhui and Cairn Gorm	41	36
Isle of Skye	24 and 33	23 and 32

A Tourist Map on similar lines has been issued for the Cairngorms, and more recently a 1:25000 Outdoor Leisure Map, HIGH TOPS OF THE CAIRNGORMS, with heights in metres. It is the best one available today, and the Ordnance Survey have been kind enough to give me the corrected heights of the Skye Peaks, fixed by Stereo-comparator, all of which now appear in the latest edition of their 6 inch sheets. A more recent issue by the O.S. is that of THE CUILLIN AND TORRIDON PEAKS, a 1:25000 Leisure Map which displays the Cuillin on one side and the Torridon Peaks on the other. It is a pity the latter does not include the Coulin and Beinn Damh Forests as these lesser peaks are of great interest to the climber. The half-inch series issued by Bartholomew have the contours at intervals of 250 feet, but the splendid layer system of colouring reveals the topography of the country with great clarity. The maps in this work are marked with the various routes to the peaks and should be of immense value to all mountaineers.

A Compass should always be carried in the hills, despite the fact that it may not be needed in clear weather if the ground is familiar. In mist, however, all mountains become wrapped in deeper mystery with the complete disappearance of well-known landmarks, and if the climber is off the beaten track he may well find himself in difficulties without one. Even in clear weather a compass is especially useful on the Scottish Peaks because many of them have tracks that are less distinct than those encountered in Lakeland and Snowdonia. A good compass is not cheap, but it is money well spent. Mountain Photographers should note that certain types of Exposure Meter containing a magnet may deflect the compass needle if the two are within a short distance of one another. Tests I have made indicate that at a distance of 9 inches N, 12 inches E, and 18 inches S and W the magnetic north is deflected, and when the exposure meter is close to the compass the needle simply spins round. Climbers should therefore test the two instruments and keep one well away from the other when in use, as in misty weather incorrect route finding might result and so lead to unforeseen difficulties. Moreover, mountaineers should remember that since much of the Coolins in Skye is built of magnetic rock, the compass needle just spins round and the instrument is useless.

An Aneroid is a most useful instrument and may be a luxury to all save the explorer. A good one is a fairly reliable forecaster of the weather, and since it approximately indicates the altitude it may be a valuable aid in misty weather by helping to locate one's position with greater accuracy. The lower-priced instruments register up to 10,000 feet. If you possess one, always remember to adjust the dial to the altitude of the starting point of your climb, if it is known with certainty, and thereafter check it at any known station. Bear in mind that when the barometer is falling the readings will be too high, and if it is rising they will be too low. In any event the error is about 100 feet for each 1/10 of an inch of rise or fall not due to change of altitude.

An Ice Axe is valuable and may be indispensable in snow climbing; moreover, it is a useful tool for glissading and its correct employment will ensure a safe and rapid descent of steep snow slopes. A thorough knowledge of its use is essential. There are numerous makes, each of which has some slight variation in design of both pick and adze. A competent dealer will advise on the most suitable type, which is largely governed by length of shaft, weight and balance. A sling is a useful adjunct and may prevent the loss of the axe if it should slip out of the hand when in use.

In conclusion, I would advise everyone venturing on the hills at any time of the year to carry the following items which could spell survival in extremely bad weather. 1, Map and Compass; 2, Torch and Whistle; 3, spare Food and Clothing, including a large polythene bag; and 4, a small First Aid Kit.

Mountaineering

The Scottish Peaks can generally be ascended without the use of a rope and do not therefore necessarily involve any rock climbing. It all depends upon how you wish to reach your summit cairn: for instance, any able bodied person can walk up to Ben Nevis by the well-trodden path from Achintee; the mountaineer can attain the same cairn by first climbing Carn Mor Dearg, then crossing the famous Arete and finally ascending the steep flanks of the great North-East Buttress; while the rock climber can reach the same objective by climbing the Tower Ridge from Coire na Ciste, or by any of the other courses that festoon the savage rock walls of this magnificent corrie. All of them must be in fit condition if they are to succeed in their quest, so it depends upon your sporting instincts, your experience, your knowledge of your mountain and on how you wish to enjoy your holiday in this superb countryside.

However, in point of fact much of the most exciting and tough mountaineering in Scotland is done under snow and ice conditions which differentiates it from the average ascents in Lakeland and Snowdonia. The Highlands are therefore an excellent training ground for the Alps and differ from them only in that the scale is more diminutive with an absence of glaciers. Snow may fall on the hills above the 3,500-foot contour at any time of the year, but it does not stay long excepting in the deep recesses of the high north-east corries. By November, the higher mountains begin to accumulate their winter raiment, but it is seldom earlier than February that heavy falls are experienced. From then on to April the great mural precipices encircling the high corries acquire a white mantle and tremendous cornices grow from the ridges and the edges of the summit plateaux, to hang over the cliffs and couloirs to an unknown depth. It is at such times that great care must be exercised in the selection of any climbing route because an otherwise easy ascent may become both difficult and dangerous. With the coming of the hot suns of May a marked disintegration of the cornices occurs and these are finally precipitated into the depths of the corries far below.

While snow remains on the hills it is always advisable to take an ice axe which is useful and may be necessary. In addition to its more general employment, it is a valuable tool as I have said for glissading and enables the glissader to control the pace of his descent by using the spike as a brake. It is always advisable to see that the terminus of a glissade is at a reduced angle and free from projecting rocks, otherwise an unpleasant collision may be experienced. An excellent place where practice may be obtained until late in the spring is immediately above the Red Burn on the western slopes of Ben Nevis which may be descended in a comparatively short time by this means.

The use of ski on the British Hills is not often possible, save in a severe winter when snow lies heavily on their slopes, and even then it is preferable to run over snow carpeting long grassy declivities rather than over boulder-strewn ground. The greater altitude of the Scottish Peaks is a decided advantage in that they are more likely to be snowbound for longer periods and so facilitate the enjoyment of this exhilarating sport. In recent years there have been notable developments in the Cairngorms, the Cairnwell and Glencoe, where the installation of chair-lifts and tows, plus exceptionally favourable snow conditions, have raised these areas to a peak of winter sport success undreamt of a few years ago. In the Glenmore district in particular a splendid team effort involving the expenditure of large sums of money has resulted in the construction of a well-graded road that runs from Aviemore, past Loch Morlich to terminate in Coire Cas at a height of 2,150 feet. Here the motorist may park his car, enjoy refreshment on the spot, and then walk uphill for a short distance to the chair-lift that will quickly hoist him to within 500 feet of the summit of Cairn Gorm itself. The topography of this peak is especially suitable for skiing, because three deep gullies flank its northern slopes and carry snow until the early summer, when the rest of the range may have been denuded by the spring sunshine. Moreover, when the whole of this massive chain is snowbound it is admirably suited for ski mountaineering, and experienced Scottish skiers are fortunate to be able to take advantage of these conditions so near their homes.

Rock climbing is a sport that is engaged in nowadays by a very large number of enthusiasts and those who live south of the border have become accustomed to regard such cliffs as Scafell, in Lakeland, and Clogwyn Du'r Arddu in Snowdonia, as the acme of perfection and difficulty. It is true enough that those Sassenachs who have climbed in Scotland are enthusiastic in their praise of the peaks of the Coolins, in Skye, the great cliffs of Ben Nevis and such Glencoe Hills as Buachaille Etive Mor and Bidean nam Bian, but these are only a few of the possible playgrounds for the rock climber in this vast mountain region where a wide variety of rock is encountered. Since this is a most important factor in the enjoyment of this sport, I append a brief list of the types met with in a few of the ranges.

Gabbro	The Black Coolins of Skye
Granite	The Cairngorms and Arran Hills
Porphyry	Ben Nevis, Buachaille Etive Mor and Bidean nam Bian
Schistose and porphyry	The Cobbler and Narnain
Sandstone and quartzite	The Torridon Peaks, An Teallach, Suilven, the Coigach Peaks and Ben More Assynt

There are thus ample opportunities for the enjoyment of this exhilarating pastime among the Scottish Peaks, but a novice should never attempt it without proper guidance and training. If you have a friend who is an experienced rock climber, ask him to explain its technique and the management of the rope, and at the first opportunity get him to lead you up some of the easy courses, when you will have the chance to put these theories into practice. If you have a steady head, good balance and can acquire the rhythm for proficiency, he will soon notice it and lead you up routes of greater difficulty until finally you tackle the severes.

Should you become keen on this fascinating sport, you may wish to apply for membership of the Scottish Mountaineering Club whose standards of admission are high, but like many of the clubs south of the border this famous club may be already full and unable to consider further applications for membership. I should mention here that it has rendered an important service to mountaineering in Scotland by the publication of a series of detailed guidebooks that cover both mainland and islands.

Munro's classification of the Peaks

The number of Scottish Peaks whose height exceeds 3,000 feet is surprisingly large. If the islands off the west coast of the mainland are included, there are 276 separate mountains and some 545 tops in all, rising above this altitude. The reason for this distinct classification is that one mountain may have two or three tops and yet be part of the same range. For instance, Carn Mor Dearg to the east of Ben Nevis, is 4,012 feet high and the culminating southernly point of a lofty ridge running roughly north–south. To the north of this summit are two excrescences on the ridge known as Carn Dearg Meadhonach, 3,873 feet and Carn Beag Dearg, 3,264 feet. These points rise above the general line of the ridge sufficiently to warrant their being named and are known as separate tops. Carn Mor Dearg is the seventh highest mountain but only the twelfth top, the other two being the 22nd and 257th respectively.

Classified lists of all the Scottish Peaks were worked out by the late Sir Hugh T. Munro and are known as Munro's Tables. There are two arrangements, the first according to districts and the second in order of altitude. In the former the county is given with a reference to the one-inch O.S. map number together with the precise position of each top and the place from which it is best ascended. The complete Munro's Tables with prefatory notes appear at the end of the General Guide Book issued by the Scottish Mountaineering Club and are now available in a separate volume. They should be consulted by those readers who are interested.

Heights of the Scottish Peaks referred to in this book arranged in order of altitude over 3,000 feet: A = separate mountain; B = top

A	B	Height	Name	Group or District
1	1	4,406	Ben Nevis	Lochaber
2	2	4,300	Ben Macdhui	Cairngorms
3	3	4,248	Braeriach	Cairngorms
4	5	4,241	Cairn Toul	Cairngorms
	7	4,095	Stob Coire Sputan Dearg	Cairngorms
	8	4,095	Sgor an Lochain Uaine—Angel's Peak	Cairngorms
5	9	4,084	Cairn Gorm	Cairngorms
6	10	4,060	Aonach Beag	Lochaber
	11	4,036	Stob Coire an Lochain	Cairngorms
7	12	4,012	Carn Mor Dearg	Lochaber
8	13	3,999	Aonach Mor	Lochaber
	16	3,983	Cairn Lochan	Cairngorms
	17	3,961	Carn Dearg	Lochaber
10	18	3,924	Beinn a'Bhuird	Cairngorms
11	19	3,883	Beinn Mheadhoin	Cairngorms
	21	3,875	Sron na Lairig	Cairngorms
	22	3,873	Carn Dearg Meadhonach	Lochaber
	26	3,856	Stob Coire an t'Sneachda	Cairngorms
16	28	3,843	Ben More	Perthshire
17	29	3,827	Stobinian	Perthshire
19	32	3,789	Cac Carn Beag	Lochnagar
20	33	3,788	Derry Cairngorm	Cairngorms
	37	3,768	Cac Carn Mor	Lochnagar
23	38	3,766	Bidean nam Bian	Glencoe
25	48	3,708	Ben Lui	Agl-Perth Boundary
26	50	3,700	Creag Meaghaidh	Loch Laggan

A	B	Height	Name	Group or District
27	51	3,700	Binnein Mor	Mamores
29	53	3,689	Ben Cruachan	Argyll
	56	3,673	Cairn Etchachan	Cairngorms
	64	3,657	Stob Coire nan Lochan	Glencoe
42	72	3,636	Meall a'Bhuiridh	Blackmount
	80	3,621	Stob Coire nam Beith	Glencoe
	82	3,611	Stob Dearg—Taynuilt Peak	Cruachan
49	88	3,602	Clach Leathad	Blackmount
50	89	3,601	Sgurr a'Mhaim	Mamores
	90	3,600	Creise	Blackmount
54	97	3,565	Stob Ghabhar	Blackmount
	102	3,552	Cuidhe Crom	Lochnagar
59	108	3,541	Ben Starav	Loch Etive
	110	3,534	Sron Riach	Cairngorms
65	119	3,505	Sgurr Fhuaran	Kintail
	124	3,497	Beinn Fhada	Glencoe
	125	3,497	Stob Coire an Lochan	Stobinian
69	132	3,483	Bidein a'Ghlas Thuill	An Teallach
	134	3,474	Sgurr Fiona	An Teallach
71	138	3,456	Spidean a'Choire Leith	Liathach
81	155	3,430	Carn an t'Sagairt Mor	Lochnagar
	161	3,424	Carn an t'Sagairt Beag	Lochnagar
91	171	3,400	Carn a'Mhaim—? 3329	Cairngorms
96	177	3,382	Am Bodach	Mamores
	179	3,380	Lord Berkeley's Seat	An Teallach
101	186	3,370	Sgurr na Ciste Duibhe	Kintail
103	191	3,362	Sgorr Dhearg	B. a'Bheithir
	192	3,360	Corrag Bhuidhe	An Teallach
	193	3,358	Mullach an Rathain	Liathach
	196	3,350	Sgurr Creag an Eich	An Teallach
106	199	3,345	Stob Dearg—Buachaille Etive Mor	Glencoe

A	B	Height	Name	Group or District
114	211	3,317	The Saddle	Kintail
	214	3,312	Drochaid Glas	Cruachan
116	215	3,309	Ruadh-stac Mor	Beinn Eighe
120	219	3,303	The Devil's Point	Cairngorms
	224	3,300	Sgor an Iubhair	Mamores
127	235	3,284	Sgorr Dhonuill	B. a'Bheithir
135	245	3,274	Stob Ban	Mamores
136	247	3,273	Ben More	Assynt
137	248	3,272	Stob Diamh	Cruachan
	249	3,272	Aonach Eagach	Blackmount
	251	3,270	Sgurr na Carnach	Kintail
	257	3,264	Carn Beag Dearg	Lochaber
145	263	3,257	Sgurr Alasdair	Skye
147	265	3,234	Sgurr Dearg— Inaccessible Pinnacle	Skye
155	284	3,232	Sgurr Mhor	Beinn Alligin
	290	3,220	Spidean Coire na Clach	Beinn Eighe
161	294	3,217	Slioch	Loch Maree
	296	3,217	Sail Mhor	Beinn Eighe
	297	3,215	Stob Garbh	Cruachan
	300	3,211	Meikle Pap	Lochnagar
167	305	3,208	Sgurr Thearlaich	Skye
	304	3,207	Stob a'Ghlais Choire	Blackmount
172	310	3,200	An Gearanach	Mamores
	312	3,200	Bidean Toll a'Mhuic	Liathach
174	315	3,196	Ben Sgriol	Kintail
178	322	3,192	Sgurr a'Ghreadaidh	Skye
	324	3,191	Meall Coire na Saobhaidhe	Lochnagar
	329	3,188	Sgurr Ban	Beinn Eighe
	337	3,176	Glas Mheall Mor	An Teallach
183	341	3,168	Sgor nam Fiannaidh	Aonach Eagach
184	342	3,167	Sgurr nan Gillean	Skye
185	343	3,166	Sgurr na Banachdich	Skye
186	345	3,164	Sgor Thuilm	Glenfinnan

Munro's classification of the Peaks

A	B	Height	Name	Group or District
	346	3,163	Sron an Isean	Cruachan
	347	3,160	Sgurr an Fhir Duibhe	Beinn Eighe
	352	3,150	Meall Dearg	Liathach
191	363	3,143	Bruach na Frithe	Skye
	369	3,140	Meall na Dige	Stobinian
	376	3,130	A'Choinneach Mhor	Beinn Eighe
199	377	3,130	Stob Dubh— Buachaille Etive Mor	Glencoe
	379	3,129	Sgurr nan Spainteach	Kintail
	385	3,125	Little Pap	Lochnagar
207	393	3,118	Meall Dearg	Aonach Eagach
210	397	3,111	Sgurr Mhic Coinnich	Skye
	401	3,108	Sgurr Sgumain	Skye
	402	3,104	Sgorr Bhan	B. a'Bheithir
	409	3,100	Sgurr na Forcan	Saddle
	412	3,100	Sail Liath	An Teallach
	426	3,085	Am Bodach	Aonach Eagach
	432	3,080	Stob Coire Leith	Aonach Eagach
	433	3,080	Glas Mheall Liath	An Teallach
230	440	3,069	Am Basteir	Skye
	455	3,058	Sgurr an Tuill Bhain	Slioch
240	456	3,058	Stob a'Choire Odhair	Blackmount
	463	3,050	Am Fasarinen Pinnacles	Liathach
	465	3,050	Corrag Bhuidhe Buttress	An Teallach
	466	3,050	Creag Dubh	Beinn Eighe
	470	3,050	Stuc a'Choire Dhuibh Bhig	Liathach
	472	3,068	Sgurr a'Fionn Choire	Skye
250	479	3,042	Blaven	Skye
	483	3,040	Stob Cadha Gobhlach	An Teallach
252	484	3,040	Ben Hope	Sutherland
255	489	3,031	Sgurr nan Eag	Skye
	507	3,021	Tom na Gruagach	Beinn Alligin

A	B	Height	Name	Group or District
270	521	3,012	Sgurr a'Mhadaidh	Skye
	525	3,010	Faochag	Kintail
272	527	3,008	Ben-a-Clee	Ben Lui
	529	3,007	Sgurr Thormaid	Skye
274	533	3,005	Bhasteir Tooth	Skye
	537	3,004	Meall Cuanail	Cruachan

The heights of the peaks below 3,000 feet are given in each monograph where applicable.

Glossary of Scottish place-names

Sassenachs usually find some difficulty in understanding and pronouncing the various Gaelic names given to many of the different topographical features in the Highlands, while several of those in Skye have always been an insoluble enigma because their spelling is frequently obscure and their correct pronunciation most perplexing. When it is realised for instance that Mhadaidh is pronounced *Vatee*, or Thuilm *Hulim*, or even the more common Dearg *Jerrag*, it will be obvious that unless the speaker is familiar with the Gaelic tongue he is scarcely ever understood by the native. The position, however, is further complicated by the number of apparently correct spellings for one and the same place; the Coolins, for example, may be spelt in a variety of ways, all of which would seem to be acceptable to the Gaelic scholar. I have therefore included a short list which I hope will be useful to visitors, but should any of them desire further information I would refer them to my *Magic of Skye* which contains an extensive monograph on Nomenclature.

Aber, *Abar*, *Obar*, mouth or confluence of a river
Abhainn, *Ambuinn*, river. Usually *Avon*
Achadh, field, park. Usually *Ach*
Ailean, a green place; plain
Airidh, sheiling
Aisir, a rocky defile or pass
Allt, burn, brook, stream. Conventional forms: *Ald*, *Alt*, *Auld*, *Ault*
Aoineadh, a steep promontory or brae

Aonach, a height, a ridge
Ard, *Aird*, a high point, promontory
Ath, a ford; also a kiln
Avon, conventional form of *Abhainn*, q.v.

Baile, town. Usually *Bal*, *Bali*
Ban, white, fair.
Barp, conical heap of stones, a chambered cairn
Barr, a point, top, extremity.
Bard, a poet, a dyke, enclosure, ward

Beag, little, small.
Conventional form, *Beg*

Bealach, breach, pass, gap, col

Beinn, a mountain.
Conventional form, *Ben*

Beith, a birch tree

Bian, a hide (of cattle)

Bidean, a pinnacle

Binnean, or *Binnein*, a pinnacle or little mountain

Blar, a plain, battlefield

Bo, plural *Ba*, cow, cows

Bodach, an old man, hobgoblin, spectre

Both, *Bothan*, a hut, booth or bothy

Braigh, top, summit. Usually *Brae*, *Bread*

Bruaich, a bank, brae, brim, steep place

Buachaille, a herdsman, a shepherd

Buidhe, yellow, golden coloured

Cadha, a pass, steep path

Cailleach, a nun, old woman, a witch

Cam, crooked, bent, one-eyed

Camas, bay, bend, channel

Caol, strait, firth, narrow. Other form *Kyle*

Caolas, alternative Gaelic form for the above

Carn, a heap of stones, cairn

Carr, broken ground

Ceann, head, headland. Usually *Ken*, *Kin*

Ceo, fog, mist

Ceum, a step

Cill, a cell, church. Usually *Kil*

Cioch, a pap, woman's breast

Clach, a stone

Clachan, stones, hamlet

Cladh, a churchyard, a burying place.

Clais, a hollow

Cleit, a ridge, reef; rocky eminence

Cluain, a field pasture, green plain, meadow

Cnap, a knob, hillock

Cnoc, a knoll. Usually *Knock*

Coill or *Coille*, a wood, forest

Coire, a cauldron, kettle, circular hollow. Other form *Corry* or *Corrie*

Creag, a rock, cliff. English form: *Craig*

Crioch, boundary, frontier, landmark

Cro, a sheep-fold, pen

Crom, bent, sloping, crooked

Cruach, stack, heap, haunch

Cul, the back, a nook

Dail, a field. In Norse, a dale

Dearg, red

Doire, grove, hollow

Druim, the back, ridge.
Usually *Drem*, *Drom*, *Drum*

Dubh, black, dark. Other form: *Dhu*

Dun, a fort, castle, heap

Eagach, notched

Ear, east

Eas, a waterfall. Other form: *Easach*, a cascade

Easg, bog, fen, natural ditch

Eilean, an island

Fad, long, e.g., *Beinn Fhada*, long mountain

Feadan, narrow glen

Fearn, an alder tree

Feith, bog, sinewy stream, a vein

Fiadh, a deer

Fuaran, a perennial spring, well

Garadh, a fence, dike, garden

Garbh, rough. Other spelling, *Garve*

Gearr, short

Geal, white, clear, bright

Gearanach, a wall-like ridge

Geodha, a narrow creek, chasm, rift, cove

Ghabhar or *Gobhar*, a goat

Glac, a hollow, dell, defile

Glais, a stream, burn

Glas, grey, pale, wan; green

Gleann, narrow valley, dale, dell; usually *Glen*

Gob, point, beak

Gorm, blue, azure, green

Gualann, shoulder of a mountain or hill

I, an island

Inbhir, confluence, place at the meeting of river and sea. Other form: *Inver*, c.f. *Aber*

Iubhair, yew tree

Kyle, see *Caol* and *Caolas*

Lag, a hollow in a hill. Usually *Logan*, *Logie*

Lairig, the sloping face of a hill, a pass

Leathad, a slope, declivity

Leathan, broad

Leithir, a slope

Liath, grey

Linne, pool, sound, channel

Loch, a lake, arm of the sea

Lochan, small loch

Lon, a marsh, morass

Lub, a bend, fold, curvature

Mam, a round or gently rising hill

Maol, headland, bald top, cape

Meadhon, middle, central

Meall, knob, lump, rounded hill

Moine or *Mointeach*, moss-land, mossy

Monadh, moor, heath, hill, mountain

Mor, great, large, tall.
  English form: *More*
Muileann, mill
Muir, the sea
Mullach, a rounded hill

Odhar, dapple, drab, dun-
  coloured, sallow
Ord, a round, steep or
  conical hill
Os, outlet of a lake or river

Pit or *Pet*, farm, hollow
Poll, a pool, pond, pit

Rathad, a road, way
Reidh, plain, level, smooth
Riabhach, drab, greyish,
  brindled, grizzled. Other
  form: *Riach*
Roinn, a point, headland,
  peninsula
Ros, a point, promontory.
  Other form: *Ross*
Ruadh, red, reddish
Rudha, promontory. Usually
  Ru, Rhu, Row
Ruigh, a run for cattle,
  sheiling, land sloping

Sail, a heel
Sean, old, aged, ancient
Sgorr or *Sgurr*, a peak,
  conical sharp rock.
  Sometimes *Scaur*
Sgreamach, rocky

Sith, a fairy. *Sithean*, a fairy
  hillock or knoll
Slochd, a deep hollow
Sneachd, snow
Socach, snout
Srath, a valley, plain beside a
  river, strath
Sron, nose, peak,
  promontory. Other form:
  Strone
Sruth, a stream, current.
  Usually *Struan*
Stac, a steep rock, conical
  hill
Stob, a point
Stuc, a pinnacle, peak,
  conical steep rock
Suidhe, sitting, resting place

Taigh or *Tigh*, a house.
  Usually *Tay, Ty*
Tairbeart, an isthmus. Other
  form: *Tarbet, Tarbert*
Tir, country region, land.
  Other form: *Tyr*
Tobar, a well, spring,
  fountain. Usually *Tober*
Tom, a hillock, mound
Torr, a mound, heap, hill
Tulach, knoll, hillock,
  eminence. Anglicized
  forms: *Tilly, Tully, Tulloch*

Uachdar, upper-land. Usually
  Auchter, Ochter
Uaine, green
Uamh, a cave, a grave

Uchd, ascent, face of a hill

Uig, a nook, bay

Uisage, water, rain

The Scottish centres

In the following list I have given the principal centres from which the Scottish Peaks cited in this book may be most conveniently climbed. But it should be borne in mind that in the remote parts of the mainland accommodation is scarce and the nearest hotel, guest house or Youth Hostel may be a considerable distance from the base of your mountain. It is therefore not surprising that camping is much favoured by climbers, and in regions like that of the Coigach Peaks a centrally placed camp would facilitate access to the surrounding hills and save much time compared with staying in Ullapool which is at least fourteen miles distant.

Even the climber who has transport is often faced with a long tramp from the nearest place he can park the vehicle to the base of his mountain. Take a peak like Foinaven in the far north, which can be reached on foot from the Rhiconich Hotel, but where the only other hotels are situated at Scourie, Durness and Kinloch Bervie. The latter is some five miles from the nearest parking place to this mountain, whose lower slopes are then reached by walking about three miles across the moor. Alternatively, a party of climbers could camp in Strath Dionard at the foot of Foinaven where no wasted time would be involved in either the traverse of its long summit ridge or the ascent of its towering cliffs.

Youth Hostelling is a pleasant, healthy and cheap way of exploring Scotland, and at the time of writing there were 80 hostels on the mainland and islands. Many of them are not only delightfully situated, and the accommodation also is admirable, but I have only cited those giving reasonable access to the peaks dealt with herein.

I have arranged the Routes from south to north of the Highlands, beginning with Arran and ending with Ben Loyal, thence followed by the Cairngorms and finally by the Coolins of Skye. For convenience of reference I have followed the same plan for the nearest centres to each range of hills.

The Isle of Arran is reached by steamer from Ardrossan or Fairlie on the mainland to *Brodick* which overlooks a beautiful bay, backed by the Arran Hills. It has several hotels and numerous cottages where accommodation may be found. These are well placed for the ascent of Goat Fell; for the walk through Glen Rosa to the Saddle; and for the traverse of the ridges from either Beinn a'Chliabhain or Beinn Nuis to Cir Mhor, *Corrie* lies on the coast some six miles to the north and is well situated for the shorter ascent of Goat Fell by way of Meall Breac, whence the ridge may be followed northwards to Coich na h'Oighe and a return made to the hotel or to one of the cottages. These are also well placed for the walk up Glen Sannox to Cir Mhor, or for the ascent of Caisteal Abhail by way of Suidhe Fhearghas and Ccum na Caillich. An additional attraction for climbers and scramblers are the four famous Boulders, all lying close to the road, of which the Cat Stone is perhaps the best known. *Lochranza* is rather distant for all the above excursions but has the nearest accommodation for the most westerly of the three Arran Ridges. There are Youth Hostels at Lochranza and Whiting Bay.

Ben Arthur, more familiarly known as **The Cobbler**, is best reached from *Arrochar* where there is a hotel, a guest house and a few cottages; or from *Tarbet*, two miles away on the shore of Loch Lomond, where there is a hotel. The Ardgartan Youth Hostel is at the head of Loch Long, two miles from Arrochar.

Ben More and **Stobinian** are most easily reached from *Crianlarich* which has one hotel and a few cottages. Strong walkers may attain the two peaks by a long tramp from *Balquhidder*, on Loch Voil, which has a hotel and other accommodation, but *Killin* on Loch Tay, and *Lochearnhead* on Loch Earn, are too far away unless transport is available. There is a Youth Hostel at Crianlarich.

Ben Lui is usually climbed from either Tyndrum or Dalmally, each of which has one hotel. The former has two starting points: 1. Tyndrum Station, and 2. a school off A82 which lies a mile from the village. The Forest Road and Cart Track eventually merge and lead to Cononish which lies at the base of the peak. The latter involves a drive of about five miles along Glen Lochy to the starting point opposite Eas Diamh, whence the route ascends the north ridge of the peak. The nearest Youth Hostel is at Crianlarich.

Ben Cruachan may be most conveniently ascended from *Loch Awe House* or nearby guest houses which overlook this beautiful lake and lie at the foot of its satellite, Ben Vourie. Transport would be necessary if staying further away at *Dalmally*, but the same point of departure could be reached from *Taynuilt* which has one hotel and a guest house.

The Blackmount may be reached from the south from the hotels at *Inveroran*, on Loch Tulla, and *Bridge of Orchy* which is some three miles further away. The range may be reached from the north from the *Kingshouse Hotel*, on Rannoch Moor. The accommodation at all three hotels is excellent.

Buachaille Etive Mor is usually climbed from the *Kingshouse Hotel* which is only a short step from the foot of the cliffs.

Bidean nam Bian can be reached from the accommodation mentioned under Aonach Eagach, but if the ascent is made from either Beinn Fhada or the Allt Coire Gabhail, then transport to their starting points would be desirable; if the descent is made from An t'Sron it shortens the walk back to the hotels.

Aonach Eagach is best climbed from the *Clachaig Inn* in Glencoe where, however, accommodation is strictly limited. It may also be reached from *Glencoe village* which has one hotel and several cottages. But when staying here transport to the foot of Am Bodach, the first top to be ascended, would be an advantage; it would be easy to walk back from Sgor nam Fiannaidh at the other end of the ridge. There is a Youth Hostel at the foot of Glencoe.

Beinn a'Bheithir overshadows the *Ballachulish Hotel* and the nearby guest house and is easily ascended from them. The village is nearly three miles away and has some cottage accommodation. Should the easterly ridge of Beinn Bhan be ascended direct its starting point is only a short step away, but if the descent is made from Creag Ghorm to the west of the range, then a long road walk is necessary to return to these lodgings. The nearest Youth Hostel is in Glencoe.

Garbh Bheinn rises in Ardgour to the west of Loch Linnhe and may be reached by car from Corran Ferry, a distance of about six miles to the starting point of the climb. There is a hotel in *Corran* and a few cottages where a bed might be found. Some climbers may prefer to stay in one of the hotels in *Onich* which is about two miles from the ferry and on the shore of Loch Leven.

The Mamores form an extensive range of hills between Loch Leven and Glen Nevis, and its eastern peaks are best reached from *Kinlochleven* which has numerous houses where accommodation might be found. The western peaks, however, are most easily climbed from Polldubh, in Glen Nevis, which may be conveniently reached by car from *Fort William*. Here several hotels, guest houses and cottages provide ample accommodation. There is a large Youth Hostel about half way down Glen Nevis, from which Polldubh and Achintee are only a short step away.

Ben Nevis dominates the busy town of *Fort William* where ample accommodation is available to suit all purses.

Creag Meaghaidh rises to the north west of Loch Laggan and the nearest hotel is at its head, just four miles from the starting point of the ascent. There are hotels at Roy Bridge and a good one to the east of it which, however, involves a drive of fourteen miles. It might be possible to get bed and breakfast at Aberarder.

The Saddle flanks the south side of Glen Shiel and its northern spurs may be reached from the cottages at *Invershiel*, or with transport from the *Kintail Lodge Hotel* on Loch Duich. However, since this peak is usually climbed by the Forcan Ridge, it is better to drive some three miles up the glen and ascend the stalker's path on the R which gives direct

access to this spectacular route. There is a Youth Hostel on
Loch Duich under two miles from Shiel Bridge.

The Five Sisters of Kintail flank the northern side of Glen
Shiel and since its terminal peak overlooks Loch Duich, it
may be climbed direct from any of the accommodation given
under the Saddle. But if the traverse of the long summit ridge
is made from east to west it is more convenient to drive some
six miles up the glen to a point on the road below Bealach na
Lapain where the ascent is shorter and over steep grass.

The Applecross Hills may be climbed from Tornapress
which is some six miles from *Jeantown* on Loch Carron,
where accommodation may be found in the hotel or in one of
the many cottages strung out along the shore of this beautiful
sea loch. The same starting point may be reached from
Shieldaig which is two miles further away and where there is a
small inn and several cottages. Moreover, the new road gives
quick access from *Torridon* where the fine hotel affords
luxurious accommodation. However, should the ridge walk
over Bheinn Bhan be planned, its cairn is only three miles
from the lofty Bealach na Ba which may be attained by road,
six miles from Tornapress and a similar distance from
Applecross where there is an inn and several cottages. The
nearest Youth Hostel is at Kishorn (Achintraid) and a more
distant one at Torridon.

Beinn Damh rises behind the Loch Torridon Hotel and the
path to it starts from its very doors, but accommodation
might be found in one of the cottages at *Annat* which is only a
short step away, or even in the more distant hamlet of *Fasag*.
There is a new Youth Hostel at Torridon.

Liathach may be reached from *Kinlochewe* where there is a
comfortable hotel, or from the Torridon Hotel on the shore of
the loch. Accommodation might be found in both *Annat* and
Fasag, or in the new Youth Hostel.

Beinn Alligin is within walking distance of *Fasag* and the new
Youth Hostel. Climbers coming by car may park the vehicle
near the stone bridge over Coire Mhic Nobuil which is the
starting point of the ascent. Accommodation as for Liathach.

Beinn Eighe rises to the west of *Kinlochewe* and may be ascended by a path that turns off to the L from the road beyond the village, where one hotel and a guest house provide the only accommodation.

Slioch may be reached by a long walk from the *Kinlochewe Hotel*, but the distance may be shortened for those coming by car either from Kinlochewe or from the *Loch Maree Hotel* by parking the vehicle at Rhu Noa and arranging for a ghillie to row the party across the lake to Glen Bianasdail where the real ascent begins.

An Teallach can be conveniently climbed only from *Dundonnell* where an enlarged hotel and a few cottages flank Little Loch Broom. The peak is best reached by a stalker's path that leaves the road about a quarter of a mile to the east of the hotel.

The Coigach Peaks are all fairly close together and any of them may be reached by car from *Ullapool*, where there are two hotels, several guest houses and a number of cottages. There is also a Youth Hostel in the village. *Drumrunie New Lodge* stands among the trees to the north of Strathkanaird and is within walking distance of Cul Beag and Ben More Coigach; the latter may be ascended from *Achiltibuie* which has a small inn and a few cottages. Stac Polly requires transport, as also Cul Mor which, however, could be reached on foot from the cottages at *Elphin* or *Knockan*. The nearest Youth Hostel is at Achininver, overlooking the Summer Isles.

Suilven can be most conveniently reached from *Lochinver* where a hotel and several cottages provide accommodation. The peak may also be reached from Little Assynt which is on the road between Lochinver and *Inchnadamph* where the hotel is useful. The nearest Youth Hostel is at Achmelvich, about four miles from Lochinver.

Quinag is too far away to be reached on foot, but climbers with transport may stay in one of the hotels at *Inchnadamph*, *Lochinver*, *Drumbeg* or *Kylesku*. The car can usually be parked off the road at any point chosen for the ascent. There is a Youth Hostel at Achmelvich.

Foinaven rises to the east of Rhiconich where the *Rhiconich Hotel* provides good accommodation. Another hotel is further away from the peak at *Kinloch Bervie*, and still more distant hotels are at *Scourie* and *Durness*; the two latter places have guest houses and are about equi-distant. There is a Youth Hostel at Durness.

Ben Hope may be reached by a wild moorland road from *Altnaharra* which has a surprisingly good hotel.

Ben Loyal rises to the south of *Tongue* which has two hotels and a few cottages. It may be reached on foot, but with transport may be climbed from the roads on either side of the peak. There is a Youth Hostel near the village.

Lochnagar may be most conveniently reached from *Ballater* where there are several hotels, many guest houses and a Youth Hostel. But since it is some fourteen miles distant the return walk would be only possible for the toughest climber. If, however, transport is available, nine miles can be saved by driving up Glen Muick to the Spittal of Glen Muick, whence a footbridge leads over the river to Allt na-Guibhsaich Lodge where the ascent of the mountain begins. *Braemar* is a possible alternative and has two hotels and several houses where accommodation may be found. It is three miles nearer the peak, but only five of the eleven miles can be saved by driving to Loch Callater, whence the path rises in six long miles to the summit of this magnificent mountain. There are also Youth Hostels at Braemar, Glendoll and Inverey.

Ben Macdhui may be reached from *Braemar* which has ample accommodation or from *Inverey* where some of the few cottages may accommodate the climber; it is four miles nearer the peak. But Mar Lodge is the nearest, where several bedrooms are available to climbers throughout the year. There is a road giving direct access to the Locked Gate for Derry Lodge and it is only two miles distant. Those who have transport should drive to the locked gate that gives access to Derry Lodge, but even so the tramp there and back to the summit cairn is a long one. It is less arduous and shorter, but less interesting to walk to it from the chair-lift on Cairn

Gorm, which can be reached by car from *Aviemore* which has two hotels and several guest houses. There is a hotel at Coylumbridge and a Youth Hostel at Inverey.

The Lairig Ghru starts at Derry Lodge and the suggested accommodation in the previous note is applicable to this long expedition through the highest pass in the country. If it is taken in the reverse direction from Aviemore, the following note will be applicable.

Cairn Gorm is easily attained from *Glenmore Lodge*, the *Dell* in Rothiemurchus, the Coylumbridge Hotel and from *Aviemore*, but all of them require transport to Coire Cas en route for the peak, which from the top of the chair-lift requires an ascent of only 500 feet to reach the cairn. There are Youth Hostels at Aviemore and Loch Morlich.

The Storr can be reached easily by road from *Portree*, which has ample accommodation in hotels, guest houses and cottages. A car may be parked off the road below this conspicuous eminence, whence grassy slopes rise to the entrance to the Sanctuary. There is a Youth Hostel at Uig.

Quiraing rises to the west of Staffin Bay, and while a bed may be found in one of the scattered cottages in the village, motorists would do better to stay at the *Flodigarry Hotel* some two miles to the north. The easiest approach to these fantastic pinnacles is by a grassy path that goes off to the right, opposite a conspicuous sheepfold, on the wild road that passes over the hills to Uig. There is a Youth Hostel at Uig on the other side of the peninsula.

Sgurr nan Gillean and Bruach na Frithe may be most conveniently climbed from the *Sligachan Hotel* at their base, or from *Sconser*, which is two miles further away from the starting point of both ascents. The Youth Hostel at Broadford is rather distant for these ascents.

The Southern Peaks of the Coolins are best ascended from *Glenbrittle* where accommodation is now very scarce and largely confined to the Memorial Hut and Youth Hostel. But the former is restricted to members of climbing clubs affiliated to the BMC and MCofS, and associated members of both these bodies, and the latter to YHA members only. However, the Campsite, with several caravans for hire, still functions and the adjoining shop is available for supplies of food etc., but Glen Brittle House no longer takes guests. Sligachan is the nearest hotel and that at Sconser is an excellent substitute when it is closed.

Mountain photography

I have already written and lectured extensively on this fascinating branch of photography, and in four of my works devoted to Scotland I included copious notes on the problems involved in securing good camera studies of many of the Bens and Glens. But since these books have been out of print for some years, it may be useful to deal more fully with the subject herein, as I have already done in its companion volumes on the Lakeland and Welsh Peaks, the Peak and Pennines, and in *Climbing with a Camera* which includes the detailed photography of most of the well-known Lakeland Fells. Moreover, I receive innumerable requests for tips from mountaineers who collect my works, and the following summary may provide the desired information and incidentally relieve me of much voluminous correspondence.

1 **The ideal camera for the mountaineer** is undoubtedly the modern miniature owing to its compact form, quick manipulation, great depth of focus, variety of lenses and thirty-six frames on each spool of film. While these instruments are represented in their best and most expensive type by the Leica, Contax, Nikon and Pentax series, it does not follow that the other less costly makes will not give good photographs. Recently I had the opportunity of making a comparative set of colour transparencies with the Leica and a camera that sells retail for about £12, and had I not been critical I should have been satisfied with the latter; for if you require a camera for your own pleasure and merely wish to show the prints or transparencies to your friends, why pay £100 or more for the instrument? In any event, I recommend that you consult your local dealer who will be happy to demonstrate the differences between the various makes and prices.

2 **The lens** is the most important feature, and the best of them naturally facilitate the perfect rendering of the subject. A wide aperture is not essential, because it is seldom necessary to work out of doors at anything greater than F/4.5. It is advisable to use the objective at infinity in mountain photography because overall sharpness is then obtained, and to stop down where required to bring the foreground into focus. It is in this connection that the cheaper camera, which is of course fitted with an inexpensive lens, falls short of its more costly competitors; for the latter are corrected for every known fault and the resulting photographs are then not only acceptable for enlarged reproduction but also yield exhibition prints of superlative quality. Three lenses are desirable in this branch of photography: 1. a 28 mm or 35 mm wide angle; 2. a standard 50 mm which is usually supplied with most cameras; and 3. a 90 mm long focus. These cover every likely requirement: the wide angle is most useful when *on* any mountain or lofty ridge; the 50 mm encompasses the average scene, such as ben and glen; and the long focus is an advantage when the subject is very distant.

An analysis of their use in this vast region is as follows:

Wide Angle	50 per cent
Standard	45 per cent
Long Focus	5 per cent

3 **A lens hood** is an indispensable accessory, because it cuts out adventitious light and increases the brilliance and clarity of the picture. Many climbers have the illusion that this gadget is only required when the sun is shining and that it is used to keep the direct rays out of the lens when facing the light source. While its use is then imperative, they overlook the fact that light is reflected from many points of the hemisphere around the optical axis, and it is the interception of this incidental light that is important.

4 **A filter** is desirable, especially for the good rendering of skyscapes. A pale orange yields the most dramatic results,

providing there are not vast areas of trees in the landscape in which all detail would be lost. It is safer to use a yellow filter, which does not suffer from this defect, and with autumn colours a green filter is very effective. The *exposure factors* do not differ materially, and in view of the wide latitude of modern monochrome film the resulting slight differences in density can be corrected when printing. *For colour work* a skylight filter, formerly known as a Wratten 1A, was useful for reducing the intensity of the blues and for eliminating haze, but from recent experiments with several makes of colour film I have found its use to be no longer necessary owing to improvements in manufacture.

5 **Panchromatic film** is to be preferred for landscapes, and the speed of modern types has been increased substantially, so much so that an ASA rating of up to 125 will yield grainless negatives providing they are processed with the developer that is recommended by the makers.

6 **Exposure and development** are co-related. From May to September with bright sunlight and well distributed clouds, films of the above speed require an average exposure of 1/250th of a second at an aperture of F/8 or 11 with a 2 × yellow filter, processed with a fine-grain developer for eight minutes at a temperature of 68°F. Such negatives should be brilliantly clear and not too contrasty, and they will print on normal paper.

7 **The best time of year** for photography among the Scottish Peaks are the months of April and May. A limpid atmosphere and fine cumulus are then a common occurrence and less time is wasted in waiting for favourable lighting. Moreover, during April many of the higher mountains are dressed in snowy raiment which adds sparkle and glamour and transforms them into peaks of Alpine splendour. Colour work at these times is also satisfactory because the landscape still reveals the reds of the dead bracken, which, however, disappear in June with the

rapid growth of the new fresh green fronds. Nevertheless, the most dramatic colour transparencies are obtained during the last week of October because the newly dead bracken is then a fiery red, the grass has turned to golden yellow, and the longer shadows increase the contrast between ben and glen.

8 **Lack of sharpness** is a problem that causes disappointment to some climbers, and they are often apt to blame the lens when the defect is in fact due to camera shake. It is one thing to hold the instrument steady at ground level with a good stance and no strong wind to disturb the balance, while it is quite another problem in the boisterous breezes on the lofty ridges of Scotland. When these conditions prevail, it is risky to use a lower speed than that indicated above, and maximum stability may be achieved by leaning against a slab of rock or in a terrific gale of wind by even lying down and jamming the elbows into the spaces between the crags. In calm weather a light tripod may be used, but in all other conditions it is too risky to erect one and have it blown over a precipice!

9 **Lighting** is the key to fine mountain photography, and the sun at an angle of 45 degrees, over the left or right shoulder, will yield the required contrasts. These conditions usually appertain in the early morning or the late evening. If possible avoid exposures at midday with the sun overhead when the lighting is flat and uninteresting. Before starting on any climb, study the topography of your mountain so that full advantage can be taken of the lighting. Moreover, never be persuaded to discard your camera when setting out in bad weather, because the atmosphere in the hills is subject to the most sudden and unexpected changes, and sometimes wet mornings develop into fine afternoons, with magnificent clouds and limpid lighting. If your camera is then back in your lodgings, you may live to regret the omission.

10 **The sky** is often the saving feature in mountain photographs since cloudless conditions or a sunless landscape

Plate 2 Skyscape taken with a 90 mm lens

seldom yield a pleasing picture. But to capture a fine cloud formation as well as the subject in the same frame often means sacrificing the foreground. This example of the Storr is typical and should be compared with plate 217 which includes Loch Fada and so misses the drama of the scene.

11 **Haze** is one of the bugbears in this branch of photography, and these conditions are especially prevalent among the Scottish Peaks during July and August. If an opalescent effect is desired, this is the time of year to secure it, but while such camera studies may be favoured by the purist, they seldom appeal to the climber who prefers to see the detail he knows exists in his subjects.

12 **Colour photography** has been simplified in recent years by the introduction of cameras in which both exposure and aperture can be automatically adjusted to light conditions, and in consequence failures are rare. Owing to the narrow latitude of colour film correct exposure is essential if the resulting transparency is to approximate in hue to that of the landscape as seen by the eye. The only certain way to achieve success in all weather conditions is to *use a meter before making each exposure* and to be sure it is pointed at the same angle as the camera. This is most important, because if more sky is included in the meter than in the lens a shorter exposure will be indicated and this will result in an under-exposed transparency in which the colour will be unduly intensified, whereas if the two operations are reversed it will be weakened. Excellent results are obtainable with most makes of colour film, whose speed has been substantially increased in recent years. ASA 10 used to be the standard, whereas today ASA 25, 32, 50, 64 and 100 are in common use. On the basis of ASA 25, an exposure of about 1/125th of a second at an aperture of F/8 in sunlight between 10 a.m. and 4 p.m. in the summer yields superlative transparencies which are viewed to greatest advantage by projection. The correct exposure for other ASA speeds may be readily calculated from a good exposure meter.

The dramatic possibilities of photographing sunsets in colour are worthy of study, and such scenes are enhanced by placing a still or slightly rippling loch in the foreground which captures the colour reflected by water as well as that already appearing in the sky. But meter readings of these subjects are often unreliable and I have found that for films of ASA 25 an exposure of 1/60th of a second at an aperture of F/4.5 gives perfect results.

13 **Design or composition** is the most outstanding feature of a good camera study; that is, one that not only immediately appeals to the eye, but rather one that can be lived with afterwards. Everything I have so far written herein on this subject comes within the scope of *Technique*, and anyone who is prepared to give it adequate study and practice should be able to produce a good negative, and from it a satisfying print.

But to create a picture that far transcends even the best snapshot requires more than this and might well be described as a flair, or if you like a seeing eye that immediately appreciates the artistic merits of a particular mountain scene. And strangely enough those who possess this rare gift usually produce a certain type of picture which is indelibly stamped with their personality; so much so that it is often possible to name the photographer as soon as his work is displayed. And, moreover, while this especial artistic trait may be developed after long application of the basic principles of composition, the fact remains that it is not the camera that really matters, for it is merely a tool, but the person behind the viewfinder, who, when satisfied with the design of his subject, ultimately and quite happily releases the shutter.

To the painter, composition is relatively easy, because he can make it conform to the basic principles of art by moving a tree to one side of his picture, or by completely removing a house from the foreground, or by inducing a stream to flow in another direction, or by accentuating the real subject, if it happens to be a mountain, by moving it or by increasing or decreasing its angles to suit his tastes. A photographer on the other hand has to move himself and his camera here and there in order to get these objects in the right position in his viewfinder. When he moves to one side to improve the position of one of them, another is thrown out of place, or perhaps the lighting is altered. In many cases, therefore, a compromise is the only solution, because if he spends too much time in solving his problem the mood may change, when his opportunity would be lost. It is just this element in mountain photography that brings it into line with sport, and, like golf, it can be both interesting and exasperating. Of course, the critic can sit in a comfortable chair by a warm fire at home and pull a photograph to pieces. He does not, perhaps, realise that the person taking the picture may have been wandering about knee-deep in a slimy bog, or that a bitterly cold wind was sweeping across a lofty ridge and making his teeth chatter, or that the light was failing, or that he had crawled out on a rocky spur with a hundred-foot drop on either side to get his subject properly composed.

Assuming, therefore, both lighting and cloudscape are favourable, what are the essential features of good composition? In the first place, you must select a pleasing object that is accentuated by tonal contrast as the centre of interest; in the second you must place this object in the most attractive position in the frame or picture space; and in the third you must choose a strong and appropriate foreground. Or, in other words, when the weather is favourable the success or failure of your photograph will depend entirely upon the *viewpoint*.

Thus, if your subject happens to be Ben Nevis I may be able to help you with a few hints about four of the illustrations in this book. Climbers generally agree that the northern aspect of this mountain is the finest because its savage cliffs enclosing Coire na Ciste can be seen from this point of the compass, and they are only illuminated on a sunny afternoon or evening. But you must first decide whether you wish to make a picture of the range, including its satellite

Carn Mor Dearg; or a similar scene with special emphasis on
its precipices overhanging the Allt a'Mhuilinn; or of its
immense bulk as seen by the average observer. If the first two
aspects are preferred, the available viewpoints are lacking in
foreground interest other than trees, whereas the third aspect
has several viewpoints with picturesque foregrounds of water
and buildings. Moreover, good camera studies of this aspect
can be made by contra jour lighting early in the day, as well as
by direct illumination in the late afternoon.

All the best viewpoints for this subject are to be found on
the Gairlochy road to the north-east of Banavie, and on the
Glenfinnan road to the west of Corpach as far as Locheilside
Station. Moreover, the former has the advantage of greater
height, by only about 200 feet it is true, but this imparts an
enhanced elevation to the peak and at the same time opens up
views of its precipitous cliffs.

Let us begin with the range itself, whose tonal contrast is
improved by side lighting in the late afternoon or evening;
whose strongest placing is in a horizontal frame, and
completely fills the upper part of the picture space; and whose
foreground is confined to trees, heather or gorse, although an
isolated cottage nearby can be used but its tangle of enclosing
trees rather mar the subject. Plate 3 was taken about five miles
from Banavie and Plate 4 some two miles distant. The former
yields a better conception of the range as a whole, and the
latter of the cliffs characterising the Ben. However, its
immensity is revealed to greater advantage from the shore of
Loch Eil and the most attractive foreground is at Corpach
where the buildings at the entrance to the Caledonian Canal
provide a strong and interesting foreground. Still water in the
loch is to be preferred, as the buildings are then reflected on
its surface as shown in Plate 5, but the same subject shown in
Plate 6, taken on a hazy morning, better captures the
picturesque qualities of the scene.

Finally, whenever you take a photograph of any of the
Scottish Peaks, remember that it will be improved not only by
placing a loch, a burn, a bridge, a figure or a group of

Plate 3 Carn Mor Dearg and the precipitous front of Ben Nevis

Plate 4 Carn Mor Dearg, the Allt a'Mhuilinn and Ben Nevis

Plate 5 Carn Mor Dearg, Ben Nevis and Sgurr a'Mhaim from Corpach

Plate 6 Morning haze and still water at Corpach

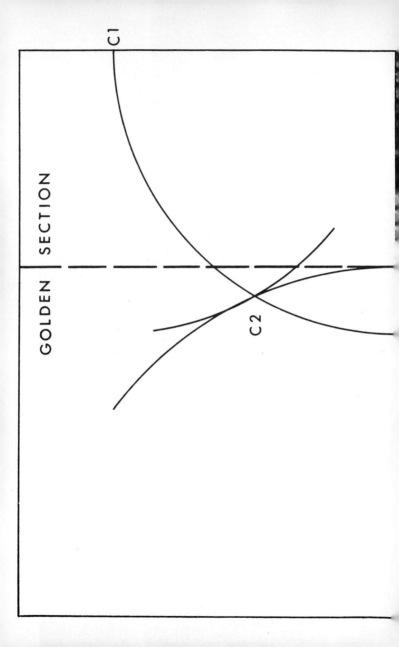

Plate 7 Stac Polly and Loch Lurgain

climbers in the foreground, but also on occasion by introducing a tree or cottage or some object whose size if known will impart both interest and scale to your picture.

Before leaving this interesting question of Design or Composition, it might be helpful to mention two systems that are used for arriving at the strongest placing of the subject in the frame. The favoured picture space measures 2×3, 4×6, 20×30 and so on, or as in the miniature camera 24×36, and when it is divided into thirds the horizontal lines cut the verticals at four points. To obtain a balance that satisfies the eye, the subject, such as a mountain peak, should be placed with its summit on one of the upper points, and an object such as a cairn, a cottage, a tree or a figure on the lower opposite point. This raises a problem when the subject is not well defined, as when a peak does not stand alone but is confused by other adjacent mountains which cannot be excluded from the picture space. In such instances the Design must be left to the photographer who will do his best to strike a balance that pleases the eye. And while it is a simple matter for anyone to guess at the thirds when looking through the viewfinder, the other system favoured by such great artists as El Greco, Leonardo, Raphael and Tintoretto, is much more difficult to position precisely, although as shown by the accompanying drawing and study of Stac Polly, it can be acquired approximately by practice and is acknowledged as the ideal in Design. In fact, placing the subject on the *Golden Section* gives a perfect visual satisfaction to the observer. There is a feeling of balance and order, even excitement in dramatic conditions—the interest is demanded.

The method of finding the approximate *Golden Section* is as follows: draw a frame measuring 4×6 inches and bisect the base line AB at C. With B as the centre and radius BC, draw an arc that intersects the vertical edge at C1. With C1 as the centre and the same radius BC intersect C–C1 at C2. From A with A–C2 as the radius, find the Golden Section where it reaches the base line at GS. This vertical line rising from GS was called the 'Divine Proportion' by no less an artist than

Leonardo, who considered the frame should be so divided in order to communicate most successfully through the eye an arrangement of shapes, dimensions and directions, mass and counter mass, that would solicit, hold and move the attention and interest.

The subject in the example is shown on the right, but is of course equally applicable on the left, and moreover, the same system can be applied to vertical frames, or to the more common whole plate, $8\frac{1}{2} \times 6\frac{1}{2}$ inches, or to exhibition prints measuring 15×12 inches or 20×16 inches.

NOTE In order to adapt the 24×36 negatives to the sizes required in this volume, it has sometimes been necessary to reduce, or even omit, the foreground appearing in the original photographs.

Photography in the different hills

I have often been asked 'What is the best view *of* such and such a mountain?' or 'What is the most striking view *from* so and so?' These are difficult questions, because the answers depend so much upon one's personal tastes, which are influenced in no small degree by atmospheric conditions on any particular occasion. The present volume seems to be a convenient medium for an attempt to offer some guidance on this very debatable question, and while there are doubtless many who will disagree with my opinions, I shall give them for what they are worth. Where possible I have appended references to appropriate examples already portrayed in one or other of my works, as follows:

SL: *Scotland through the Lens*
HH: *Highland Holiday*
NH: *The North Western Highlands*
CC: *A Camera in the Cairngorms*
MS: *The Magic of Skye*
EH: *Escape to the Hills*
SP: *The Scottish Peaks* (the present work)

The number indicates the plate in the particular volume, to which I have added the most suitable time of day (G.M.T.). It should be noted that the examples given were not necessarily taken at the best time or season.

The suggestions are arranged according to the grouping system adopted throughout this work and under two headings: (1) The best pictorial views *of* the range, their dominating peaks or their separate tops; (2) The most striking views *from* the range. After what I have already written herein it will be obvious that foreground interest is of paramount importance since it bears a direct relationship to the pictorial rendering of the subject.

The best pictorial views *of* the range

The Arran Hills
From the Clauchland Hills to the south of Brodick before noon. HH 3; EH 80; SP 8

The Cobbler
From the lower corrie before 11 a.m. HH 34; EH 95; SP 21.

Ben More
From Strath Fillan or Glen Dochart at any time of day. SP 25.

Ben Lui
From Coninish before noon. HH 55; EH 99; SP 26.

Ben Cruachan
From the road on the south side of Loch Awe at any time of day. HH 69; SP 31.

The Blackmount
(*a*) Stob Ghabhar from Loch Tulla before noon. SL 4; SP 40.
(*b*) The range to Meall a'Bhuiridh from Lochan na h'Achlaise before noon. SP 42.
(*c*) Sron na Creise from Kingshouse before 10 a.m. SL 7; EH 106; SP 43.

Buachaille Etive Mor
From Kinghouse in the early morning. EH 107; SP 44.

Bidean nam Bian
(*a*) The range from Aonach Eagach before noon. EH 118; SP 50.
(*b*) Aonach Dubh from Clachaig in the afternoon. SL 13; EH 111; SP 51.

Aonach Eagach
(*a*) From the River Coe opposite Clachaig up to 4 p.m. SL 10 & 11; EH 117; SP 58.

(*b*) From the summit of Aonach Dubh up to 4 p.m. EH 112; SP 59.

Beinn a'Bheithir
From North Ballachulish morning or evening. SL 30; EH 122 & 124; SP 68.

Garbh Bheinn
From Druim an Iubhair before noon. SP 73.

The Mamores
From Glen Nevis in the evening. SL 48, 53, 54 & 56; EH 133; SP 75.

Ben Nevis
(*a*) From Corpach in the evening. SP 5.
(*b*) Coire na Ciste from Carn Mor Dearg before noon. SL 60, 61, 62, 63; EH 136 & 137; SP 83.

The Saddle
From Glen Shiel in the morning. NH 20; SP 87.

The Five Sisters of Kintail
(*a*) From Mam Rattachan in the afternoon. NH 25; SP 89.
(*b*) From Loch Duich in the afternoon. NH 24.

The Applecross Hills
(*a*) From Loch Carron at any time of day. NH 49.
(*b*) From Loch Kishorn in the morning. NH 43; SP 93.
(*c*) The Corries from Kishorn Lodge in the morning. NH 45; SP 95.

Beinn Damh
(*a*) From Lochan an Loin at any time of day. SP 100.
(*b*) From the Diabaig Road in the early evening. SP 101.

Liathach
(*a*) From Loch Clair in the morning. NH 51, 54; SP 1 & 106.
(*b*) From Beinn Alligin in the afternoon. NH 66; SP 117.
(*c*) From the New Road at any time of day.

Beinn Alligin
From the southern side of Upper Loch Torridon in the morning. NH 64; SP 113.

Beinn Eighe
(*a*) From Kinlochewe up to noon. NH 52; SP 119.
(*b*) From Loch Coulin at any time of day. NH 53; SP 120.

Slioch
From Loch Maree at any time of day. NH 69; SP 125.

An Teallach
From the Road of Destitution up to noon. NH 72; SP 126.

Ben More Coigach
(*a*) From Ardmair Bay up to 4 p.m. NH 81; SP 131.
(*b*) Sgurr an Fhidhleir from Lochan Tuath in the morning. NH 86; SP 132.

Cul Beag
From Loch Lurgain in the afternoon. NH 84; SP 137.

Cul Mor
(*a*) From Stac Polly at any time of day. NH 90; SP 139.
(*b*) From Ledmore in the morning. SP 140.

Stac Polly
(*a*) From the eastern end of Loch Lurgain in the morning. SP 7.
(*b*) From the lower southern slopes of the peak in the late afternoon. NH 85; SP 146.

Suilven
(*a*) From Elphin at any time of day. NH 97; SP 154.
(*b*) From the northern shore of Loch Inver in the late afternoon. NH 105; SP 155.

Quinag
(*a*) From the head of Loch Assynt up to noon. NH 102; SP 165.
(*b*) From the foot of Loch Assynt in the afternoon. NH 103; SP 166.
(*c*) From Loch Cairnbawn, opposite Kylesku, in the late afternoon. NH 117; SP 168.

Foinaven
(*a*) From a small lochan near Rhiconich at any time of day.
(*b*) From above Loch Laxford at any time of day. SP 176.

Ben Hope
From near Hope Lodge in the late afternoon. SP 183.

Ben Loyal
From Lochan Hacoin in the afternoon. NH 127; SP 184.

Lochnagar
(*a*) From the Spittal of Glen Muick at any time of day. CC 4; SP 186.
(*b*) From the Old Bridge of Dee at Invercauld in the afternoon. CC 21; SP 187.
(*c*) The Corrie from Meikle Pap before noon. CC 8.

Ben Macdhui
From Black Bridge at any time of day. CC. 30; SP 192.

The Lairig Ghru
From opposite the Devil's Point at any time of day. CC 54; SP 205.

Cairn Gorm
From the northern shore of Loch Morlich in the late afternoon. CC 74; SP 210.

The Storr
From Loch Fada in the morning. MS 8; SP 217.

Quiraing
From the Prison up to noon. MS 37; SP 221.

Sgurr nan Gillean
(a) From Sligachan up to 11 a.m. MS 116 & 134; SP 228.
(b) From the South East Ridge up to 4 p.m. MS 118 & 119; SP 230.
(c) The Pinnacle Ridge from Sgurr a 'Bhasteir between 3 and 4 p.m. MS 126 & 127; SP 237.

Bruach na Frithe
From Sgurr Bhairnich in the afternoon. MS 109; SP 234.

Sgurr Dearg
(a) From Eas Mor in the morning. MS 88; SP 241.
(b) From Sgurr Sgumain or Sgurr Alasdair in the afternoon. MS 87.

Sgurr Alasdair
(a) From Sgurr nan Eag up to 2 p.m. MS 81; SP 245.
(b) From Sgurr Dearg in the late afternoon. MS 91; SP 244.

The most striking views *from* the range
The Arran Hills
Cir Mhor, the Peak of the Castles and the Carlin's Leap from North Goat Fell up to 3 p.m. HH 16; EH 84; SP 20.

The Cobbler
The Last Overhang from the ridge in the afternoon. HH 35; EH 94; SP 22.

Ben Cruachan
(*a*) The Panorama to the North at any time of day.
(*b*) The Summit Ridge from Drochaid Glas at any time of day. HH 96 & 97; SP 38.

Buachaille Etive Mor
The vast expanse of Rannoch Moor and Shiehallion in the afternoon.

Bidean nam Bian
(*a*) Stob Coire nan Lochan from Aonach Dubh before 11 a.m. SL 14. SP 52.
(*b*) Lochaber from Stob Coire nan Lochan at any time of day. SL 21; SP 53.
(*c*) Aonach Eagach from Aonach Dubh up to 4 p.m. EH 112; SP 59.

Aonach Eagach
(*a*) Bidean nam Bian before noon. EH 118; SP 50.
(*b*) Glencoe and Loch Achtriochtan from Am Bodach before 11 a.m SL 25; SP 61.

Beinn a'Bheithir
Sgorr Dhearg from Sgorr Bhan before noon. SL 33; EH 125 & 126; SP 69.

The Mamores
(*a*) Am Bodach from Sgurr a'Mhaim before noon. SL 41; SP 77.
(*b*) The Devil's Ridge from Sgurr a'Mhaim before noon. SL 42; SP 76.
(*c*) Stob Ban from Sgurr a'Mhaim before noon. SL 47; SP 78.
(*d*) Stob Ban from the Devil's Ridge before noon. EH 128.

Ben Nevis
(*a*) The vast panorama in all directions.
(*b*) The Tower Ridge from the plateau in the afternoon. SL 73; EH 143; SP 85.

The Five Sisters of Kintail
(a) Sgurr na Ciste Duibhe from Sgurr nan Spainteach before 11 a.m. NH 34; SP 90.
(b) Ben Nevis and the intervening ridges from Sgurr Fhuaran in the afternoon. SP 91.

The Applecross Hills
(a) Skye from the Bealach na Ba in the morning.
(b) Torridon, Ben Damph and Coulin Forests from Beinn Bhan in the afternoon.
(c) Coire na Poite from the Ridge. SP 97.

Beinn Damh
(a) The sea and Torridon Peaks at any time of day.
(b) The peaks of Ben Damph and Coulin Forests.

Liathach
The summit ridge from Spidean a'Choire Leith at any time of day. NH 62 & 63; SP 109 & 110.

Beinn Alligin
The Peaks from Coir an Laoigh. SP 114.

Beinn Eighe
(a) The summit ridge from Sgurr an Fhir Duibhe up to 3 p.m. NH 59; SP 123.
(b) Coire Mhic Fhearchair after 7 p.m. NH 60; SP 124.

Slioch
The northern panorama at any time of day.

An Teallach
(a) The pinnacle ridge from Bidean a'Ghlas Thuill up to noon. NH 71; SP 127.
(b) Beinn Dearg Mhor from Corrag Bhuidhe up to noon. SP 129
(c) Toll an Lochain up to 11 a.m. NH 74; SP 130.

Ben More Coigach
Stac Polly from Sgurr an Fhidhleir at any time of day. NH 87; SP 133.

Cul Beag
Stac Polly up to noon. SP 138.

Cul Mor
Suilven at any time of day. NH 94; SP 143.

Stac Polly
(*a*) Suilven at any time of day. NH 89; SP 151.
(*b*) Cul Mor at any time of day. NH 90; SP 139.
(*c*) Cul Beag, Loch Lurgain and the Pinnacles in the afternoon. NH 91.
(*d*) Ben More Coigach and Beinn Eun in the late afternoon. NH 77.

Suilven
Meall Mheadhonach from Caisteal Liath at any time of day. NH 109; SP 163.

Quinag
The head of Loch Assynt from Spidean Coinich in the afternoon. NH 111. SP 170.

Foinaven
The eroded central spur of A'Cheir Ghorm, backed by Ben Hope after 2 p.m. SP 179.

Lochnagar
(*a*) The vast panorama of the Cairngorms beyond Deeside at any time of day.
(*b*) The Corrie from Meikle Pap up to noon.

Ben Macdhui
(*a*) Cairn Toul from Sron Riach before noon. CC 34; SP 201.
(*b*) The ridge and corries from Cairn Toul to Braeriach before noon. CC 39 & 40; SP 197 & 198.

Cairn Gorm
The view of Loch Morlich and Glenmore Forest at any time of day.

The Storr
The mainland peaks and the Old Man from the summit ridge up to 4 p.m. MS 22; SP 219.

Quiraing
The sea and Trotternish ridges from the Table in the afternoon. MS 38, 43 & 44; SP 224.

Sgurr nan Gillean
(*a*) Blaven and Glen Sligachan in the afternoon. MS 121.
(*b*) Looking down the Western Ridge in the afternoon.
MS 122; SP 232.

Bruach na Frithe
The Three Bends in the Main Ridge in the late afternoon.
MS 114; SP 235.

Sgurr Dearg
Sgurr Alasdair in the late afternoon. MS 91; SP 244.

Sgurr Alasdair
(*a*) The Dubhs in the late afternoon. MS 71.
(*b*) The Main Ridge from Sgurr Dearg to Sgurr nan Gillean at any time of day. MS 70.
(*c*) The Thearlaich-Dubh Gap from Sgumain in the afternoon. MS 85.

Notes on the Routes

I have arranged the Scottish Peaks from south to north for the sake of convenience and easy reference. They commence with the Arran Hills, and then continue from the Cobbler to Ben Loyal in the far north of the mainland. The Cairngorms follow and the work terminates with Trotternish and the Coolins in the Isle of Skye.

Ascents. When there is more than one route to the dominating peak in a group of hills, I have described the most popular one first, followed by the alternatives, in which case the reversal of one of them could be used for the *Descent*.

The Panorama from the reigning peak in each group is always noted at the termination of its first ascent. But many of the routes involve the traverse of subsidiary tops and the conspicuous features revealed from them are mentioned in passing, despite the fact that there may be a similarity in the views when they are near together. Climbers will notice that in many parts of Scotland the panoramas do not clearly disclose any individual peaks, save those near at hand, and this is accounted for by the peculiar geological origin of the Highlands. For although this part of the mainland is usually considered to be a mountainous country, it is in fact the remnant of a dissected plateau having a general fall to the east. This strange feature can be observed from the summits of Ben Nevis and Bidean nam Bian, and is well illustrated by plate 91 taken from the summit of Sgurr Fhuaran, when it will be noticed that the panorama spread out at one's feet consists of ridge upon ridge and peak after peak, all of which rise to a general level above the intervening straths and glens, dominated however in the far distance by the bold summit of Ben Nevis. In general such a panorama is best appreciated in clear weather, but if the mountaineer is fortunate enough to stand by the summit cairn of one of these hills when the valleys are hidden by mist and the tops of the ridges and peaks only protrude from the protecting shroud, then the origin of the Highlands is more clearly revealed; for if the valleys were filled in, a large tableland would appear sloping gently from west to east.

Traverses. Several of the ranges in Scotland are so immense that in some of them it is an advantage to traverse all the peaks in one expedition; as in that of the Five Sisters of Kintail where the ascent is made at one end of the chain and the descent at the other, even though it is possible but more arduous to climb Sgurr Fhuaran direct from Glen Shiel.

Distances and times

These questions always involve a certain amount of speculation in mountaineering and I have purposely omitted any detailed reference to them in this work. *The Distances* may be calculated approximately from the maps, which are about one inch to the mile, but it should be remembered that a map mile may in fact be considerably more than that owing to the undulating nature of the ground. *The Times* depend not only upon the pace and rhythm of each climber, but also upon the topography of the mountain as well as weather conditions. The best way to calculate them is to use the formula of Naismith, which allows one hour for each three map miles, plus half an hour for every 1,000 feet of ascent. This is fairly accurate for ordinary hill walking under favourable conditions, and while it includes reasonable halts for food and for viewing the grandeur of the mountain scene, it does not allow for bad weather, snow, rock climbing or photography, since the latter often involves much delay in finding the most effective foreground for any particular picture and for awaiting favourable lighting.

To make the application of this system clear, I will illustrate it by calculating the distance and time required for the long traverse of the Five Sisters of Kintail, which is described and portrayed herein, on the assumption that transport has been used in Glen Shiel to reach the point on the road immediately below the Bealach an Lapain which is the best starting point on this lofty ridge.

It is seven map miles from Glen Shiel over the Five Sisters to Loch Duich, and according to the above formula will take about two and a half hours. Since the starting point on the road is at a height of 558 feet, this must be subtracted from the altitude of the Bealach an Lapain, 2,371 feet = 1,813 feet, whence there is a rise of 758 feet to Sgurr nan Spainteach = 2,571 feet. There is another rise of 457 feet from the next bealach to Sgurr na Ciste Duibhe = 3,028 feet; 487 feet from the next to Sgurr na Carnach = 3,515 feet; 649 feet from the next to Sgurr Fhuaran = 4,164 feet; 274 feet from the next to Sgurr nan Saighead = 4,438 feet; and finally 442 feet from the last bealach to Sgurr na Moraich = 4,880 feet in all. According to the above formula this adds about another two and a half hours, thus allowing five hours for the complete traverse in favourable weather. However, as no account has been taken of halts for viewing the scenery from the six tops, or for food, or for snow climbing, or for photography, at least one hour should be added, making six hours a good time for a fit and strong pedestrian. In fact, the last time I did it I was alone, when the snow on the rocky summits slowed me down and I spent a lot of time on photography. I left the Kintail Lodge Hotel by car at 9 a.m. and got back at 5 p.m.—thus taking eight hours in all and the weather was perfect. The descents from all peaks total 5,438 feet, which added to 4,880 feet of ascent, makes a grand up and down aggregate of 10,318 feet! Readers who have "walked" over the Snowdon Horseshoe will find the five graceful Sisters a much tougher proposition.

Route finding in mist

In these not uncommon conditions it is imperative to know with certainty your exact location on the map when mist comes down to engulf you in gloom and to immediately note the direction to be taken. If you are on a well-cairned track no difficulties should be encountered, but when this is not the case you must estimate the distance to the next known point and set a course accurately by using your companion as a sighting mark. Keep him in view ahead while frequently referring to the compass and use your aneroid to check the rise and fall in the ground. If you are familiar with the gradient this will help to control your direction, but take nothing for granted; always trust the compass excepting when among magnetic rocks, basaltic and gabbro formation such as exist in the Coolins of Skye, and pay no attention whatsoever to gratuitous advice as to the direction from compassless companions. Avoid contouring a slope; if you do this, you will no longer be master of your direction. It is always advisable to go straight down and never diverge from a supposed obstacle, because mist exaggerates both size and distance.

Should you be in the unhappy position of having no compass but *are familiar with the terrain* work your way down slowly over grass but never enter a ravine or gully or endeavour to descend a series of steep crags, whereas if you are on a ridge keep to its declining crest and if it forks make sure you take the known branch. If, on the other hand, you are alone on an uncairned track and also unfamiliar with the ground, stay put until the mist clears sufficiently for you to find your way. In these conditions you are in a very dangerous situation, because mist sometimes persists for days in mountainous country. It is much better to practice map and compass reading in clear weather so that in mist you will have a reasonable chance of finding your way to safety.

Accident procedure

Distress signal. *Six* long flashes or *six* long blasts of a whistle in quick succession followed by a pause of one minute. This is repeated again and again until assistance is forthcoming. **The reply** to this signal is in similar vein; that is *three* flashes or blasts of a whistle followed by a pause of one minute, repeated again and again.

The Mountain Rescue Committee maintain Mountain Rescue Posts in all mountainous areas in Scotland. All venturing on Scottish Hills are advised to purchase the official handbook issued by the above committee annually and make themselves acquainted with the location of the nearest Rescue Post in the area where they are climbing. This is especially essential to leaders of school and youth parties.

Brocken Spectres

These remarkable phenomena are usually confined to hill country, and in consequence may, with luck, be observed by any climber on the Scottish Peaks, especially if he happens to be on a lofty ridge enclosing a corrie filled with mist. They appear as gigantic shadows on the surface of the mist and were first observed on the Brocken in Germany, hence the name, but are said to be an optical illusion because the shadow is quite close and of actual size. It is usually only possible for each climber to see his own spectre.

Glories

These appear as a coloured ring round the shadow cast by the climber on the mist in similar circumstances. Each member of a climbing party can see only his own glory. Readers who have flown in an aeroplane will have often seen the shadow of the plane ringed by a variegated circle on the clouds beneath them.

The Arran Hills

Goat Fell	2,866 feet	874 metres
Caisteal Abhail	2,817 feet	859 metres
Beinn Tarsuinn	2,706 feet	825 metres
Mullach Buidhe (Goat Fell)	2,687 feet	819 metres
North Goat Fell	2,659 feet	810 metres
Cir Mhor	2,618 feet	797 metres
Beinn Nuis	2,597 feet	792 metres
Mullach Buidhe	2,368 feet	722 metres
Beinn Bharrain	2,345 feet	715 metres
A'Chir	2,335 feet	712 metres
Beinn Bhreac	2,333 feet	711 metres
Ceum na Caillich	2,300 feet	701 metres
Bealach an Fhir-Bhogha	2,250 feet	685 metres
Beinn a'Chliabhain	2,217 feet	676 metres
Am Binnein	2,172 feet	662 metres
Coich na h'Oighe	2,168 feet	661 metres
Suidhe Fhearghas	2,081 feet	634 metres
Meall Breac	1,900 feet	579 metres
Meall nan Damh	1,870 feet	570 metres
The Saddle	1,413 feet	430 metres

The island of Arran lies in the Firth of Clyde and is almost kidney-shaped; its longer north-south axis covers some twenty miles, while it is ten miles across from east to west. A road follows the coast round the island and is about fifty-six miles in length. The magnetic charm of Arran is concentrated in its splendid hills which occupy the northern half of the island and are easily accessible from the roads in the vicinity of Brodick and Corrie, a village lying about six miles to the north. Large expanses of heather-clad moorland occupy the main part of the southern half of the island, with here and there farmlands at the lower levels. The coast-line is charming and Brodick

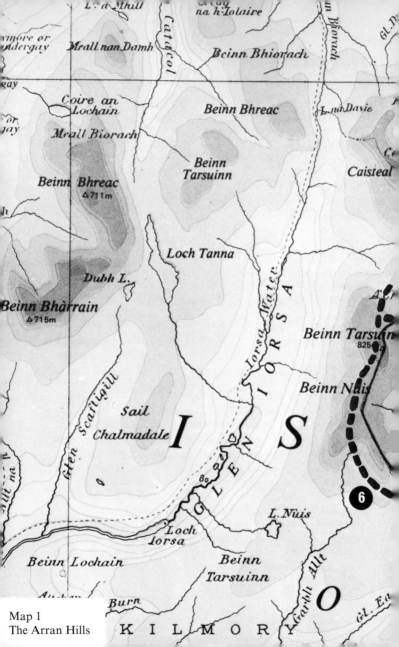

Map 1
The Arran Hills

Bay, with its lovely sweep of sands backed by forests of Larch and Spruce and dominated by the peak of Goat Fell, provides a picture of exquisite beauty.

Nevertheless, the finest profile of the peaks clustered about Goat Fell is obtained from the Clauchland Hills which rise to the south of Brodick. The graceful lines of their grey granite, joined by the serrated intervening ridges, make an attractive skyline at any time of day, but when they are silhouetted against the sunset glow of evening, these magical lights impart a mysterious quality of atmosphere and purple majesty which is only equalled by the Coolins in Skye. These enchanting hills present a picture of inaccessibility when seen from afar, but with the exception of A'Chir and the Carlin's Leap they have no great difficulties for the climber. In fact any fit person can walk over them with ease, but if the crests of the ridges are strictly adhered to, there are places where the granite pinnacles require the use of the hands to pass them in safety. Possibly their finest asset is the proximity of the sea, which can be observed from them in almost all directions.

The Arran Hills are composed mainly of granite which has been forced upwards through beds of sandstone and slate. Great whin dykes are a notable feature and are conspicuous on A'Chir, where they form the gullies and chimneys splitting the face of the granite masses. The fantastic pinnacles crowning the ridges and the amazing Cyclopean walls supporting them are also a remarkable feature. Perhaps the most striking example of erosion is to be seen on the pinnacled ridge rising from the Saddle to North Goat Fell, where disintegration is so far advanced that the granite forms vast areas of rough golden sand, much of which is washed down the burns descending from each side into the valleys beneath.

The topography of the Arran Hills is very simple. there are roughly three ridges, each running approximately north–south and separated by well-defined glens. The most westerly is the Beinn Bharrain—Meall nan Damh group, with Mullach Buidhe reaching an altitude of 2,368 feet. Then comes Glen

Plate 8 The Arran Hills seen from above Brodick Bay

Iorsa between these hills and the Central Ridge, which stretches from Beinn Nuis to Suidhe Fhearghas, with Caisteal Abhail as the highest summit, rising to 2,817 feet above sea level. Glens Rosa and Sannox separate this group from the Goat Fell Massif, which dominates the island at 2,866 feet.

Route 1. Brodick and Goat Fell. Leave by the Corrie road which skirts the bay and golf course. After passing the Standing Stone take the path on R which crosses the stream to rejoin the road, whence, beyond the Home Farm and before reaching Brodick Castle, turn L up the road that rises through the trees. On reaching the open moorland, follow the path that winds along beside the Cnocan Burn and then rises across the boulder-strewn ground to Meall Breac, the eastern shoulder of Goat Fell. On attaining the ridge bear L and keep to the path which leads to the summit of the island's reigning peak. If you are thirsty after the ascent, you will find pools of water in the hollows of the rock.

On a clear day the panorama from Goat Fell is one of the most entrancing in all Scotland. It is a marvellous combination of fantastic mountain scenery so near, sunlit seas far below, and the isles away to the west that makes this prospect so unique. To the east lie the glimmering waters of the Firth of Clyde in which seemingly float the Cumbraes near the mainland, backed by the low hills of Renfrew. To the south-east the eye skims across the surface of Brodick Bay to rest finally upon Holy Island in Lamlash Bay. To the south the rocky cone of Ailsa Craig is a conspicuous object some twenty-six miles distant. To the south-west rise the Beinn Nuis-Beinn Tarsuinn ridges with the lower summit of Beinn a'Chliabhain intervening and the floor of Glen Rosa over 2,000 feet below. To the west stands the ridge of A'Chir and to the north-west the colossal obelisk of Cir Mhor with the Saddle at its feet. Swinging round to the north are the Peak of the Castles, the Carlin's Leap and Suidhe Fhearghas which enclose Glen Sannox, while nearer at hand runs the ridge of the Goat Fell Massif. Those who wish to pick out more

Plate 9 **Route 1**—Holy Island, Lamlash and Brodick Bays from Goat Fell

distant landmarks should study the Mountain View Indicator nearby.

Now walk due north along the crest of the ridge and if you do not wish to traverse the pinnacles take the sheep tracks round them. On reaching North Goat Fell note the magnificent prospect of the Caisteal Abhail group on the L, and just before attaining Mullach Buidhe examine the gigantic Cyclopean buttress on the L, perhaps the most remarkable on the island. Then continue to the end of the ridge and look down on Coich na h'Oighe which is very narrow and whose cliffs on the R flank the famous Punch Bowl. Unless you are an experienced mountaineer do not attempt to traverse this ridge and descend into Glen Sannox as it is at all times a dangerous venture.

Cir Mhor → Caisteal Abhail →

Plate 10 **Route 1** — A pinnacle on the Goat Fell Ridge

Plate 11   **Route 1** —Cyclopean Buttress overhanging Glen Sannox

Plate 12 **Route 1**—Coich na h'Oighe and the Punch Bowl on the right

Route 2. Corrie and Goat Fell. Walk south along the road to Brodick until you come to the Corrie Burn. Turn R on to the open moor and follow it into the mouth of the Corrie. Then bear L up the slopes of Meall Breac, where join Route 1 to the summit of Goat Fell.

Route 3. Glen Rosa, the Saddle and Goat Fell. Leave the String road near the Auld Kirk and pass the many charming cottages in the lane which ends at the farm standing at the well-wooded entrance to Glen Shant. Walk beside the Rosa Burn with the sharp peak of Beinn Nuis ahead, and when the glen bears R note the ridge of Beinn a'Chliabhain on the skyline, with a glimpse of A'Chir over its R shoulder. A grass-covered terminal moraine is soon encountered, above which on R appears the well-known Pinnacle which has been climbed and is about 40 feet high. A little further along Glen Rosa turns sharply to the north and is dominated by Cir Mhor which stands in splendid isolation at its head. Hereabouts a path goes off to the L to give easy access to the Beinn Nuis Ridge. Now cross a wooden bridge over the turbulent Garbh Allt, a torrential stream coming from this direction, and then continue ahead beside the burn over considerable stretches of boggy ground. On reaching the last tree in the glen, which overhangs a pretty cascade, pause for a moment to admire the fine prospect of Cir Mhor with the Carlin's Leap on R beyond the Saddle. Thence the barren glen is a scene of sombre desolation, but you must plod on bravely until you attain the Saddle, whence bear R and climb the shattered and pinnacled ridge to North Goat Fell. Here you turn R and follow the ridge to the reigning peak.

Plate 13 **Route 3**—Looking up Glen Rosa to Cir Mhor and Ceum na Caillich

Route 4. Glen Sannox, the Saddle and Goat Fell. Leave the coast road at Sannox Bay and walk along the cart track beside the golf course and cemetery until you reach the Barytes mine. Here you are confronted by a wilderness of bog and tangled heather through which you must make your way as best you can, following the burn almost to its source. Ahead rises the magnificent pyramid of Cir Mhor, flanked by 1,200 feet of precipitous cliffs that are riven by gullies, ridges, caves and pinnacles, all of which are the treasured playground of the rock climber, and the finest on the island. To the L of them reposes the Saddle, and on approaching it you must exercise care while you climb until you reach a conspicuous whin dyke which is the key to your route and terminates on its R crest. Now turn L and follow Route 3 to Goat Fell.

Route 5. Beinn a'Chliabhain and Caisteal Abhail. Follow Route 3 to the fork in the Glen Rosa path, and take the L branch which gives access to the south ridge of your first peak. Its ascent is easy and the steep gradient continuous, but on attaining its narrow, wall-like crest you will find it paved with immense flat slabs, akin to a lofty flagstone pavement, which is flanked here and there with granite pinnacles between which on R you will obtain a dynamic prospect of North Goat Fell. On the L there are revealing views across Coire Bhradain of both Beinn Nuis and Beinn Tarsuinn. Now walk down to the col, with close views ahead across Coire Daingean of the great whin dykes splitting the eastern flanks of A'Chir. Then turn R and keep to the track low down on its Iorsa side, which presents a formidable appearance of the great overlapping granite slabs overhead. Continue ahead until you reach the col below Cir Mhor.

A party of experienced climbers may prefer to traverse the sharp ridge of A'Chir, which is the most entertaining scramble on the Arran Hills. It is attained by a scree gully on R running up to the skyline which consists of unbroken towers and massive walls of granite. Beyond its summit there is a sharp and difficult descent to the famous *mauvais pas* which displays

Suidhe Fhearghas

Caisteal Abhail

Cir Mhor

Plate 14 **Route 4**—A hazy morning in Glen Sannox

a definite hiatus in the ridge. Its traverse requires a steady head owing to the precipices on each side, whence the going is easier all the way to the aforementioned col.

Now, walk up the easy slopes to the summit of Cir Mhor, noting on R the Rosa Pinnacle with its superb granite slabs. Pause for a moment to admire the vistas along both Glen Rosa and Glen Sannox, and then retrace your steps and turn north for the summit of the Peak of the Castles, passing en route a cairn that marks a spring of ice-cold water.

The splendour of the panorama from Caisteal Abhail has to be seen on a clear day to be believed. The first object to catch the eye is the tapering peak of Cir Mhor which is one of the most impressive spectacles on the island. To the south-east there is a grand prospect of the Goat Fell Massif terminating with Coich na h'Oighe; to the south you look back to A'Chir and the Beinn Tarsuinn group; to the west across Glen Iorsa and its western ridges the eye skims across the glimmering sea to its islands; while to the north-east your gaze is held by the ridge to Suidhe Fhearghas and the gloomy stretches of Glen Sannox, to rest finally upon the familiar Firth of Clyde and the more distant mainland.

Plate 15 **Route 5**—North Goat Fell from Beinn a'Chliabhain

Beinn Nuis →   Beinn Tarsuinn →

B.a'Chliabhain ↓

Plate 16 Beinn 5 and 6 seen from the summit of Goat Fell

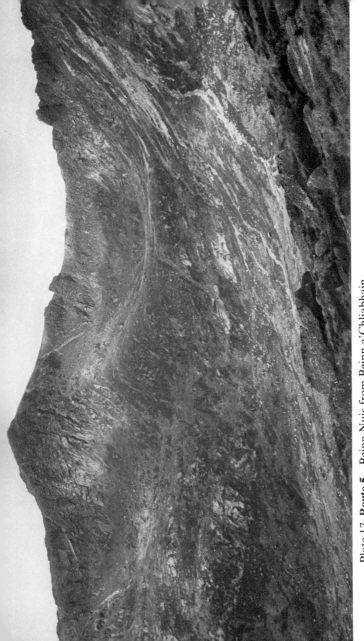

Plate 17 **Route 5**— Beinn Nuis from Beinn a'Chliabhain

PLATE 10. Beinn Torran from Beinn a'Chliabhain

Plate 19 **Route 5**—The granite walls and Whin Dykes of a'Chir

Route 6. Beinn Nuis and Caisteal Abhail. Follow Route 5 to the fork and take the L branch, whence ascend the L bank of the Garbh Allt. Cross the moor ahead to the south-east shoulder of Beinn Nuis and continue the tramp to its summit. Observe on R the 500 feet of precipices, split by gullies, all of which are the resort of the keen rock climber. Then, after delighting in the spacious views, skirt the cliffs and stroll along the grassy, moss-covered ridge to Beinn Tarsuinn, which also unfolds grand prospects of hill and sea. Thereafter descend to the Bealach an Fhir-Bhogha and bear R to pick up Route 5 for Caisteal Abhail.

Route 7. Suidhe Fhearghas and Caisteal Abhail. Your first peak is a prominent landmark when seen from Sannox Bay, and to attain it you must make your way across the moor in a westerly direction. Flanked with crags, its crest presents no difficulties and you continue south-westwards along the lofty ridge for Ceum na Caillich. Unless you are an experienced climber do not attempt the direct descent of its 150 feet of granite slabs to the col, but on approaching the peak descend slightly on its North Sannox slopes and traverse round ledges of rock and turf to reach the 15-foot wide saddle. Thence, leaving behind the Carlin's Leap, climb steadily up the broadening ridge to the Peak of the Castles.

Climbers will observe that some of the above Routes may be combined to make a long and invigorating tramp. Nos. 6 and 7 afford the finest traverse in Arran, and photographers should walk from south to north, to take full advantage of the lighting. Interested readers will find further details and photographs in the author's *Highland Holiday*.

Ceum na Caillich →

Plate 20 Terminal sections of **Routes 5, 6** and **7** seen across the Saddle from North Goat Fell

Ben Arthur

The Cobbler   2,891 feet   881 metres

This conspicuous mountain rises to the north-west of Loch
Long, from the head of which the well-known road over Rest
and Be Thankful passes below it and through Glen Croe to
Loch Fyne. It is inferior in height to its neighbour, Ben Ime,
but its weird, serrated profile at once stamps it as the most
striking peak in the Southern Highlands. Known familiarly as
the **Cobbler**, it is well seen from the railway in the vicinity of
Arrochar, from which station it is readily accessible. And
while this mountain has a great attraction for the hill walker,
it is chiefly of interest as a rock climbing venue within easy
reach of Glasgow. It displays three separate and well defined
tops, of which the central peak only is properly called the
Cobbler. That to the south of it is affectionately known as
Jean or the Cobbler's Wife, while that to the north, with its
spectacular overhangs, is the Cobbler's Last. And strange as it
may seem, the latter is the only top that can be easily attained
by the pedestrian; for the other two require some experience
in rock climbing if their summits are to be reached in safety.

Route 8. From Arrochar. Leave the station by the road round
the head of Loch Long, and after crossing the bridge spanning
the turbulent waters of the river flowing down Glen Loin,
take the road on the R for Succoth. Now cross a stile opposite
the farm and attain the Forestry Road above it by another
stile. Turn L and after a few hundred yards turn R up a track
formed partly of concrete slabs; this leads uphill to a level
path that gives direct access to the Allt a'Bhalachain, or
Buttermilk Burn. Now keep to its L bank until you reach a
collection of large boulders on the slopes of Narnain, whence
cross the main stream and follow its tributary on the L that

The Cobbler →　→

Plate 21　**Route 8**—The Cobbler seen from the approach to the Upper Corrie

Map 2
Ben Arthur

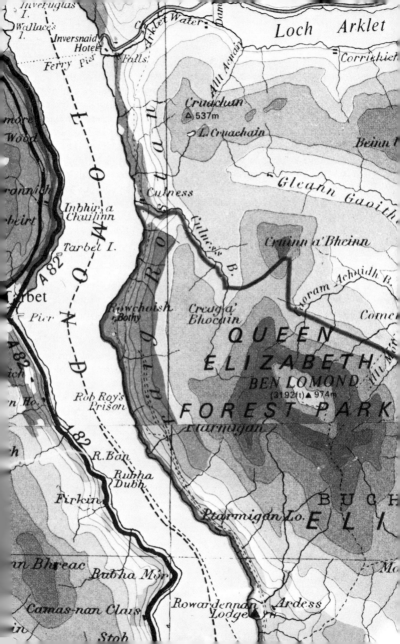

descends from the main corrie, whence a rough path leads steeply to the immense depression between the north and centre peaks. There are two variations to this route, one at the start and the other at the finish. The former begins on the west side of the Buttermilk Burn at the point where it enters Loch Long, but as the path is very muddy it is seldom used nowadays. The latter follows the main stream from the Narnain Boulders as far as its source in a small lochan, whence the track turns sharp L and climbs to the north peak, from which the ridge may be followed to the summit tower. On a clear day the panorama from the Cobbler is very fine and includes all the surrounding hills, but the most striking landmark is Ben Lomond whose shapely lines appeal to the eye and dominate the intervening blue of Loch Lomond.

Route 9. From Glen Croe. Leave the road beyond the plantations and climb the L bank of the stream, and eventually its R tributary which has its source beneath the crest of Ben Arthur. This ascent is steep but not difficult, and since it is lacking in interest it is seldom used.

Route 10. From Upper Inveruglas. This is the longest and most picturesque approach to the Cobbler. Follow the new road to a point beyond Coiregrogain and turn L by the Burn of the same name. Climb beside it to its source on the col between Ben Ime and Narnain, whence make for the North Peak by joining Route 8 near the lochan.

Plate 22 Spectacular overhangs of the North Peak

Plate 23 Centre Peak of the Cobbler

Plate 24 The South Peak

Ben More Group

Ben More	3,843 feet	1,171 metres
Stobinian (Am Binnein)	3,827 feet	1,166 metres
Stob Coire an Lochain	3,497 feet	1,066 metres
Meall na Dige	3,140 feet	951 metres
Stob Creagach	2,966 feet	904 metres
Meall Monachyle	2,123 feet	641 metres
Caisteal Corrach	1,997 feet	603 metres

This beautifully shaped mountain is a conspicuous landmark throughout the length of Glen Dochart and Strath Fillan, and together with its equally graceful neighbour, Stobinian, affords one of the easiest ascents in Perthshire, providing always the atmosphere is clear and it is not snowbound. It is the highest peak in Britain south of Strathtay and in consequence discloses a stupendous panorama on a clear day.

Route 11. Ben More from Benmore Farm. This is the most favoured starting point for the ascent as it is only two miles from Crianlarich. However, do NOT go through the farm but walk east along the road until you reach a stile on the R. Cross it and follow the waymarked route: climbers coming from Luib leave the road some three miles further to the east. The 3,300 feet of steep, grassy slopes have a foreshortened aspect and as a result the climb seems endless. And aside from the shallow "corrie", which is passed on the R, there are no features to rivet the eye until the summit cairns are attained, when the rewarding panorama bursts upon the view.

Owing to the dominating altitude of Ben More the prospect is extensive, and on a clear day the Cairngorms can be seen far away to the north-east. The southern arc is impressive, as both Edinburgh and Glasgow can be picked out, while to the west Rhum and Jura can be distinguished on the glistening sea.

Plate 25 **Routes 11** to **13**—Ben More and Stobinian from Strath Fillan

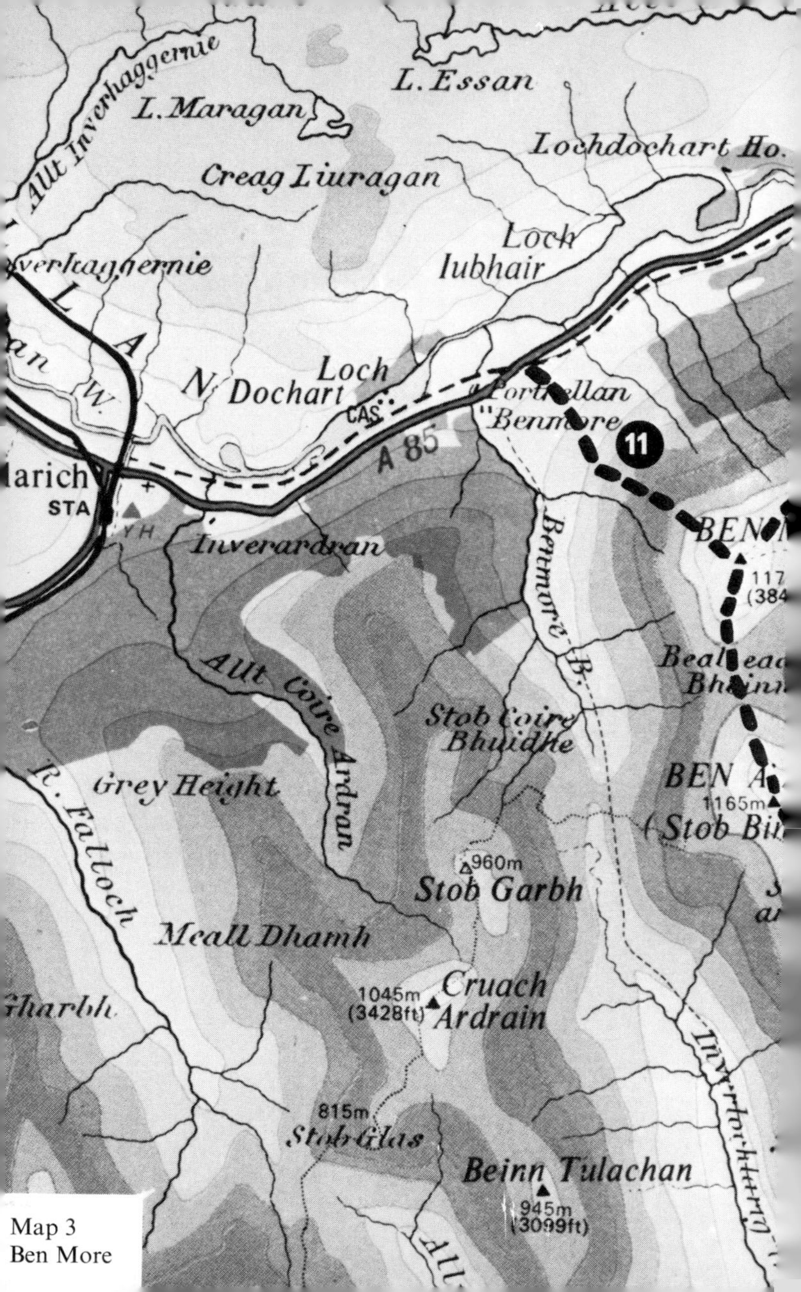

L. Essan

Allt Inverhaggernie

L. Maragan

Lochdochart Ho.

Creag Liuragan

Loch Iubhair

verhaggernie

Loch Dochart

Portnellan "Benmore"

CAS.

⑪

A 85

L A N

N

W.

BEN

arich

STA

117
(384

Inverardran

Benmore B.

Y·H

Bealleach
Bhainn

Allt Coire Ardran

Stob Coire
Bhuidhe

BEN A
1165m
(Stob Bi

R. Fattoch

Grey Height

△960m

Stob Garbh

Meall Dhamh

harbh

1045m
(3428ft) ▲

Cruach
Ardrain

815m

Stob Glas

Beinn Tulachan

945m
(3099ft)

Map 3
Ben More

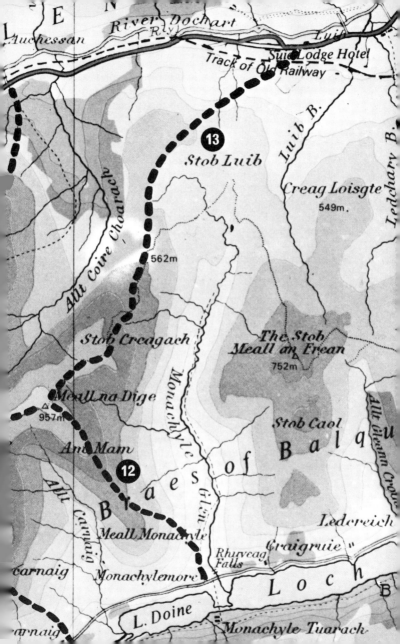

Strong walkers may wish to continue along the summit ridge to Stobinian, but it should be borne in mind that it falls about 1,000 feet to the Bealach-eadar-dha Beinn and rises again almost as much to the second top, so making a long and strenuous expedition before the climber reaches his lodgings in the evening.

Route 12. Stobinian from Balquhidder. This approach is subject to two variations: the first starts from Monachylemore and the second from Glen Carnaig. Both of them open up splendid views of the adjacent tops and ridges, and are more interesting than Route 11. To reach the starting points, drive to the end of Loch Voil for the former and continue to Loch Doine for the latter, a distance of about five miles. If desired both of them may be combined for the ascent and subsequent descent.

From Monachylemore climb the steep slopes of Meall Monachyle to gain the ridge, and then walk along it past Am Mam to Meall na Dige where observe the fine prospect of Stobinian and the corrie to its south. Now descend sharply to the tiny lochan on the col to the east and ascend Stob Coire an Lochain, whence it is only a short step to Stobinian. From Glen Carnaig, skirt the eastern slopes of Stob Invercarnaig to reach the ridge and then climb its gradually rising crest to Stob Coire an Lochain, thence to Stobinian.

Route 13. Stobinian from Luib. Proceed from the station in a south-westerly direction and pass Creag Sasunnaich on the L. Make for the first top above it, descend to Garbh Bhealach and then climb steeply to Caisteal Corrach. Now continue along the crest of Leacann Riabhach to the rocky top of Stob Creagach, whence make your way over the shattered rocky ridge to Meall na Dige. Here join Route 12 for Stobinian.

Ben Lui

Ben Lui (Beinn Laoigh)	3,708 feet	1,130 metres
Ben a Clee (Beinn a'Chleibh)	3,008 feet	917 metres

When garbed in white and seen from the railway between Crianlarich and Tyndrum on a sunny winter or spring morning, the Alpine splendour of this twin-topped peak commands the attention of all passengers and affords an unforgettable picture to all mountaineers. Its great north-eastern Coire Gaothach, guarded on the R by the satellite peak of Stob Garbh, will be noticed as the chief topographical feature of the mountain. The western aspect of Beinn Laoigh is of less interest, but is a conspicuous landmark in all the eastern prospects from Loch Awe. It is most famous for the snow ascents of the great corrie, and under good winter conditions it is no unusual sight to observe a party of enthusiasts forcing their way to the summit ridge through the massive snow cornices that overhang the precipices to the north-east of its crest. In favourable conditions the ascent of this peak has no great difficulties, and there are three good routes, of which the first one described herein is the most interesting and revealing.

In recent years the Forestry Commission have planted vast areas of conifers in the vicinity of this mountain, through which there is access by Routes 14 and 16, although the latter reaches the skyline below the summit of Beinn a'Chleibh. The unsolved problem concerns direct access from Glen Lochy, which by Route 15 involves a walk of nearly two miles from the Crossing. However, the Forestry Commission have agreed to erect a footbridge opposite the mouth of Eas Diamh and at the time of writing were awaiting permission to cross the railway. Moreover, they have made a car park for twenty vehicles on the busy road opposite which is located between

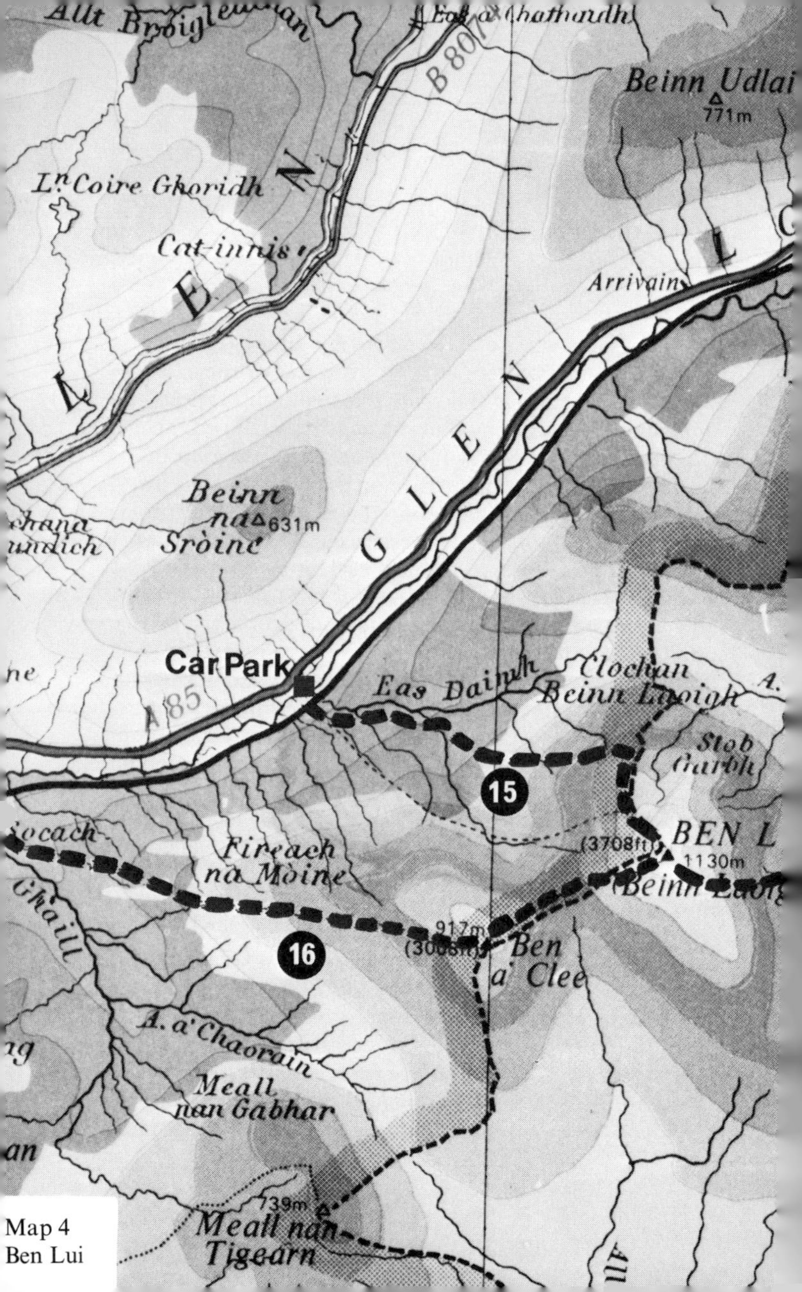

Map 4
Ben Lui

Altr Broigleachan

Eas a'Chathaidh

B 807

Beinn Udlai
△ 771m

Ln Coire Ghoridh

Cat-innis

G L E N L O

Arrivain

G L E N

L E

chana undich

Beinn na Sróine △ 631m

A 85

Car Park

Eas Daimh

Clochan Beinn Laoigh A.

A 85

15

Stob Garbh

Fireach na Móine

BEN L

(3708ft)
1130m

Beinn Laoig

iocach

16

917m
(3008ft)

Ben a' Clee

Chaill

A. a'Chaorain

Meall nan Gabhar

739m

Meall nan Tigearn

Plate 26 **Route 14** — Ben Lui from above Cononish

Plate 27 **Route 14**—The summit ridge of Ben Lui

the A85 and the River Lochy, just to the north of where the Eas Diamh joins the Lochy. Hence, for the time being this route remains with little alteration, but in the meantime I hope climbers will be able to ford the river if it is low and so shorten the ascent.

Route 14. Tyndrum and Ben Lui. Leave by A82 and drive as far as the school on the R, which is about one mile from the village. Park your car nearby. Now walk along the cart track to Cononish, a distance of about 2½ miles, with magnificent views ahead of your mountain. Continue in a south-westerly direction with the River Cononish on your L and walk along the cart track that leads to the old mine workings, but desert it L when facing the corrie. Drop down to the Allt an Rund, and after crossing the stream make for the south ridge of the corrie. Climb it steadily and be careful in its higher reaches because the rock is often loose and much shattered. You will soon attain the short, flattish summit ridge where there are two cairns; that to the south is the higher. The panorama is extensive and the first object to catch the eye on a clear day is the massive range of Ben Cruachan that frowns upon the glittering surface of Loch Awe. In the opposite direction Ben More and Stobinian are prominent, while to the north Ben Nevis tops the skyline of peak after peak.

Since Cononish is the key to this route, it may now be reached by an easier variation which starts at Tyndrum Station. Beyond the locked gate on the railway a forestry road follows the line of the original path, now planted with conifers, but keeps to the contours higher up the flanks of Meall Odhar. After about one mile it emerges from the plantations and bends to the R to reveal Ben Lui and Cononish ahead, whence it descends in long curves to merge with the rough cart track from the school.

Route 15. Glen Lochy and Ben Lui. Pending direct access from the Glen, possibly by the erection of a footbridge over the river opposite the mouth of Eas Diamh, the key to this route

Plate 28 The terminal stretches of **Route 15**

Ciochan Beinn Laoigh

Eas Morag

Beinn Lui

at the time of writing was still Glenlochy Crossing which is six miles from Tyndrum and a similar distance from Dalmally. In any case after crossing the railway you must walk beside it for 1¾ miles until you reach Eas Diamh and follow the stream to the beautiful fall of Eas Morag. Thence, bear R and pick up the burn coming down from Fionn Choirean, and when the plantation begins to thin out cut across to the L to the fine North Ridge with splendid views ahead of the summit of your mountain.

Route 16. Dalmally and Beinn a'Chleibh. Drive towards Tyndrum and on reaching Corryghoil turn R up the road to Succoth Lodge. To the east of the farm the broad ridge rises to Beinn a'Chleibh which is largely covered by a plantation with a space on the L reserved for a Nature Conservancy. Make your way through the trees by a path and on attaining the ridge bear L for the first top, whence drop down to the col and scale the rocky ridge to the summit of Ben Lui.

The finest walk is to ascend Route 14 and descend by Route 16, returning to Tyndrum by road or rail.

Plate 29 Ben Lui and Glenorchy Forest from the new car park, 1978

Photo 20. Cloud over Ben Lui and Beinn a'Chliabhain

The Cruachan Range

Ben Cruachan	3,689 feet	1,124 metres
Taynuilt Peak (Stob Dearg)	3,611 feet	1,101 metres
Drochaid Glas	3,312 feet	1,009 metres
Stob Diamh	3,272 feet	997 metres
Stob Garbh	3,215 feet	980 metres
Sron an Isean	3,163 feet	964 metres
Meall Cuanail	3,004 feet	916 metres
Beinn a'Bhuiridh	2,941 feet	896 metres
Monadh Driseig	2,098 feet	639 metres

Ben Cruachan is the highest of the eight tops crowning this great mountain range, which is bounded on the north by the deep rift of Glen Noe and on the south by the Pass of Brander and Loch Awe. It covers an area of about twenty square miles and forms a horseshoe stretching some four miles from east to west. The lower slopes of its two southern spurs are shagged with woods, but the higher parts are bare, and great smooth slabs of granite characterise the ridges. To obtain any real conception of its fine topography it is necessary to walk over the low hills between Cladich and Port Sonachan, some six miles to the south, where many of its salient features can be clearly discerned. Stob Dearg is the top on the extreme L and is usually known as the Taynuilt Peak. A narrow ridge about half a mile long connects it with Ben Cruachan, the dominating peak on the R. A long rounded hill known as Meall Cuanail rises in front of it and forms the western wall of the vast Coire Cruachan on the R. From Ben Cruachan a narrow shattered ridge sweeps across the skyline for about a mile to the east and terminates with Drochaid Glas. It then falls to a windy col and rises again to Stob Diamh, immediately to the south of which stands Stob Garbh. In Plate 31 this top is seen behind the L shoulder of the massive

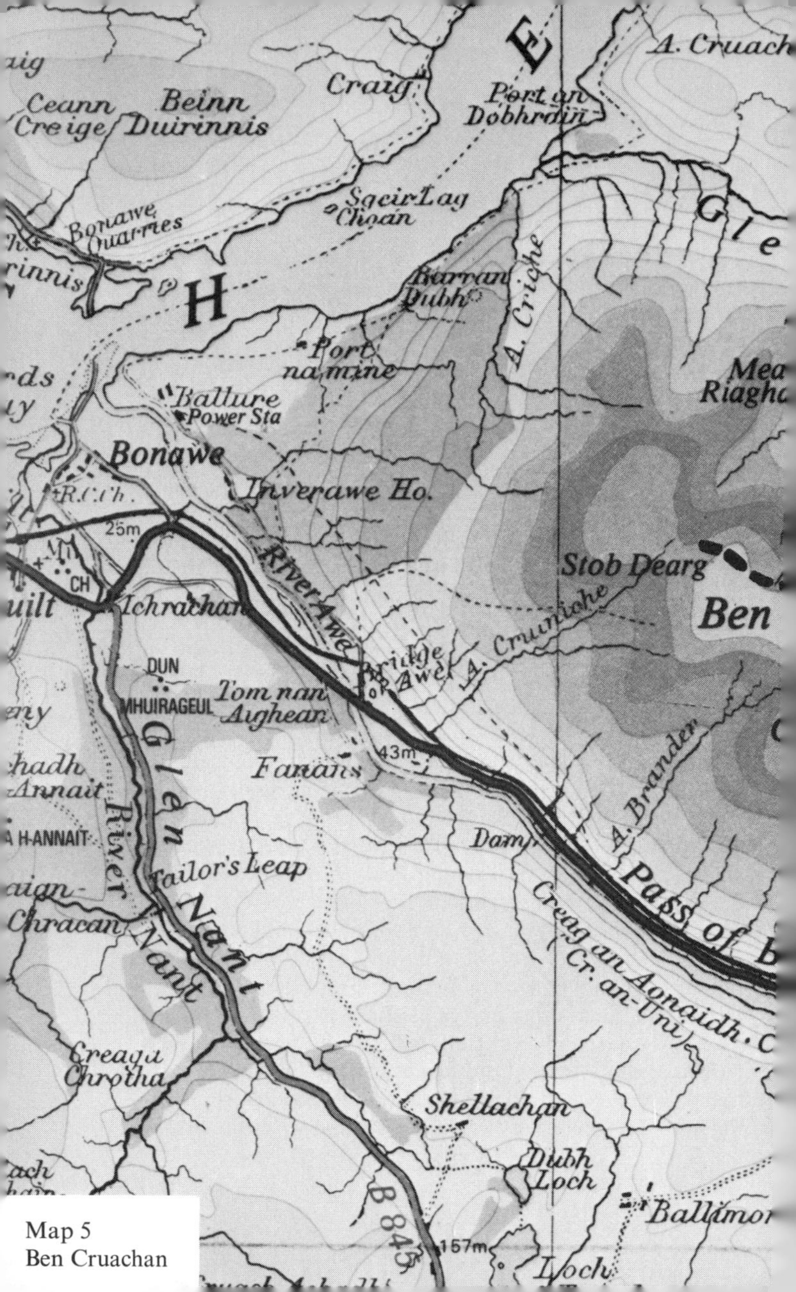

Map 5
Ben Cruachan

Beinn a'Bhuiridh, commonly known as Ben Vourie. To the north-east of Stob Diamh there is another subsidiary top called Sron an Isean, which stands at the head of Glen Noe. This latter group is well seen from the east, and particularly so from Ben Lui on a clear day. There are no difficulties encountered in the climb to any point on the ridge, but the finest expedition is to traverse the whole of it from east to west, which in favourable conditions is a rewarding experience for the mountain photographer.

Route 17. Coire Cruachan and Ben Cruachan. This vast gloomy hollow now cradling a reservoir, forms the first step in the direct ascent of the reigning peak, and it may be reached by a new road which ends at the Dam completed in 1965. It turns R off the highway about a mile to the west of Loch Awe House, but is not accessible by car. The vehicle may be parked on the L near a locked gate, but climbers can use the road which rises gradually for three miles round the flanks of Beinn a'Bhuiridh and reaches the Dam at a height of 1,315 feet. During the walk there are splendid views of the Pass of Brander far below on the L. Here you are surrounded on three sides by lofty ridges, whence make for the broad ridge ahead which rises to Meall Cuanail. The ascent is continuously steep until you attain the cairn, then walk down to the col and ascend the easy final slopes of your peak. On reaching the lofty cairn you should walk along the ridge to the L, keeping to the edge of the precipices until you attain the Taynuilt Peak.

The panorama from both these tops is of the first order, but the view round its northern arc will hold your gaze because it reveals the full length of Loch Etive, bounded on the east by the graceful peak of Ben Starav. On a clear day you can pick out many of the familiar Glencoe hills beyond the head of the loch, some of the tops of the Mamore Forest still further away, and your eye will rest finally upon the great dome of Ben Nevis in the far north. To the south, east and west rise a perfect galaxy of peaks, with here and there the glint of light

Plate 31 The Cruachan Range and Loch Awe from Cladich

on the many lochs and lochans that add charm to this delectable landscape. Immediately to the east of Ben Cruachan there is a magnificent prospect of the ridge which slants down to the two tops and falls precipitously on the L into the depths of Glen Noe.

Plate 32 The Pass of Brander from the first section of **Route 17**

Meall Cuanail   Ben Cruachan

Plate 33 The dam in Coire Cruachan is the key to **Route 17**

Plate 34 **Route 17**—The Taynuilt Peak and Ben Cruachan from the Cuanail-Cruachan col

Route 18. The Traverse of the Cruachan Ridges. Walk
eastwards from Loch Awe Station until you reach the end of
the plantations, and then turn L to climb the steep slopes of
Monadh Driseig. Continue along the crest of the rising ridge
to Ben Vourie, from whose crags you will obtain a fine view
of Ben Cruachan across the depths of the intervening corrie.
Now turn R and descend sharply to the col from which a steep
climb will place you on the summit of Stob Garbh. Thence
after a slight ascent you step on to the summit of Stob Diamh,
which is a commanding viewpoint for the main ridge
stretching westwards, and as it is only a short walk to Sron an
Isean you may wish to make this diversion for the splendid
vista along Glen Noe. Returning to Stob Diamh, you descend
to the col and then climb to Drochaid Glas, known as the
Grey Bridge, which opens up a superb prospect to the final
section of the ridge, crowned by both Ben Cruachan and the
Taynuilt Peak. Since the next mile is very narrow in places
you must advance with care, eventually to stand beside the
summit cairn of the reigning peak. When you have rested
from the ardours of the ascent and admired the splendour of
the panorama, walk over to the Taynuilt Peak and then
retrace your steps to join Route 17 for the descent, visiting the
cairn on Meall Cuanail en route.

Other routes to the main ridge from Taynuilt can be
worked out from the map, but they are just hard grinds and
lacking in interest compared with the two routes already
described.

Plate 35 **Route 18**—Ben Cruachan from Beinn a'Bhuiridh

Plate 26. **Route 18**. Ben Cruachan and Drochaid Glas from Stob Diamh

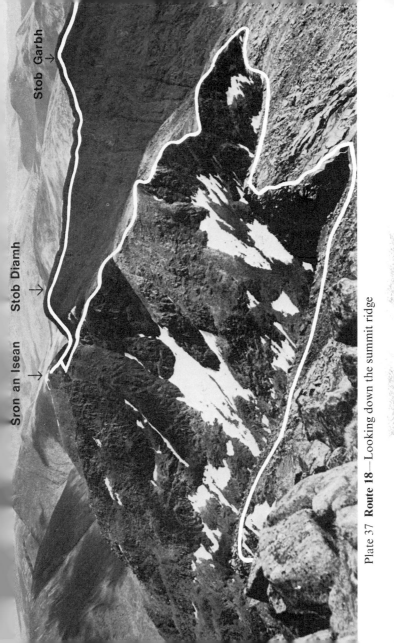

Stob Garbh

Stob Diamh

Sron an Isean

Plate 37 **Route 18**—Looking down the summit ridge

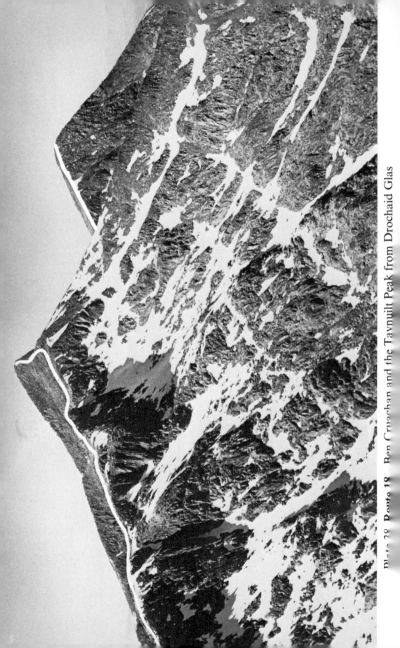

Plate 20 **Route 38** Ben Cruachan and the Taynuilt Peak from Drochaid Glas

The Blackmount

Meall a'Bhuiridh	3,636 feet	1,108 metres
Clach Leathad	3,602 feet	1,097 metres
Creise	3,596 feet	1,096 metres
Stob Ghabhar	3,565 feet	1,087 metres
Mam Coire Easain	3,506 feet	1,069 metres
Aonach Eagach	3,272 feet	997 metres
Sron a'Ghearrain	3,240 feet	988 metres
Stob a'Ghlais Choire	3,207 feet	978 metres
Sron nan Giubhas	3,174 feet	967 metres
Stob a'Bhruaich Leith	3,083 feet	940 metres
Stob a'Choire Odhair	3,058 feet	932 metres
Sron na Creise	2,952 feet	900 metres
Aonach Mor	2,839 feet	865 metres
Bealach Fuar-chathaidh	2,320 feet	707 metres

Plate 39 The old Glencoe road

Map 6
The Blackmount

Any mountaineer who has driven over the new Glencoe road will have been impressed by the magnificent array of peaks that come into view on the L after passing the foot of Loch Tulla and extend in an unbroken line all the way to Kingshouse. The old Glencoe road wound its way across their flanks, but was too near to open up such grand prospects of them as are now revealed across the many glittering blue lochans that deck the wayside across Rannoch Moor. The range is known as the Blackmount, which, however, strictly speaking includes Ben Starav, referred to in the last monograph. It includes thirteen other separate tops, but in the course of their traverse from Inveroran to Kingshouse, which is usually regarded as a classic among the many expeditions in the Central Highlands, it is customary to visit only seven or eight of them. The first peak to be climbed is Stob Ghabhar in the south, and the last Sron na Creise in the north; the map distance between them is about five miles and the lowest point the Bealach Fuar-chathaidh. Given favourable weather in summer, when no snow should be encountered, the walk from start to finish, allowing for halts for food and to view the scenery, and also for photography, will occupy a whole day. Its total length is eleven map miles. However, when climbers make this traverse from south to north IN MIST the only difficulty is to locate with certainty the exact spot on Aonach Mor, at 2,839 feet approx. where the spur on the R descends to the Bealach Fuar-chathaidh. Hence, the erection of a large cairn at this key point would be welcomed and a small one has been built recently by Mr Ian McMillan.

It should be noted that the following Route 19 may be shortened by turning R at Mam Coire Easain for Meall a'Bhuiridh, whose lower slopes may be descended from 2,090 feet by the White Corries Chairlift. The station is only just over a mile from the greatly improved Kingshouse Hotel.

Route 19. From Inveroran to Kingshouse. Leave the Inveroran Hotel and walk for half a mile along the old Glencoe road to Victoria Bridge, beyond which motor traffic is impossible.

Turn L along the private road that follows the course of the river, and in about a mile turn R up the path beside the Allt Toaig. On reaching the 1,000 feet contour cross the burn and bear L to ascend the south-east ridge of Stob Ghabhar. On attaining the cairn note the rock-bound corrie of the R which cradles a shining lochan and beyond it the vast prospect of Rannoch Moor, dappled with innumerable lochans as far as the eye can see. Keeping to the edge of the precipices, walk downhill to Sron nan Giubhas and continue along the ridge of Aonach Mor. This rises gently in a north-westerly direction and discloses Coireach a'Ba on the R, with a glimpse of Ba Bridge on the old Glencoe road some three miles to the east. Less than a mile ahead bear R and descend the spur that leads down some 500 feet to the Bealach Fuar-chathaidh, the lowest point on the ridge. Then tackle the steep declivities of some 1,200 feet rising to Clach Leathad, and on reaching the cairn pause for a moment to admire the wild prospect in which Meall a'Bhuiridh is prominent to the north-east and the long crest of Buachaille Etive Mor to the north-west. Now walk due north for nearly two miles over the almost level ridge, passing Mam Coire Easain and Creise to attain Stob a'Ghlais Choire, which suddenly discloses Kingshouse on the moor far below. Now make your way through the crags to Sron na Creise, the terminal point on the ridge, and descend to the L of its long shoulder to pass the buttress in safety. Here you will find scree which terminates in a track beside a burn. This eventually goes over to the R and then straight down to the grassy bank of the river. If the water is low, cross to the road and turn R for Kingshouse; if it is high, keep to the L bank of the river for one mile to the road bridge.

In severe winter conditions of heavy snow this long traverse should only be undertaken by a properly equipped party of experienced mountaineers.

Plate 40 **Route 19**—Stob Ghabhar from Loch Tulla

Plate 41 **Route 19**—Clach Leathad and Meall a'Bhuiridh from Ba Bridge

Plate 42 **Route 19**—Clach Leathad and Meall a'Bhuiridh from Rannoch Moor

Plate 43 **Route 19**—The terminal peaks of the Blackmount seen from Kingshouse

Buachaille Etive Mor

Stob Dearg	3,345 feet	1,020 metres
Stob na Doire	3,250 feet	991 metres
Stob na Broige	3,120 feet	951 metres
Stob Coire Altruim	3,065 feet	934 metres

On passing the watershed on the new Glencoe road, above
Kingshouse, the whole of this mountain comes into view
across Rannoch Moor and reveals three of its four tops, as
follows: Stob na Broige on the L; Stob na Doire in the centre
hides Stob Coire Altruim; and Stob Dearg on the R. However,
the beautiful elevation of the latter peak is not disclosed until
the Kingshouse Hotel is reached, when it becomes clear that
Stob Dearg is the most attractive of all the mountains
frowning upon the vast wilderness of the moor. It presents the
appearance of a broken, reddish-black symmetrical rock cone
and in one sweep rises from the level moor, its lines
converging on the Crowberry Ridge and North Buttress
immediately below the summit. The view of it is most
arresting when seen by early morning sunlight, because it
throws into sharp relief all its main topographical features. It
will be noticed that its northern and eastern flanks are split up
into numerous buttresses and gullies which have become
famous as a treasured playground for the rock climber. The
first recorded ascent was in 1894, but today the whole façade
is festooned with courses of varied difficulty, all of which are
described in detail in the excellent Scottish Mountaineering
Club *Guide to the Central Highlands*. On the Glen Etive side,
the Buachaille Etive as it is familiarly called, contains a wild
rift, known as the Chasm, which for many years had the
distinction of being the longest gully climb on the mainland;
its only rival was the Water Pipe Gully in the Coolins of Skye.
However, more recently the Clachaig Gully on Aonach

Plate 44 Buachaille Etive Mor from Kingshouse, as it was in 1942

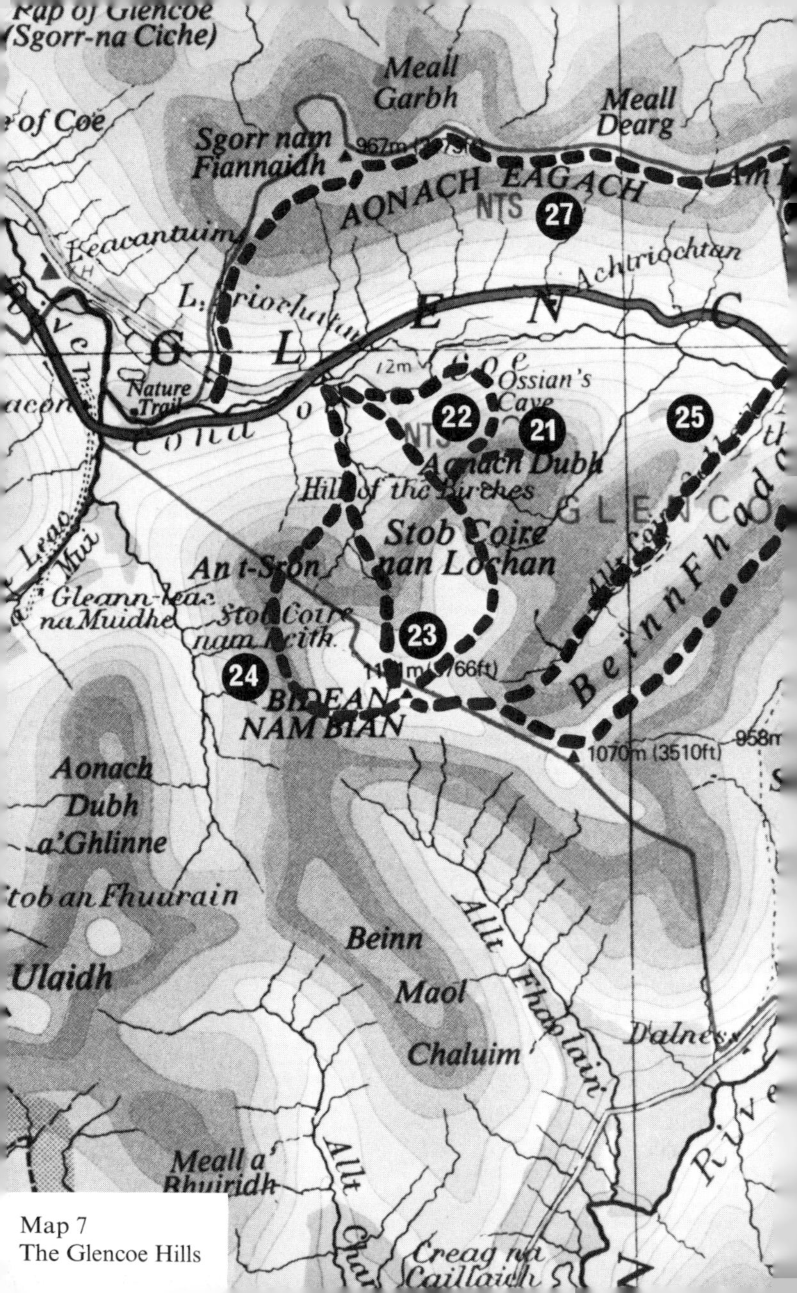

Map 7
The Glencoe Hills

Sròn Coire Odhair-bhig
Stob Eoin Mhic Mhartuin
Altnafeadh
Stob Beinn a'Chrulaiste
L.na Fèithe
308m
A82
Stob nan Cabar
DALNESS
Stob Coire Raineach
R. Coupal
NTS
20
Stob Dearg
Buachaille Etive Beag
Buachaille Etive Mór
Stob na Doir
FOREST
Stob na Brogie
180m
Alltchaorunn
Beinn Mhic Chasgaig
Sròn Creise
Stob a'Ghlais Choire
997m
CREISE
1100m
(3608ft)
Mam Choire Easain
1069 m
Grianan Deirdire
(Sunny Peak)
Clach Leath

Eagach has superseded it and is now acknowledged as the longest gully climb in Scotland. Buachaille Etive Mor is almost surrounded by the River Coupall which rises in the adjacent Lairig Gartain, swings round to the east beside the road and then turns south in Glen Etive to fall into the sea at Loch Etive. Bounded on the east by the Blackmount, this glen is thirteen miles in length and one of the loveliest in Scotland. Both climber and tourist will be charmed by the artificial lochan and its rhododendrons, about half way down on the L, whereas the former will make for the Slabs of Beinn Trilleachan on the R, above the derelict pier at the head of Loch Etive.

Route 20. Kingshouse and Stob Dearg. In view of the precipitous nature of the peak it does not offer the ordinary pedestrian a choice of routes to its summit. The most interesting is to first walk about three miles along the road to Altnafeadh, turn L to cross the River Coupall by a footbridge, and then make for the mouth of Coire na Tulaich opposite. Follow the burn and continue the rough scramble over steep scree and boulders to attain the lip of the corrie, whence turn L and walk up the remaining half-mile of slopes to the summit cairn. The panorama is disappointing owing to the lack of any interesting features on the nearer peaks. The only compensation is the view of Schiehallion which dominates the vast solitudes of Rannoch Moor to the north-east. A less interesting ascent can be made from a point about two miles down Glen Etive by way of Coire Cloiche Finne, but in bad weather it is best left alone.

Plate 45 Buttresses and gullies flank the northern front of Stob Dearg

Plate 46. Buac 20. Stob Dearg and Coire na Tulaich from Altnafeadh

Plate 47 Lochan Creag na Caillaich in Glen Etive

FIG. 48. The Lobster of Peirao Triller, here seen from the Pier

The Bidean nam Bian Range

Bidean nam Bian	3,766 feet	1,148 metres
Stob Coire nan Lochan	3,657 feet	1,115 metres
Stob Coire nam Beith	3,621 feet	1,104 metres
Stob Coire Sgreamhach	3,497 feet	1,066 metres
Beinn Fhada	3,120 feet	951 metres
Aonach Dubh	2,849 feet	868 metres
An t'Sron	2,750 feet	838 metres
Gearr Aonach	2,500 feet	762 metres

Bidean nam Bian is the dominating peak in the great range of hills bearing its name, and the crowning glory of Argyll. It hems in the south side of Glencoe and from the highest point on the old road, near the Study, its three northern spurs, well known as the Three Sisters, exhibit a remarkable pendent profile, but the real grandeur of the whole group is not seen to advantage from such a close viewpoint. While it assumes a striking elevation when seen from the adjacent ridge of Aonach Eagach, its real dominance of the landscape is best observed from some of the peaks in the Mamore Forest and on a clear day even from the distant summit of Ben Nevis. In the vicinity of Clachaig, the actual summit of Bidean is hidden by its satellite, An t'Sron which encloses, with Stob Coire nan Lochan, the deep rift of Coire nam Beith. From the bridge over the River Coe at the junction of the old and new roads, the Diamond and Church Door Buttresses can be seen through the entrance to this corrie but they again hide the summit itself. Furthermore, owing to the close proximity of the eight tops which rise from the ridges of this massive group, none of them assumes any individual beauty when seen from afar, but when viewed from closer range the graceful lines of Stob Coire nan Lochan immediately attract the eye

Beinn Fhada   Stob Coire nan Lochan   Gearr Aonach   Aonach Dubh

... and Stob Coire nan Lochan from the Old Road

Plate 50 **Routes 21, 25** and **26** are seen to advantage from Aonach Eagach

and stamp it as the Queen of this mountain range.

Bidean nam Bian may be ascended without difficulty from several points within easy reach of the Clachaig Inn, but the usual approach is either by way of An t'Sron when the ridge may be followed over Stob Coire nam Beith to the summit or the cairn may be attained directly from the corrie below. The finest ridge walk, however, is to climb one of the Three Sisters of Glencoe, take in Bidean on the way, and descend from An t'Sron. This means a longer expedition which can be accomplished in an easy day and is more than repaid by the variety of views obtained en route.

Route 21. Aonach Dubh and Stob Coire nan Lochan. The finest prospect of Aonach Dubh is obtained from Clachaig by afternoon sunlight which throws into sharp relief the innumerable buttresses and gullies that split its western front. The Dinner Time Buttress is the most conspicuous feature and rises in an unbroken line in the centre of its immense façade. On the extreme L, a great gash known as Ossian's Cave looks like a dark keyhole just below the summit when seen from the road and immediately below it a deep gorge rises in an almost straight line from the glen. This gives access to the sloping ledge below the cave and is the key to our route which is for the experienced climber only and should be severely left alone by the ordinary pedestrian. Cross the bridge that gives access to Loch Achtriochtan, skirt its southern shore and continue below the cliffs until you reach the mouth of the gorge. Turn sharp R to enter it and scramble up its steep floor, using one or other of its retaining walls to facilitate progress, or, as an alternative, climb its right bank. On emerging on the broad sloping ledge turn R below the Cave, skirt the Porphyry Buttress on the L and beyond it climb the first short gully on the L to attain the rocky summit of Aonach Dubh. From the cairn note the dynamic prospect of Aonach Eagach on the other side of Glencoe and then turn your steps to ascend the broad ridge rising to Stob Coire nan Lochan, noting on the L the four fine rock buttresses that

Aonach Dubh →

Buttress →

Plate 51 **Routes 21, 22, 23** and **24** — The slopes of An t'Sron are on the right and hide Coire nam Beith

support the ridge and peak. On attaining the cairn, pause for a moment to admire the superb northern panorama, where the eye skims over Aonach Eagach and then the Mamores, to rest finally upon the dominating peak of Ben Nevis. Now continue your climb by traversing the narrow but easy ridge that rises to the cairn on the summit of Bidean nam Bian, noting on the R the Diamond and Church Door Buttresses with Collie's Pinnacle at their feet.

The panorama is stupendous and the first section of note lies to the south where Loch Etive leads the eye past Ben Starav on the L to the Cruachan Range, then to the R to the western seas, Mull and the hills of Ardgour. The northern section is not so good as that from Stob Coire nan Lochan, but to the east it is possible on a clear day to pick out the tapering cone of Schiehallion immediately above Buachaille Etive. The cairn stands at the junction of three supporting ridges, all of which look easy, but unless the climber is familiar with their topography it is best to leave them alone and descend by Route 24.

Plate 52 **Route 21** —Stob Coire nan Lochan from Aonach Dubh

Plate 53 **Route 21** — Ben Nevis, the Mamores and Aonach Eagach from Stob Coire nan Lochan

Plate 54 **Route 21**—Bidean nam Bian from Stob Coire nan Lochan

Route 22. The Dinner Time Buttress. This rib is such a prominent feature of Aonach Dubh that after crossing the bridge near Loch Achtriochtan you make direct for its base. Ascend the grassy centre of the buttress until you reach the crags and then climb them by the easiest variation until you emerge on the skyline. Here bear L for the cairn and join Route 21 for Bidean.

This route can be dangerous in snow or mist, when it should be avoided.

Route 23. Coire nam Beith. Start by Route 22 but make for the mouth of the corrie ahead where the burn cascades down through its narrow opening. Then ascend the scree towards the Church Door Buttress, pass to the R of it and climb to the Saddle where turn L for Bidean.

Route 24. An t'Sron and Stob Coire nam Beith. Follow Route 23 to the mouth of the corrie and climb through the scanty trees on the R. Then make for the long gully splitting the north face of An t'Sron and ascend its west side to the cairn. Now contour round to the R and follow the track rising to the summit of Stob Coire nam Beith, whence keep to the lip of the corrie all the way to Bidean.

Route 25. Allt Coire Gabhail. Leave the Glencoe road opposite Gearr Aonach, the prominent rocky central buttress of the Three Sisters, and descend the path to the bridge over the River Coe. Pass the pools and then climb steeply beside the burn, making your way through the maze of boulders piled one on top of another in its higher reaches, with the hidden stream gurgling away out of sight beneath them. When you step on to the grassy floor of the corrie, which is littered with gigantic boulders, go straight ahead and climb the grassy tongue on the R of the scree to the saddle at the head of the glen and to the L of Bidean. Then turn R and walk up the ridge to its summit.

Plate 55 **Routes 23** and **24** — Bidean, the Diamond and Church Door Buttresses from Stob Coire nam Beith

Route 26. Beinn Fhada and Stob Coire Sgreamhach. Leave the Glencoe road near the waterfall at its head and follow the Allt Lairig Eilde for a short distance. Then bear R and make your way through the crags that deck the northern slopes of Beinn Fhada. Continue along its lofty ridge with splendid views on the R of Bidean and Stob Coire nan Lochan, and after passing its two tops climb some 400 feet to reach the summit of Stob Coire Sgreamhach. Here turn R and ascend the narrow ridge to the cairn on the reigning peak.

Plate 56 **Route 24**—Stob Coire nam Beith from the summit of Bidean

Plate 57 **Route 24**—Stob Coire nam Beith

Aonach Eagach

Sgor nam Fiannaidh	3,168 feet	966 metres
Meall Dearg	3,118 feet	950 metres
Am Bodach	3,085 feet	940 metres
Stob Coire Leith	3,080 feet	939 metres
A 'Chailleach	2,938 feet	895 metres
Sron Garbh	2,857 feet	871 metres
Garbh Bheinn	2,835 feet	864 metres
Pap of Glencoe (Sgor na Ciche)	2,430 feet	741 metres

This is the name given to the Notched Ridge surmounting the
north wall of Glencoe and stretches for over five miles from
the Devil's Staircase in the east, to the Pap of Glencoe in the
west. Although it comprises eight tops in its entirety, the
narrowest part of the ridge from which its innumerable
pinnacles project is under two miles in length and lies between
Am Bodach in the east and Stob Coire Leith in the west. The
south side of Aonach Eagach is most spectacular and
stretches in one unbroken line along the north of Glencoe, but
a more realistic view of its amazing structure is obtained from
the cairn on Aonach Dubh on the other side of the glen. To
mountaineers it is famous for its ghostly pinnacles, all of
which have to be climbed in the traverse of the ridge; it is the
narrowest and most sensational on the mainland. The
quickest way to see the best part of it is to ascend Am Bodach
from the Keeper's cottage opposite Gearr Aonach and
descend to the West of Stob Coire Leith. The highest top to
be traversed is Meall Dearg which is about half way along.
This ridge is often referred to as the Chancellor and is known
to local keepers as the Ptarmigan Ridge as these beautiful
birds are often encountered on its lofty crest.

Route 27. The Traverse of the Ridge. Park your car in a lay-by below the Keeper's Cottage in Glencoe, and begin the ascent of Am Bodach at the Warning Notice to the west of it. There are several rocky outcrops on the higher slopes of this peak which are best avoided on the R. The ascent is steep all the way and on reaching the cairn you must linger for a while to admire the views of the glen far below, the great yawning gullies that split the face of the cliffs which are a characteristic feature of this sentinel when seen from the glen, and the dynamic prospect of Bidean nam Bian and its supporting ridges which are revealed to greater advantage from this lofty coign of vantage. You will also note the central peak of Meall Dearg in the north-west, and to reach it you must exercise care in descending to its connecting ridge from Am Bodach, where you will find ample hand and footholds on its precipitous northern face. On attaining this summit you get a splendid conception of the line of pinnacles stretching away to the west, and to reach the first of them you descend the track that meanders in and out of the rocks on its south side. About half way along you will encounter the Crazy Pinnacles, three of which stand at the top of gullies falling down both sides of the mountain. On a wild day the wind shrieks through this narrow gap in the ridge, but with a steady head you should have no difficulty in passing them, whence you climb a steep little chimney to set foot on the next pinnacle. Here you should pause to admire the retrospect, which reveals your last pinnacle standing boldly between Meall Dearg on the L and Am Bodach on the R, with immense precipices sweeping down on either side. On and on you go with no way of escape until eventually you reach the last two pinnacles which are the narrowest and most sensational of them all. You must again exercise the utmost care and balance to traverse them in safety until you encounter the Stone Shoot at the next col which descends on the L just below Stob Coire Leith. Thence the wider ridge is grassy all the way to Sgor nam Fiannaidh and ultimately to the Pap of Glencoe at its terminus. But few climbers take in these two tops as they are less interesting

Am Bodach

Plate 58 **Route 27**—Aonach Eagach from Glencoe

Plate 59, Photo 37. Aonach Eagach from the summit of Aonach Dubh

after the delights of the narrower ridge. *If you are experienced in descending rolling scree* you will hasten down the Stone Shoot, soon to set foot on the road in the glen, whence turn R for Clachaig. If, however, you prefer a grassy way down, turn L off the ridge beyond the next top, but it is better to go on to the col just short of Sgor nam Fiannaidh and walk down the easier slopes beside the burn to the bridge over the River Coe, so to end one of the most entertaining traverses in the Highlands.

Special warning. Climbers have reported considerable difficulty on descending the Stone Shoot and several parties have had to be rescued. It is advisable to avoid this dangerous descent and to leave the ridge beyond Stob Coire Leith as suggested above.

Plate 60 **Route 27**—Warning sign

Plate 61 **Route 27**—Loch Triochatan from Am Bodach

Sgor nam Fiannaidh   Stob Coire Leith

Plate 62 **Route 27**—Looking west along the narrowest section of the ridge

Meall Dearg →   Am Bodach →   Stob Dearg →

Plate 63 **Route 27** — Looking east along the crest of Aonach Eagach

Plate 64 **Route 27** — The last pinnacle but one in the Western Traverse

Sgor nam Fiannaidh →   **Stob Coire Leith** ⟍

Plate 65 Descent of **Route 27** seen from the last pinnacle on the ridge

Plate 66 **Route 27** — Retrospect of the last pinnacle on Aonach Eagach

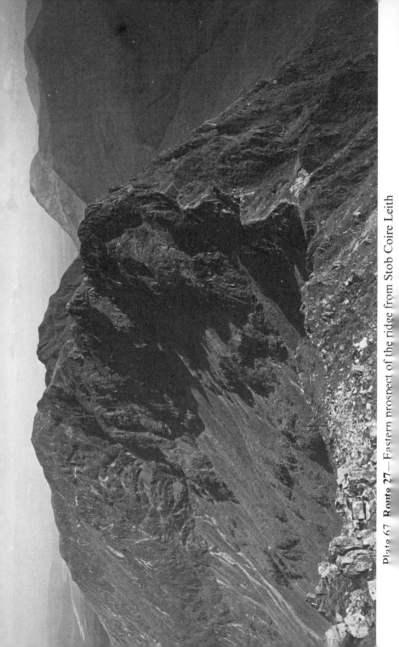

Plate 67 **Route 27**—Eastern prospect of the ridge from Stob Coire Leith

The Beinn a'Bheithir Group

Sgorr Dhearg	3,362 feet	1,025 metres
Sgorr Dhonuill	3,284 feet	1,001 metres
Sgorr Bhan	3,104 feet	946 metres
Sgorr a'Chaolais	2,700 feet	823 metres
Creag Ghorm	2,372 feet	723 metres

This beautiful group of hills rises to the south of Loch Leven and forms a great horseshoe which extends from above the village of Ballachulish and ends above the wooded slopes, a mile west of the new Bridge. It exhibits three well-defined peaks, Sgorr Bhan, Sgorr Dhearg and Sgorr Dhonuill. A rocky spur extends to the north from the latter and is known as Sgorr a'Chaolais. It forms a horn-shaped peak which is a prominent feature when seen from the Bridge. The western ridge is broad and dappled with a collection of small lochans; it terminates in the summit of Creag Ghorm, and its lower slopes, together with those of the more easterly ridges, are surrounded by dense plantations. The fine topography of this magnificent range is well seen from the hills to the north of Loch Leven, and even better from the westerly peaks of the Mamore Forest. No problems will be encountered during the traverse of the ridges where the going is easy and the views attractive. But it might be as well to warn climbers that the direct descent through the plantations from Creag Ghorm is fraught with difficulties. It is advisable, therefore, to come down from the col to the west of Sgorr Dhoniull and follow the path through the woods in Gleann a'Chaolais, or to descend from this peak in a westerly direction to Kentallen and so avoid the plantations.

Route 28. The Traverse of the Horseshoe. Turn R off the road about a mile to the east of the new bridge and follow the path through the trees enclosing the Allt Giubhsachain. On emerging from the leafy canopy bear L and climb the steep slopes leading to the ridge of Sgorr Bhan, which follow in a southerly direction until you attain the cairn, noting on the L the subsidiary spur of slate that falls to the east. The view of the adjacent peak of Sgorr Dhearg is always attractive, but especially so under snow when the graceful curves of its ridge delight the eye. It swings round to the R for about half a mile to end by the cairn on this dominating peak, which unfolds a fine panorama. A pleasant feature is the prospect to the north-east of the whole of the Mamores beyond the blue of Loch Leven, while to the west across the intervening bealach Sgorr Dhonuill assumes a magnificent profile; to reach it from the col involves a steep ascent of 800 feet. When you attain its cairn, pause for a moment to scan the retrospect which discloses the zig-zag pattern of the ridge you have just descended, with the sharp little peak of Sgorr a'Choise peeping over its R shoulder. To the north you look over the craggy top of Sgorr a'Chaolais to the narrow entrance of Loch Leven below, but to the west Creag Ghorm obscures the broad stretches of Loch Linnhe, above which Garbh Bheinn rises into the sky above Ardgour. Now walk down the slopes of this peak, and if you do not elect to turn R at the col to descend into Gleann a'Chaolais and so directly to the bridge, continue along the broad plateau with its tiny lochans which sweeps round to the north to Creag Ghorm, whence turn L and go down its slopes to Kentallen with spacious views ahead of Loch Linnhe.

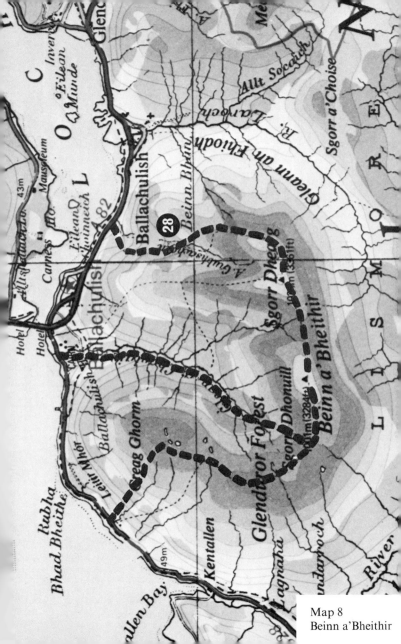

Map 8
Beinn a'Bheithir

Sgorr Bhan   Sgorr Dhearg   Sgorr Dhonuill

Plate 68 Beinn a'Bheithir seen across Loch Leven

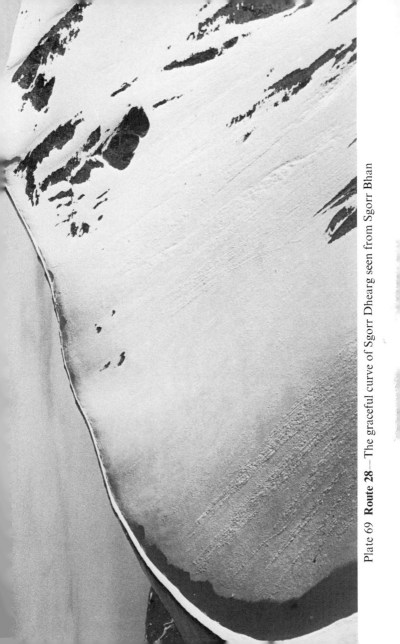

Plate 69　**Route 28**— The graceful curve of Sgorr Dhearg seen from Sgorr Bhan

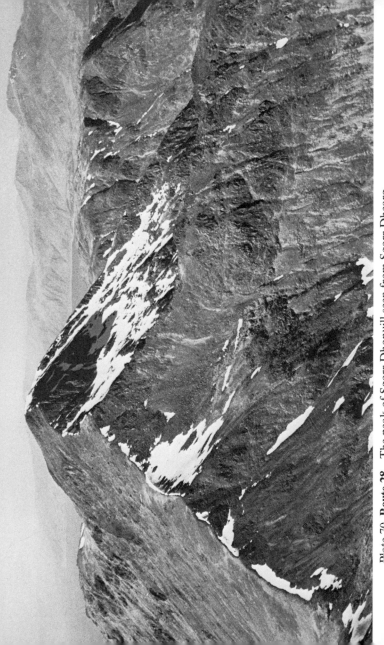

Plate 70. Route 28. The peak of Sgorr Dhonuill seen from Sgorr Dhearg

The Garbh Bheinn Group

Garbh Bheinn	2,903 feet	885 metres
Sron a'Gharbh Choire Bhig	2,671 feet	814 metres
Beinn Bheag	2,387 feet	728 metres
Meall a'Chuillin	2,228 feet	679 metres
Sgor Mhic Eacharna	2,130 feet	649 metres
Bealach Feith'n Amean	1,753 feet	534 metres
Druim an Iubhair	1,600 feet	481 metres

When seen from Corran Ferry, the magnificent rock peak of
Garbh Bheinn is a conspicuous feature in the western
prospect of Ardgour, and may be reached by following the
narrow road skirting Loch Linnhe to Inversanda, whence the
R fork leads to a bridge over the river flowing down Glen
Iubhair. This is the starting point of the three following
routes, all of which are interesting but longer than they seem,
and a car may be parked in the large Passing Place
immediately to the east of the bridge. The mountain flanks the
northern side of Glen Tarbert, along which the road continues
to Loch Sunart. Looking back from the vicinity of Strontian
discloses a splendid view of its immense rocky declivities
dominating the head of the loch. On closer acquaintance
Garbh Bheinn is revealed as a superb rock peak whose eastern
front is riven by ridges, buttresses and gullies, of which the
Great Gully is a prominent feature cleaving the face of the
mountain. It is hemmed in on the L by the Great Ridge, and
further to the R by the Pinnacle Ridge, beyond which the
North-East Buttress falls steeply to the Bealach Feith'n
Amean and its lonely Lochan Coire an Iubhair. To the L of
the peak a bealach separates it from Sron a'Gharbh Choire
Bhig, and its lofty ridge falls to the bridge, flanked by
immense slabs of rock which are well seen from the other side
of the glen. The best way to see the topographical features of

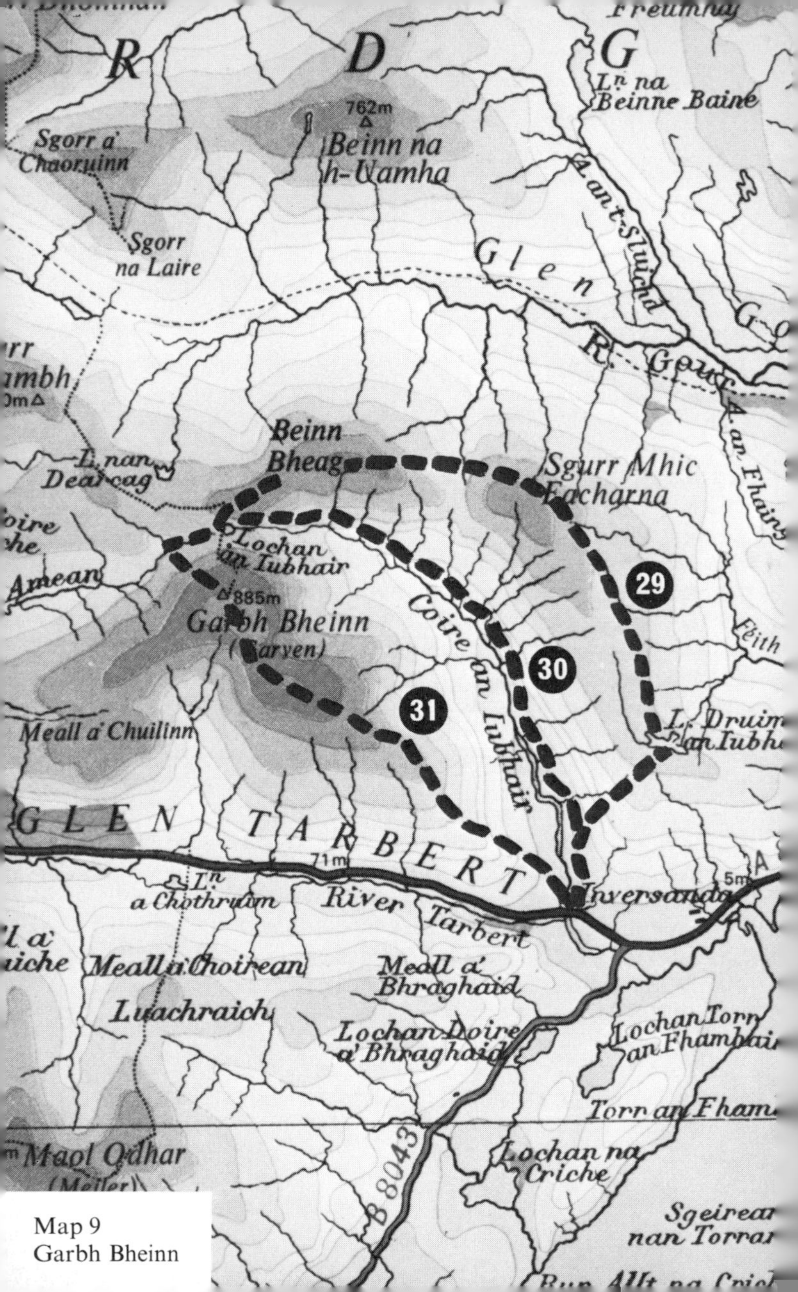

Map 9
Garbh Bheinn

Dubh

U · R

Beinn

A 861

Sgurr na
h-Eanchainne
730m

LO

nan Muc

Meall Breac

Keil

Church

Ardgour Ho.

Ardgour Hotel

Pier

Corran

Hotel
Linnres

Loch nan
Gabhar

Clovullin

Sallachan 13m

Corran Narrows

Keppanich
19m

Camas
Shallachain

Cuilcheanna Ho.

Or

hain

Rubha
Cuilcheanna

CLACH-A-CHARRA

Salachan
Point

Rubha Ruadh

Gearradh

Rubha
Bhad Bheithe

L · I · N · N · H · E

da

Kentallen Bay

Creic

48m

Ardsheal House

Kentallen

Back
Settlement

A 828

Glendurор

Lagnaha

this great peak is to combine Routes 29 and 31 which keep to the skyline of Glen Iubhair, ascending by the former and descending by the latter. But even under favourable conditions this is a long and arduous expedition, totalling over seven map miles, with 4,300 feet of ascent, and should only be undertaken by climbers in very fit condition.

Route 29. By Sgor Mhic Eacharna. Cross the fence near the large boulder lying beside the road and make your way through bog, tangled heather and crags in a north-easterly direction. After climbing about 1,300 feet you set foot on the gradually rising Druim an Iubhair, where a small lochan can be seen on the R. Continue along the flattish ridge and note the great slabs of rock flanking the glen on the L, and when just short of the first top observe the fine elevation of Garbh Bheinn on the L. After passing Sgor Mhic Eacharna descend to the col and thence climb to the narrow crest of Beinn Bheag. This opens up a view of the Bealach Feith'n Amean and its blue lochan, above which rise abruptly the precipitous northern slopes of your peak. Descend sharply to the lochan and note the great rock buttresses ahead which seemingly halt your progress, but do not attempt to climb them or their adjacent gullies. Go further to the R until you encounter a long talus slope which terminates in a narrow stone shoot high above. Scramble up this to enter the little north-west corrie and so gain the main ridge near the top of the Pinnacle Ridge on the L. Then walk up to the summit cairn which is perched almost on the rim of the Great Ridge. The stupendous panorama from Garbh Bheinn is breath-taking in its magnificence, with the crags dropping away at your feet to Glen Iubhair far below. Its eastern arc will hold your gaze as it unfolds the splendour of Ben Nevis, the Mamores, the Glencoe Hills and Beinn a'Bheithir across the glimmering stretches of Loch Linnhe. To the west Ben Resipol is a prominent landmark, and to its L your eye will skim over the shining surface of Loch Sunart to Ardnamurchan and the sea, with, in the south-west, vistas over Movern to the hills of Mull.

Garbh Bheinn →

Plate 71 Garbh Bheinn from Corran Ferry

Route 30. By Glen Iubhair. Follow the sketchy track beside the burn descending the glen, which peters out after about a mile. Then continue over boggy ground along its north bank and eventually climb the rough heathery slopes to its source on the bealach, observing the fine views of the immense crags on the L. There join Route 29 for the summit of Garbh Bheinn.

Route 31. By Sron a'Gharbh Choire Bhig. Cross the bridge over the river and make your way through a maze of tangled heather and grass to the foot of the ridge that rises on the L of the glen. Keep the precipitous crags on your R as you climb and make your way in and out of the many slabby outcrops. The going is steep and strenuous, but on reaching the top of your first objective you will be rewarded by a close view of the magnificent Great Ridge that falls in one unbroken sweep from the summit of Garbh Bheinn, on the other side of the intervening bealach. Now descend to it and climb the 500 feet of steep rock to the cairn on the reigning peak of the group.

From Glen Tarbert there is a wild prospect up the steep rock walls enclosing Coire a'Chothruim, which is the source of the Carnoch River. Its ascent looks tempting, but is best left alone by all save the experienced rock climber.

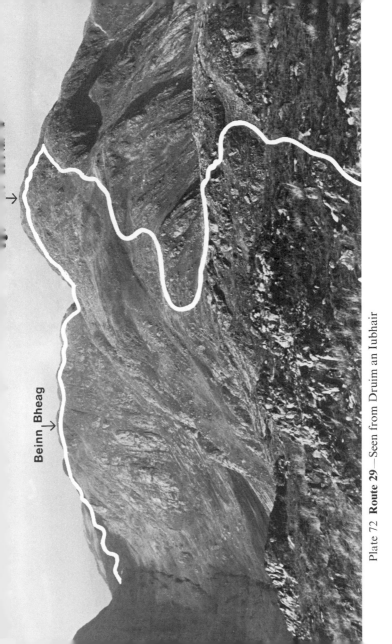

Beinn Bheag

Plate 72 **Route 29**—Seen from Druim an Iubhair

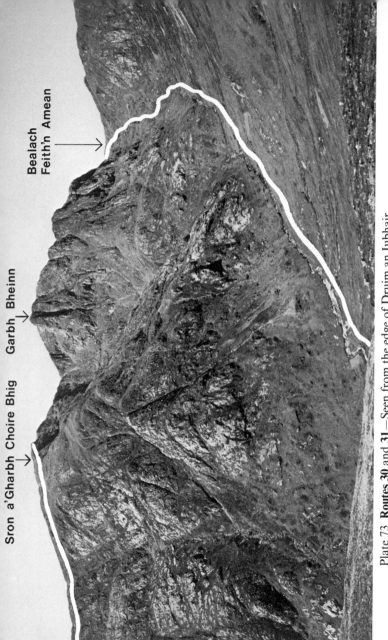

Sron a'Gharbh Choire Bhig   Garbh Bheinn   Bealach Feith'n Amean

Plate 73 **Routes 30 and 31**—Seen from the edge of Druim an Iubhair

The Mamores

Binnein Mor	3,700 feet	1,128 metres
Sgurr a'Mhaim	3,601 feet	1,098 metres
Na Gruagaichean	3,442 feet	1,049 metres
Am Bodach	3,382 feet	1,031 metres
Sgur an Iubhair	3,300 feet	1,006 metres
Sgurr Eilde Mor	3,279 feet	999 metres
Stob Ban	3,274 feet	998 metres
Stob Coire a'Chairn	3,219 feet	981 metres
An Gearanach	3,200 feet	975 metres
Sgurr Eilde Beag	3,140 feet	957 metres
Binnean Beag	3,083 feet	940 metres
Mullach nan Coirean	3,077 feet	938 metres

This delightful range of hills stretches from east to west for nearly ten miles and is bounded on the north by Glen Nevis and on the south by Loch Leven. On a clear day the whole of it can be seen from Beinn a'Bheithir and Aonach Eagach in the south, and although the views of it are against the light when observed from the north, Ben Nevis and Aonach Beag have the advantage of proximity and superior height as coigns of vantage for its appraisal. The group comprises a main ridge about seven miles in length, with three well defined northern spurs, and includes several shapely conical tops; it is therefore ideal terrain for the ridge wanderer. White quartzite is well distributed on the ridges, but is most noticeable on the summits of Sgurr a'Mhaim and Stob Ban. Both these peaks are a conspicuous feature of the views looking up Glen Nevis. Some of the peaks can be reached from Glen Nevis in the vicinity of Polldubh, or from its remote stretches between Steall and Tom an Elte, and on the south side the Old Military Road gives easy access throughout its entire length.

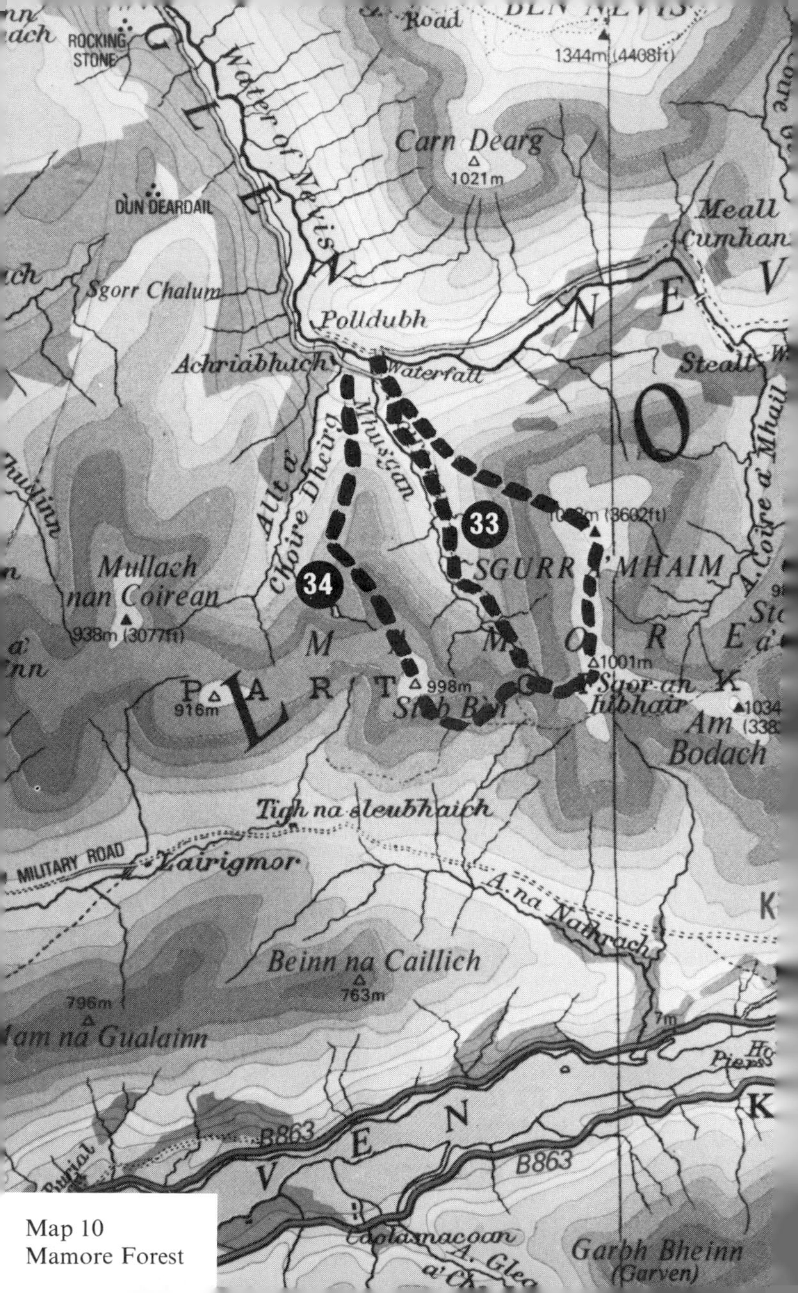

Map 10
Mamore Forest

The more westerly tops are usually climbed from the former and the more easterly from the latter. Strangely enough the most picturesque peaks are clustered round Sgurr a'Mhaim, and include the superb elevations of Stob Ban, Am Bodach and the Devil's Ridge.

Glen Nevis is one of the most beautiful in Scotland and should be seen by all climbers as well as walkers. The finest section begins at Polldubh and increases in splendour as you walk east, but its most spectacular feature is only revealed where the path turns to the right beyond the cataract. Here you are confronted by a scene of wild grandeur, with Steall Waterfall coming into view beyond the narrow gorge where it descends the steep and rugged slopes of An Gearanach. With favourable lighting it makes a superb subject for your camera.

Plate 74 An Gearanach and the gorge of Glen Nevis

Route 32. Binnein Mor from Kinlochleven. Leave the town by the path that skirts the shoulder of Meall an Doire Dhoraich, and after crossing the Old Military Road continue round the flanks of Na Gruagaichean, with views on the R of Loch Eilde Mor. Follow the path that rises round the crags of Sgurr Eilde Beag on the L until the lochans are reached, then bear L again to ascend the rough scree to the saddle due south of your peak. Since this is the highest top in the Mamores the panorama is extensive and to the west reveals most of the range in which the wall-like ridge of An Gearanach is prominent. Ben Nevis and its easterly satellites stretch across the skyline to the north and disclose their extremely steep declivities to advantage. Aonach Eagach does not look so formidable from this viewpoint and is crowned by the indented skyline of Bidean nam Bian in the south. To the south west glimpses of Loch Leven lead the eye to Loch Linnhe, backed by the hills of Ardgour.

Route 33. Sgurr a'Mhaim from Polldubh. While this peak can be climbed direct by its north-west ridge rising straight to the summit, it is more interesting to walk up the Allt Coire a'Mhusgain to the saddle and then turn L to attain Sgor an Iubhair. Now turn L again and traverse the Devil's Ridge which leads to the summit, passing *en route* the little peak of Stob Coire a'Mhail. The views from the cairn are magnificent and include the three features already noted.

Route 34. Stob Ban from Polldubh. This peak is usually ascended without difficulty by its north ridge, but again it is more interesting to follow Route 33 to the saddle as it opens up grand prospects of the precipitous buttresses supporting its summit. Turn R at the saddle and scramble up the rough quartzite scree to the cairn.

Stob Ban

Allt Coire a'Mhusgain

Plate 75 **Routes 33** and **34** are seen to advantage from Glen Nevis

Plate 76. **Route 23.—Sgor an Iubhair and the Devil's Ridge from Sgurr a'Mhaim**

Plate 77 **Route 33**— Am Bodach from Sgurr a'Mhaim

Bidein Druim nan Ramh and Mhallach nan Coireon from Sgurr a'Mhaim

Ben Nevis Range

Ben Nevis	4,406 feet	1,343 metres
Aonach Beag	4,060 feet	1,237 metres
Carn Mor Dearg	4,012 feet	1,223 metres
Aonach Mor	3,999 feet	1,219 metres
Carn Dearg North	3,961 feet	1,201 metres
Top of Achintee Path	3,900 feet	1,188 metres
Carn Dearg Meadhonach	3,873 feet	1,180 metres
Carn Mor Dearg Arete	3,750 feet	1,143 metres
Lowest point of Arete	3,475 feet	1,059 metres
Carn Dearg-South	3,348 feet	1,020 metres
Carn Beag Dearg	3,265 feet	995 metres
Meall an Suidhe	2,322 feet	708 metres

Ben Nevis is the highest mountain in Scotland and also the Monarch of our British Hills. It frowns upon the busy town of Fort William, but is obscured by its satellite, Meall an Suidhe. Its smooth and steep western flanks completely belie its hidden grandeur, but its rugged southern slopes, crowned by Carn Dearg and well seen from Polldubh, are an indication of its real magnificence. When viewed from Corpach across the glittering blue of Loch Linnhe, Ben Nevis reveals some of these features, but the main impression is that of its immense bulk, whereas the more easterly coign of vantage of Banavie opens up a glimpse of its towering cliffs that enclose the precipices of Coire na Ciste, a secret that is hidden from the average tourist but well known to the legions of rock climbers who visit this delectable playground. Facing the north-east, this superb display of buttress, ridge, gully and couloir is hemmed in by the lofty ridge crowned by Carn Mor Dearg, whose altitude is only about 400 feet less than its peer, and to which it is joined by the famous Arete, a feature that is unique in the Munros. Between these two peaks lies the Glen of the

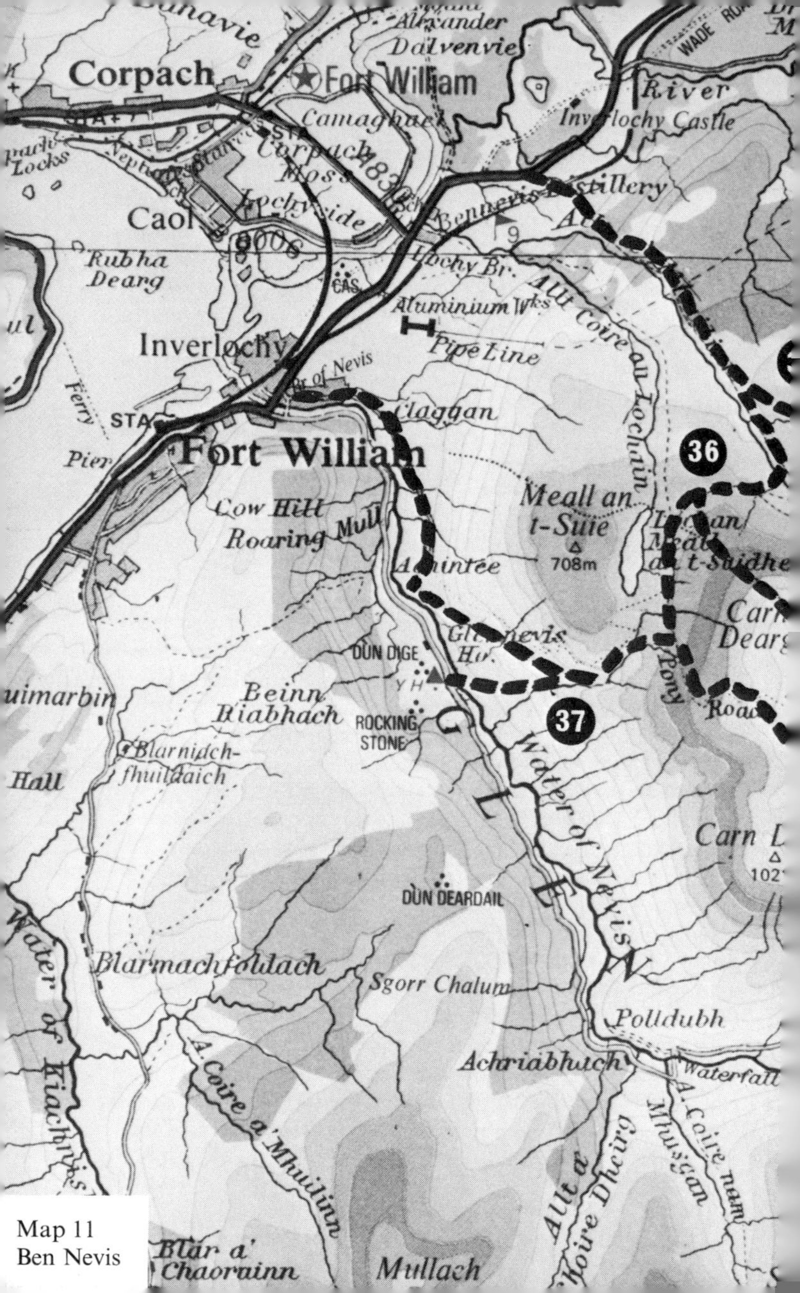

Corpach

Bunavie

Alexander
Dalvenvie

Fort William

Camaghael

River

Inverlochy Castle

Corpach 83

Neptunes Stair

Caol

Lochy-side

Rubha
Dearg

Ben nevis

Distillery

Lochy Br.

Aluminium Wks

Pipe Line

Inverlochy

Allt Coire an Lochain

STA

Br. of Nevis

Claggan

36

Pier

Fort William

Cow Hill
Roaring Mull

Meall an
t-Suie
△ 708m

Carn
Dearg

uimarbin

Hall

Beinn
Riabhach

Blarnidich-
fhuildaich

DUN DIGE

Achintee

Glen nevis
Ho.

Y.H.

ROCKING
STONE

37

Water of Nevis

Carn L
△ 102

Blarmachfoldach

DUN DEARDAIL

Sgorr Chalum

Polldubh

Achriabhach

Waterfall

Water of Kiachnish

A' Coire a' Mhuilinn

Blàr a'
Chaorainn

Mullach

Allt a'
Choire Dheirg

Allt a' Coire nam Muscan

Map 11
Ben Nevis

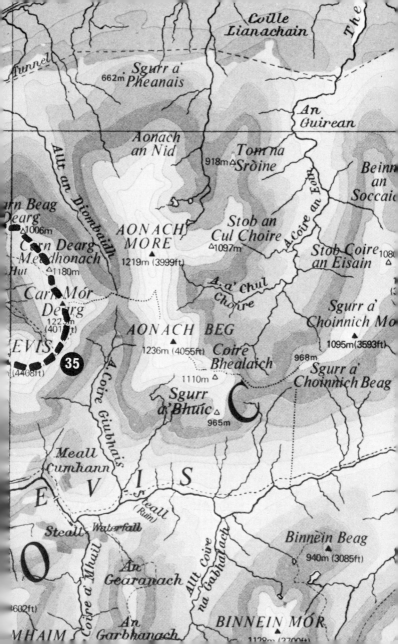

Allt a'Mhuilinn, which is the usual line of approach for the climber, and at its head stands the remote Hut of the Scottish Mountaineering Club, protected from the gales that sweep across the nearby summits and a welcome retreat for the mountaineer. Owing to its dominating altitude, Ben Nevis is often snowbound during both winter and spring, when great cornices overhang the lip of the corry to an unknown depth, and in whose north-eastern gullies it sometimes lingers on into the summer. This great mountain, therefore, has everything to offer the climber and in consequence is perhaps the most powerful magnet in the Highlands. But, since it has the reputation of being curtained by cloud for as much as 300 days each year, those who wish to enjoy to the full its glorious scenery must choose a day for the climb with discretion, savoured with luck, and the best opportunities for success are in April and May. Pedestrians who are content to gaze in wonder upon the towering precipices with as little effort as possible should stroll up the Allt a'Mhuilinn into Coire na Ciste, or if they are more energetic could walk up the uninteresting Tourist Route from Achintee, whence they may wander at leisure along the rim of the summit plateau and see at their feet the splendours of the mountain. But the experienced climber will select the only route that displays its charms to perfection; by first ascending Carn Mor Dearg, then crossing the sensational Arete, and finally wending his way along the plateau, and if the weather is calm and sunny he will see Ben Nevis in one of its most gentle moods.

Route 35. By Carn Mor Dearg. Start at the Ben Nevis Distillery by walking through the grounds to the railway bridge and then follow the path to the British Aluminium Tramway. Bear L and pick up the path through the heather which slants across the slopes to the brow of the moor, where the Allt a'Mhuilinn chatters away merrily as it plunges through a little gorge. Cross the burn and keep to the more level but often boggy path on its R bank, and after about a mile strike up to the L in the direction of Carn Beag Dearg,

Plate 79 **Route 35**—The summit of Carn Dearg Meadhonach

the first top on the ridge. The going is very arduous until it is attained, whence the walk along the lofty ridge is a revelation; as it gradually unveils Coire na Ciste on the R and the massive Aonachs on the L. Pass Carn Dearg Meadhonach to reach the shapely top of Carn Mor Dearg, which is a viewpoint without compare in this region, since it reveals the whole of Coire na Ciste from the North-East Buttress on the L to Carn Dearg on the R. Ahead the ridge falls to the Arete, with beyond its graceful sweep splendid prospects of the Mamores, among which Sgurr a'Mhaim and its little corrie are conspicuous. Then begin the traverse of the Arete, moving along its rocky crest with care until you come to the last section where the steepest rise is some 700 feet to the top of the North-East Buttress. Should this last section be under snow, exercise the utmost alertness and make use of your ice axe to ensure stability of each step, as a slip and slide backwards would precipitate you into the depths of Coire Leis. Having safely passed this lofty sentinel, the rest of the route is easy, with first a close view of the derelict Observatory, and then the many attractive topographical features of Coire na Ciste, in which the Gardyloo Gully, the Tower Ridge and Trident Buttress are prominent. On a clear day the summit panorama from Ben Nevis is stupendous, with the distant sea and its islands to the west, and in all other directions peaks and ridges, enlivened by the glint of light on lochs and lochans, as far as the eye can see. In an atmosphere of exceptional clarity you may be able to pick out such well-known landmarks as Ben Wyvis to the north; the Cairngorms to the north-east; Ben Lawers and Schiehallion to the east; Ben Lomond and the Cobbler to the south-east; Ben Cruachan, the Paps of Jura and the sea to the south; Mull over Loch Linnhe to the south-west; the Coolins of Skye to the west with Ben Attow and Mam Soul to the north-west. And beyond the summit plateau you look into the wide green valley where the River Lochy leads your eye to the R into the Great Glen which ends at Inverness. Having now gained many varied impressions of and from this peak, you will turn your steps homewards, descending by Routes 36 or 37 according to your destination.

Plate 80 **Route 35**—Carn Mor Dearg

Plate 35 **Route 25**   Sgurr a'Mhaim seen across the Arete from Carn Mor Dearg

Plate 82 **Route 35**—The twin ridges of Ben Nevis from Carn Mor Dearg

Route 36. By Carn Dearg. Follow Route 35 until you can pick out a line of cairns on the R slopes of the glen. Cross the burn and climb the rather indistinct track beside them until Lochan Meall an t'Suidhe appears ahead. Then turn L and pick your way over the scree and through the crags that deck the slopes of Carn Dearg, whence, on passing its summit, continue along the rising rim of the plateau to the cairn on Ben Nevis.

Route 37. By Achintee. Leave the farm and follow the well-worn pony track, now known as the Tourist Route, that rises diagonally round the steep flanks of Meall an Suidhe until you come to the ruins of the Half Way House. Then climb the seemingly endless stony zig-zags until the lip of Coire na Ciste is reached, whence turn R for the summit of the mountain. This route may be reached by the path from the Youth Hostel in Glen Nevis.

Plate 83 **Route 36**—Coire na Ciste and Carn Dearg from Carn Mor Dearg

Plate 84. **Photos 36 and 37**—Snow cornices overhang the precipices of Ben Nevis

Plate 85 **Routes 36** and **37** — The Tower and the final section of its ridge

Creag Meaghaidh Range

Creag Meaghaidh	3,700 feet	1,128 metres
Puist Coire Ardair	3,592 feet	1,095 metres
Creag Mhor	3,496 feet	1,066 metres
Poite Coire Ardair	3,460 feet	1,055 metres
Beinn a'Chaoruinn	3,437 feet	1,048 metres
Meall Coire Choille-rais	3,299 feet	1,006 metres
Carn Liath	3,298 feet	1,005 metres
An Cearcallach	3,250 feet	991 metres
Sron Garbh Choire	3,250 feet	991 metres
The Window	3,200 feet	975 metres
Meall an-t-Snaim	3,180 feet	969 metres
A'Bhuidheanach	3,177 feet	968 metres
Stob Choire Dhuibh	3,002 feet	915 metres
Carn Dearg	2,955 feet	901 metres
Lochan Coire Ardair	2,046 feet	624 metres

Creag Meaghaidh dominates the massive group of rounded hills that extend for some 12 miles along the entire north-western border of Loch Laggan. When seen from the lakeside road they display little of interest to the climber, other than an invigorating traverse of the ups and downs of the lofty connecting ridges. But, hidden away in the deep fastnesses of the range lies a wild corrie that is hemmed in on the south and west by immense cliffs that drop precipitously for about 1,500 feet to Lochan Coire Ardair. This is the most spectacular prize of the group and may be reached by a stalkers' path which starts at the farm of Aberarder; it is some four miles in length and takes about two hours of easy going to attain the lochan.

The path rises sharply from the moorland as far as the first group of scattered trees, at a height of about 1,800 feet, whence it levels out and contours round the northern slopes of the vast corrie. But when about a mile from the cliffs it descends slightly to the burn and follows its L bank to the shore of the lochan. Photographers should note that even during the summer months the light goes off the cliffs about 1 p.m., so that it is essential to get there by mid-day if satisfactory shots are to be secured.

The cliffs were first explored by rock climbers as long ago as April 1896, but in recent years they have received more attention and a hut now stands behind an immense boulder at the foot of the Pinnacle Buttress. The most popular ascents are the three Buttresses and the three 'Posts' or gullies that cleave them. To the north the cliffs diminish in height and finally merge with the rising ground leading to the lofty Pass, known as the Window.

Loch a' Bhanain

Coire a' Bhanain

Be Bh

Sròn Garbh Choire

A' nan Luibhean

River Roy

Meall a' Mheanbhchruidh
△ 818m

L. Roy

Poite Coire Ardair

Allt Coire

Uisge nam Fichead

L. Uaine

Coire Ardair

Lochan a'
• Hut

Creag
△ 1065m

CREAG MEAGHAIDH
1130m (3707ft)

Puist
Coire Ardair

G

Coire Buidhe

Meall a' Bharnish

Meall Coire
Choille-rais

45m
△

Coire na h-Uamha

Moy Burn

993m
△

An Cearcallach

Beinn a' haorainn
▲ 1053m (3455ft)

A. na h-Uamha

Creag an Cailliche

Meall Badanach

Creag Mhór
Moy

Moy

Lublea
• 254m

Tey

Craigbeg

Moy

N

Map 12
Creag Meaghaidh

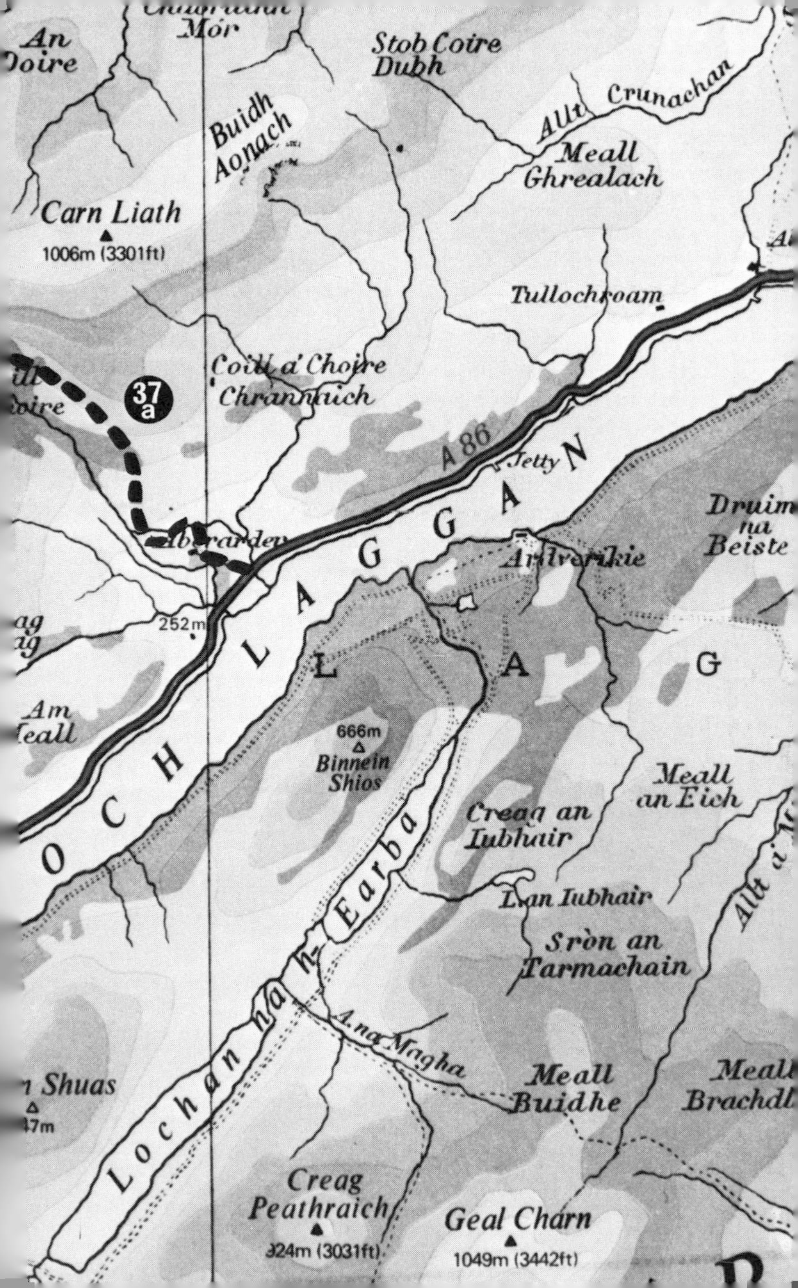

An Doire
Cùl Raithe Mòr
Stob Coire Dubh
Allt Crunachan
Buidh Aonach
Meall Ghrealach
Carn Liath
1006m (3301ft)
Tullochroam
Coill a' Choire Chrannuich
37a
A 86
Jetty
LAGGAN
Druim na Beiste
Aberarder
Ardverikie
L
A
G
Am Meall
252m
ag ig
OCH
666m
Binnein Shios
Creag an Iubhair
Meall an Eich
Lochan na h-Earba
Lon Iubhair
Sròn an Tarmachain
Allt a' M
A na Magha
n Shuas
7m
Meall Buidhe
Meall Brachdl
Creag Peathraich
324m (3031ft)
Geal Charn
1049m (3442ft)

Route 37a. Climbers who stay at the Loch Laggan Hotel need to drive only four miles to reach Aberarder, whereas those who prefer the comforts of Glenspean Lodge Hotel will have to drive fourteen miles to reach it. Turn up the side road to the farm and park your car on the R where there is space for several vehicles. After changing into climbing boots, pass through the gate at the back and turn L to follow the wall to a sheepfold. Go through it to the top gate and pick up the track on the R beside a stone wall. About two hundred yards ahead turn sharp L and climb steeply through the boulders as far as the scattered trees on the skyline. A short cut may be made across the moor from the farm, but this involves the crossing of a high stone wall when it may be difficult to locate the path; hence while the former approach is slightly longer it is free from possible error. Beyond the trees the rough track levels out and swings round to the L along the contours of the corrie. Hereabouts the cliffs at its head come into view and reveal the sharp dip on their right, already referred to as the Window. The last mile of the ascent seems endless until finally the lochan suddenly appears at your feet. The scene is magnificent and the epitome of sombre desolation, with only the music of the burn to break the profound silence, save on occasion the sudden flight of a brace of Ptarmigan with their chicks fluttering away to seek cover. Should you wish to scale Creag 'Meggie', as it is familiarly known to climbers, walk up to the Window and turn L to ascend the final slopes to its summit cairn.

Plate 86 **Route 37a** — Pinnacle Buttress and the 3 Posts from Lochan Coire Ardair

The Saddle Group

The Saddle	3,317 feet	1,011 metres
Sgurr na Forcan	3,100 feet	945 metres
Sgurr na Sgine	3,098 feet	944 metres
Spidean Dhomhuill Bhric	3,082 feet	942 metres
Sgurr Leac nan Each	3,013 feet	918 metres
Faochag	3,010 feet	917 metres
Sgurr na Creige	2,850 feet	869 metres
Bealach Coire Mhalagain	2,291 feet	698 metres
Sgurr a'Gharg Gharaidh	2,252 feet	686 metres

The finest elevation of this graceful, tapering peak comes into view during the long descent of Glen Shiel, and for about two miles it dominates the scene, framed by the rugged enclosing slopes of the narrowest part of the glen. It only disappears from view on reaching Bridge of Shiel, whence the road skirts its flanks almost to the head waters of Loch Duich. In this classic view of the mountain, Faochag appears on the left as a sharp, well defined peak, and it is customary to portray the two together, when, in snowy raiment, the beauty of one is complimentary to that of the other. Moreover, when seen from Sgurr na Carnach on the other side of the glen, the serrated eastern ridge of The Saddle charms the eye and is a prominent feature of the view. The two peaks are separated by the lofty Bealach Coire Mhalagain, which is the starting point for the most sporting ascent of The Saddle. This is really the culminating point of a U-shaped group of hills, to the east of which extends the rocky spur of Sgurr na Forcan. It affords an interesting scramble of which about 1,000 feet are very steep, but should not be scaled by inexperienced climbers as the knife-edge section is sensational and yields the summit only by way of a short narrow gully. In severe winter conditions this ascent would rank as a major expedition. The two northern ridges are in part narrow and characterised by precipitous rock faces, with here and there knife-edges and pinnacles. But the main ridge proper is about one and a half miles in length and extends due east-west from Sgurr na Forcan to Spidean Dhomhuill Bhric. The ascent of the two northern ridges can be made without difficulty and the best plan is to climb Sgurr na Creige and descend by Sgurr a'Gharg Gharaidh. Two wild corries flank the Sgurr na Criege ridge; Coir' Uaine lies to the west and is the finer, with a small lochan at its head almost directly below The Saddle, whose face hereabouts is cleaved by a great gully. Coire Caol lies to the east and is of less interest.

Map 13
Kintail Hills

Route 38. By Sgurr na Forcan. Leave Glen Shiel about three quarters of a mile south-east of Achnangart and follow the stalkers' path to the west which winds its way uphill across the moor to the broad ridge south of Biod an Fhithich, then turn L in the direction of the above mentioned bealach. To the R of it rises the Forcan Ridge that is supported on the L by shattered, precipitous cliffs of menacing aspect. Climb to the R of its crest, then cross the knife-edge and scale the gully that will place you at the foot of the rocky cone carrying the summit cairn. The panorama is extensive but shut in to the north-east by the Five Sisters of Kintail. To the south-east a veritable sea of peaks and ridges lead the eye on a clear day to Ben Nevis. To the west Ben Sgriol is prominent by reason of its proximity, and to the L of it there are glimpses of Loch Hourn, while to the R the blue arms of the sea, backed by the distant Coolins of Skye, make a beautiful and attractive vista.

Route 39. By Sgurr na Creige. Leave Shiel Bridge and follow the path up the Allt Undalain as far as the fork in the burn; cross it and climb the slopes of Sgurr na Creige ahead. This ascent is steep and strenuous, and continues for about 1,500 feet, but the going may be facilitated by taking a wide zig-zag course. The sharp nose of the peak appears on the skyline, but after passing it the angle eases off and good progress can be made along the ridge and over its narrow sections to the cairn on The Saddle.

Route 40. By Sgurr a'Gharg Gharaidh. Follow Route 39 but keep to the path all the way to the col above Loch Coire nan Crogachan, with striking views on the L of Coir' Uaine. Turn L at the col and traverse the crest of the ridge all the way to the reigning peak, noting on the R glimpses of Loch Hourn far below.

Plate 87 Faochag and The Saddle from Glen Shiel

Plate 88 **Route 38** The Saddle, Sgurr na Forcan and the connecting ridge

The Five Sisters of Kintail

Sgurr Fhuaran (Scour Ouran)	3,505 feet	1,068 metres
Sgurr na Ciste Duibhe	3,370 feet	1,027 metres
Sgurr na Carnach	3,270 feet	997 metres
Sgurr nan Spainteach	3,129 feet	954 metres
Sgurr nan Saighead	2,987 feet	910 metres
Sgurr na Moraich	2,870 feet	875 metres
Bealach an Lapain	2,371 feet	723 metres
Sgurr an t'Searriach	1,886 feet	575 metres

This mighty range of hills dominates the head of Loch Duich
and its conspicuous, well defined tops can be picked out
among its cluster of lofty neighbours from many points to the
west. Its finest elevation is revealed from the crest of Mam
Rattachan where the view includes the blue of Loch Duich
below, but a good idea of its topography is also obtained
from the Youth Hostel on the shore of the loch. A reference
to the map will show that there are actually six peaks in this
range, but since Spainteach is hidden behind Ciste Duibhe in
the above prospect, the impression is gained of only five,
hence the name. As mentioned earlier in this volume, the
complete traverse of the range is a considerable undertaking,
even with transport to a point in Glen Shiel immediately
below the Bealach an Lapain. But in the walk from east to
west a saving can be made by omitting the last top, Moraich,
and following the burn down from the last bealach. And
moreover, since it involves over 10,000 feet of ascent and
descent, an early start should be made if the members of the
party wish to be back at their lodgings in time for dinner.

Fig. 88. The Five Sisters of Kintail and Loch Duich from Mam Rattachan

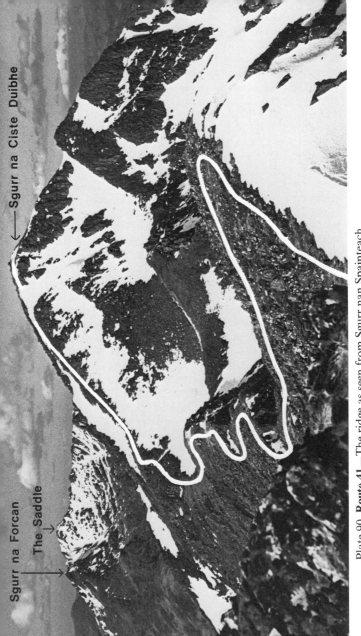

Sgurr na Ciste Duibhe

Sgurr na Forcan

The Saddle

Plate 90 **Route 41** — The ridge as seen from Sgurr nan Spainteach

Route 41. The Traverse of the Ridge. Drive up Glen Shiel to the gap in the plantations below the Bealach an Lapain and climb the steep grassy slopes to attain it. Turn L and ascend the long approach to Spainteach, noting the view to the R of Fhuaran across the depths of Coire Domhain. One of the best views of the ridge is disclosed on reaching the cairn, with Ciste Duibhe ahead and a glimpse over its L shoulder of the more distant Saddle. Continue along the rocky crest of the ridge to this top, with a bird's eye view of the glen below on the L, and then cross the next bealach to climb Carnach. This peak opens up a superb vista of Loch Duich below and of the fine eastern ridge of The Saddle, together with Sgurr na Forcan, on the other side of the glen, and also unveils the real dominance of Fhuaran to the R. Now cross the deep bealach and scale its slopes, resting awhile by the cairn to admire the magnificent panorama which is one of the most celebrated in all Scotland. There is such a galaxy of peaks in this region that it is difficult to pick out any one of them for special mention, save perhaps that of Beinn Fhada on the other side of Gleann Lichd. But far away to the south-east and above the long skyline of peaks and ridges appears the dome of Ben Nevis, which is most clearly perceived in a limpid atmosphere when carrying a mantle of snow. Now commence the descent to the next bealach, which is the longest and steepest in this range, noting on the approach to the triple-peaked Saighead its fine supporting cliffs that drop away into the depths of Gleann Lichd on the R. Walk round the rim of the corrie to attain its chief cairn, and then proceed over easier ground to Moraich, your last top, whence descend its grassy slopes eventually to reach the shore of Loch Duich.

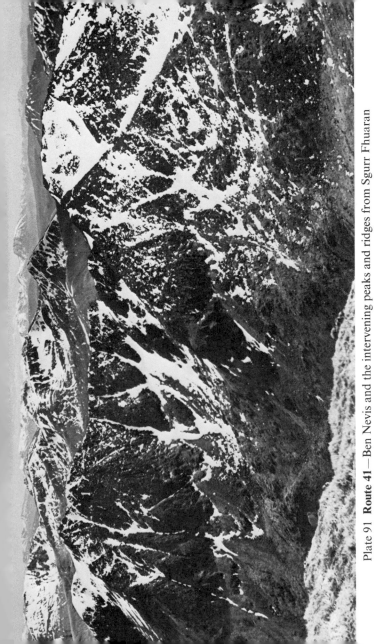

Plate 91 **Route 41** — Ben Nevis and the intervening peaks and ridges from Sgurr Fhuaran

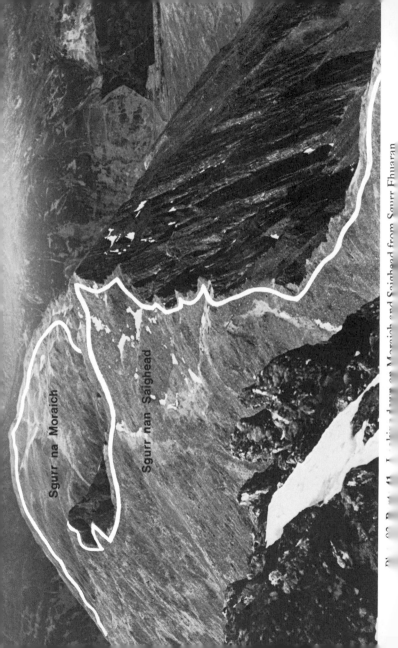

Sgurr na Moraich

Sgurr nan Saighead

Looking down on Moraich and Saighead from Sgurr Fhuaran

The Applecross Hills

Beinn Bhan	2,936 feet	895 metres
Sgurr a'Chaorachain	2,600 feet	792 metres
Meall Gorm	2,325 feet	709 metres
Bealach na Ba	2,053 feet	625 metres

Seen from Skye, the Applecross tableland presents an
unattractive appearance as its western slopes of bare, broken
sandstone fall gradually to the tree-fringed shore of the Inner
Sound between Toscaig and Applecross Bay. But when
observed from the wild hill road connecting Jeantown on
Loch Carron with the charming fishing village of Shieldaig
these hills assume an entirely different aspect, and on
proceeding downhill to Loch Kishorn the scene unfolded is
one of the most dramatic in Scotland. For ahead rises the
dominating southern satellite of Sgurr a'Chaorachain whose
precipitous front of purplish-red sandstone is stratified
horizontally and flanked on the L by the deep glen that carries
the road over to Applecross, and on the R by its dynamic
outlier, the Cioch. At Tornapress there is a fork in the road
which is the starting point for one of the most spectacular
drives in Britain. In a distance of only six miles this L branch
rises from sea level to a height of 2,053 feet at the Bealach na
Ba, where there is now a large car park, ascending *en route*
the wild glen of the Allt a'Chumhaing and ending with a series
of zig-zags at a gradient of 1 in 3. On a clear day its cairn-
littered crest reveals a splendid distant prospect of the peaks
of Rhum and the Coolins and Red Hills of Skye, with on their
R a glimpse of the Storr and on their L the ranges that extend
southwards from Loch Duich. Some two miles to the north of
Tornapress the four great corries of Beinn Bhan come into
view on the L. They face the north-east and their mural
precipices fall vertically for about 1,500 feet; each corrie is
separated by a castellated spur and the whole provides a

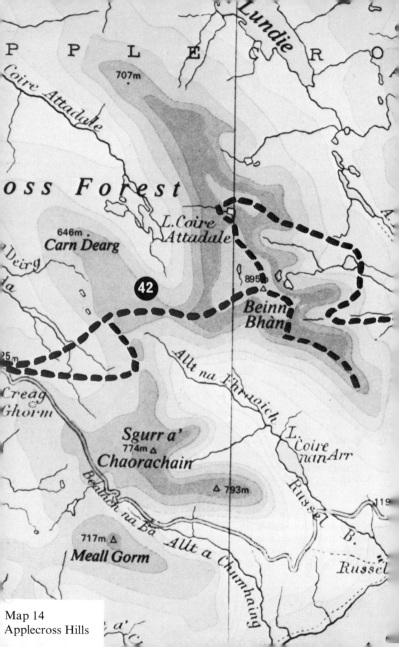

Map 14
Applecross Hills

Treudaich
Meall na Saobhaidhe
368m
Strath a'Bhathaich
Ceann-loch damh
Abhainn Deary
94m
L. Coultrie
Meall Gobhar
A. Meall nan Gobhar
Allt a' Ghiubhais
Glaschnoc
Coille Dhubh
L. an Loin
Sgorr a'Gharaidh
730m
Ln. Meall na Caillich
Rassal Ashwood
Kishorn
Allt a' Chuirn
Tornapress
Cearcall Dubh
A 896
Works
Kishorn
Glenmore
Abhainn
Ardarroch
L. a' Choire Leith
An Sgurr

picture of mountain grandeur that completely belies the uninteresting western aspect of the whole plateau. From L to R the four corries are: Each; na Feola; na Poite and nan Fhamhair.

The new road encircling the Applecross Peninsula has now been completed, and motorists who have driven up to the Bealach na Ba should continue downhill to the village of Applecross where it begins at sea level. Here you turn R to enjoy miles of sea and mountain scenery where the views unfolded in rapid succession are some of the finest in Scotland. The engineering of the road is marvellous and has a smooth tarmac surface; it goes up and down hill, sometimes beside the sea and often right up into the wild hills, eventually to join the road to Kenmare which was completed some years ago. By taking the drive in this direction, the light is most favourable for both colour and monochrome photography. Based on a start and finish at the Loch Torridon Hotel, the total distance of the drive is about 60 miles.

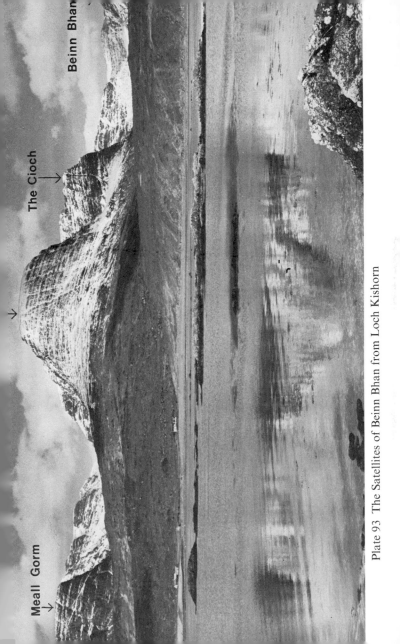

Plate 93 The Satellites of Beinn Bhan from Loch Kishorn

Plate 94 Looking down to Loch Kishorn from the zig-zags of the Bealach na Ba

Plate 95 The four corries of Beinn Bhan from Kishorn Lodge

Route 42. Beinn Bhan from Bealach na Ba. To reach the
dominating cairn of the group involves a very rough tramp of
about three map miles but with a rise of less than 1,000 feet.
On looking north-east from the Bealach na Ba, the
configuration of the ground is obvious; for a horizontal ridge
connects the northern slopes of Sgurr a'Chaorachain with the
saddle which is in line with Beinn Bhan, whence gently rising
ground leads to the cairn on the skyline. However, while this
may seem the best line of approach, the broken character of
the connecting ridge, supported on its north side by 1,000-foot
precipices, is not clearly revealed from this distance and on
closer acquaintance will be found to consist of great inclined
slabs of sandstone with considerable drops between them. It is
therefore advisable to take a direct line for the saddle, first
going downhill to the floor of the immense intervening corrie
and thereafter climbing to the summit by a sketchy cairned
track over less broken ground but returning by the ridge and
slopes of Sgurr a'Chaorachain. To view the corries it is best to
turn R from the summit and to keep to the crest of the ridge as
far as na Feola, with sensational vertical drops on the L and
splendid prospects on a clear day of the vast panorama round
the eastern arc. Then, retrace your steps and continue to the
end of nan Fhamhair, noting in passing the awesome vertical
buttress and deep gully that separates it from na Poite. The
latter, with its two gleaming green lochans far below, affords
the most dramatic scene of all. The first peak to rivet the eye
in the panorama is Beinn Damh, whose undulating ridge
stretches for some three miles and reveals the Stirrup Mark
below its highest top, and with below it a glimpse of Loch
Damh. Beinn Alligin, Beinn Dearg and Liathach appear to
the L, and form the skyline, while further to the R rise the
many peaks of the Ben Damph and Coulin Forests. To the
south-east there is a perfect galaxy of peaks with Ben Sgriol
prominent in the south, then to the L The Saddle and an end-
on-view of the Five Sisters of Kintail. Skye is disclosed to the
west and on a clear day the Outer Hebrides in the far north-
west.

Beinn Bhan

Plate 96 **Route 42**—Seen from the new car park on the summit of Bealach na Ba

Route 43. The Corries of Beinn Bhan. Leave Tornapress and cross the stone bridge over the River Kishorn. Turn R at the building and pick up the stalkers path that skirts the south-eastern shoulder of Beinn Bhan. This rises gradually in the direction of the Allt Loch Gaineamhach, but should be deserted when in sight of the corries which are reached over rough heather and steep boulder-strewn ground. In misty weather it is safer to keep to the stalkers' path as far as the plank bridge spanning the burn coming down from Coire na Feola. Here turn L and ascend the sketchy path which rises along the R bank of the stream and ends at the poised boulder shown in the foreground of plate 98. Walk into each corrie in turn to admire the splendour of their perpendicular mural precipices, all of which look most impressive under snow and might well be courses of Cyclopean masonry, and note the spectacular spurs that remind of Titanic Castles. Go as far as the lochans cradled in Coire na Poite and then continue over easy ground to the ridge on the R of the fourth corrie. Climb this with care and then bear L along the crest for the cairn on Beinn Bhan.

It should be noted that the former Route and much of the latter are exceedingly rough, since both of them are decked with thousands of red sandstone boulders through which the easiest way has to be found, meanwhile keeping an alert eye on the objective ahead.

Routes 42 and 43 may be combined to make a most enjoyable round, but it is best to start from the Bealach na Ba and return to be picked up at Tornapress.

Plate 97 **Route 42** — Looking into Coire na Poite from the ridge

Plate 43. The Mural Precipices of Coire na Feola

Plate 99 **Route 43**—The last of the Four Great Corries—Coire nan Fhamhair

Beinn Damh

Beinn Damh	2,957 feet	901 metres
Sgurr na Bana Mhoraire	2,251 feet	686 metres

Ben Damph House, now the luxurious Loch Torridon Hotel, is superlatively situated for the exploration of this mountain and its adjoining peaks, and may be reached conveniently from Loch Carron by the new road running from Shieldaig on the south side of Upper Loch Torridon, or from Kinlochewe by the old, single-track road down Glen Torridon. The twin summits of Creag Sgorach, known also as Sgurr na Bana Mhoraire, stand at the northern extremity of the lofty ridge of Beinn Damh, and overhang the hotel to dominate the foreshortened view of the Forest. And while the whole mountain, together with its strange Stirrup Mark immediately beneath the highest top, are seen at their best on a clear day from Beinn Bhan, or from the Shieldaig Road near Lochan an Loin, the many peaks of the Forest, together with those of the adjacent Coulin Forest, are revealed at their finest from the Diabaig Road on the north side of Loch Torridon late on a sunny afternoon. One of the great charms of Ben Damph Forest is that it is threaded by a maze of well preserved stalkers' paths, which reveal more intimately its several peaks as they come into view, and moreover, are so easily graded that they can be ascended with equal facility by old and young.

Ben Damph Forest and the adjacent Coulin Forest are strictly guarded deer-forests, where climbers are regarded with little favour during the late summer months. No objection, however, is raised during April, May and June, but should the visitor wish to explore these regions in the autumn, the best plan is to consult the head ghillie as to the movements of local stalkers, otherwise he may be accidentally shot!

Sgurr na Bana Mhoraire

Plate 100 The long ridge of Beinn Damh is well seen from Lochan an Loin

Map 15
Beinn Damh and Liathach

Spide an Coire nan Clach
972m
NTS
Allt a Choire Dhuibh Mhoir
Spidean an a' Choire Leith
L. Coire na Caime
Stuc a'Choire Dhuibh Bhig
1054m (3458ft)
1023m
LIATHACH
45
Glen Torridon
NTS
Lochan an Iasgaich
River Torridon
Seana Mheallan
436m
Lochan Odhar
Abhainn Thraill
L. an Neimhe
L. Meall a' Ghuail
L. an Uillt-bheithe
L. an Diona
Meall Dearg
Bealach Ban
Bealach na Lice
Sgurr na Lochan Uaine
925m (3035ft)
Sgurr Ruadh
960m (3150ft)
933m (3061ft)
Meall a'Chinn Deirg
L. Coire Fionnaraich
Eaglaisse
an Eoin

Beinn na h-Eaglaise →   Maol Chean - Dearg →   Beinn Damh →

Plate 102 Beinn Damh from the same viewpoint with a telephoto lens

Fig. 100. The Avenue of Rishis

Plate 104 **Route 44**—A distant view from Upper Loch Torridon

Route 44. Beinn Damh from the Hotel. Follow the new road to
the bridge spanning the tumultuous Ben Damh Burn, and just
beyond it on the L pass through a gate to gain the stalkers'
path threading the forest. This rises at an easy gradient on the
L bank of the stream, and on emerging from the leafy canopy
note the fine waterfall in the deep gorge on the L. Continue
along the path, with views ahead of your mountain, until you
reach the small cairn marking its terminus; it is situated
immediately below the spacious saddle on the skyline. Now
make your way uphill over heather, bent and moss to the
second cairn, whence continue more steeply through bog and
boulders to the saddle, meanwhile noting on your L the vast
stony corrie that deeply penetrates the mountain and is
dominated on the L by Creag na h-Iolaire. On gaining the
ridge turn R and ascend its broad crest, noting the precipitous
crags on the L overhanging Loch Damh far below. The twin
tops of Creag Sgorach unfold magnificent vistas round the
north-western arc, in which Liathach, Beinn Alligin and Beinn
Bhan are prominent, but it is the blue sea with its islands and
rocky coastline that will hold your gaze, backed by the Outer
Hebrides. Now retrace your steps to the saddle and climb the
steeper ridge to the highest top, observing on the L the
remarkably bold elevation of Maol Chean-Dearg, the highest
peak in Ben Damph Forest, and to the L of it the more distant
Sgurr Ruadh, the crowning peak of Coulin Forest. To the
south-west observe the wonderful vista along Lochs Kishorn
and Carron to Scalpay and the Red Hills of Skye, backed by
the sharp peaks of the Coolins. If time is not pressing, encircle
the wild corrie of Toll nam Biast until you reach the strange
flat-topped Stuc Toll nam Biast, which is a superlative
viewpoint for the appraisal of the peaks of Ben Damph
Forest, for the glittering lochans between them, and for the
whole of the vast panorama round the southern arc.

NOTE. The descent may be shortened by walking down the
ridge on the R to Creag na h'Iolaire.

Plate 105 A view of **Route 44** from Beinn Damh

Liathach

Spidean a'Choire Leith	3,456 feet	1,054 metres
Mullach an Rathain	3,358 feet	1,024 metres
Bidean Toll a'Mhuic	3,200 feet	975 metres
Am Fasarinen	3,050 feet	930 metres
Stuc a'Choire Dhuibh Bhig	3,000 feet	913 metres
Meall Dearg	2,606 feet	855 metres
Sgorr a'Chadail	2,297 feet	700 metres

Climbers who know this great mountain will agree that it is the mightiest and most imposing in all Britain. On leaving Kinlochewe to drive down Glen Torridon, you first skirt the quartzite slopes of Beinn Eighe, but on reaching Loch Clair it suddenly bursts upon the view across the moor, its eastern ramparts falling almost vertically and its impending cliffs of red sandstone stretching as far as the eye can see. As you continue your drive beneath them you cannot fail to be impressed by their extreme steepness and horizontal bedding, as they hem in the north side of the glen for no less than six miles, to end suddenly above Torridon House. On a clear sunny morning you will also notice the glittering cap of white quartzite which has often been mistaken for snow and is the crowning feature of the lofty ridge. When driving eastwards from Shieldaig by the new road, Liathach appears ahead on topping the first rise and continues to dominate the whole scene until the grim portals of Glen Torridon are entered. On the north side this mountain is even more precipitous, and the perpendicular cliffs enclosing Coire na Caime are some 2,000 feet high. Such a mountain not only commands admiration but also respect, both of which are heightened as you walk along the narrow sections of its summit ridge. Liathach should be traversed from east to west on a favourable day, and it requires a good two-hour scramble to attain the eastern

Plate 106 A majestic prospect of Liathach from the end of Loch Clair

end of the ridge by one of two steep gullies that split the upper section only of this face. After visiting the nearby eastern top for the close view of Beinn Eighe, you retrace your steps and climb steadily over two subsidiary tops before setting foot on the reigning peak. The views throughout are spectacular and especially so of the corries on the north side of the mountain, but it is only on reaching Spidean a'Choire Leith that both sections of the ridge are revealed to your gaze. The absence of quartzite to the west will be noticed, but as compensation there is the bird's-eye view of Am Fasarinen and a fine prospect of Mullach an Rathain. This is the last top to be visited by most climbers, who on reaching the Stone Shoot on the L used to run down its 2,000 feet of scree to quickly reach Fasag. But in recent years there has been considerable deterioration in the scree and it is no longer a safe route of descent. Hence, it is better to leave the ridge to the south-east of Mullach an Rathain and to go due south down the grassy tongues into a wide grassy corrie. Thence follow the course of the Allt an Thuill Bhain, either directly to Glen Torridon or when the sandstone bands appear descend westwards along the sloping terraces to the road near the camp sites.

The standard time for the Liathach traverse by a fit and experienced climber is 8 hours; split up as follows: 2 hours up to the ridge from the glen; 4 hours over the summit from Stuc a'Choire Dhuibh Bhig to Mullach an Rathain, which allows time for lunch and photography; and 2 hours down to the road.

It whould be noted that the traverse of Liathach is a considerable undertaking and is for the experienced climber rather than for the ordinary pedestrian, by whom it should be severely left alone. However, it is possible for the latter to reach Sgorr a'Chadail, the most westerly top on the ridge, by following the stalkers' path in Coire Mhic Nobuil for about a mile and to then take a diagonal course up the north western slopes of the mountain. Thence, the summit ridge may be followed safely to Mullach an Rathain and the descent made as described above.

Plate 107 **Route 45** begins with a relentless ascent of Stuc a'Choire Dhuibh Bhig

Since the road threading Glen Torridon runs along the actual base of the southern front of Liathach, the foreshortened aspect of its cliffs is misleading and gives no true conception of their angle or immensity. Climbers who are interested should make the easy ascent of Beinn na h'Eaglaise on the opposite side of the glen and in the late afternoon, when the westering sun clearly delineates every detail, they will obtain the most spectacular prospect of the mural precipices of this mighty peak.

Route 45. The Traverse of Liathach. Park your car off the road about a mile west of the ruined cottage in Glen Torridon, or in the new car park nearby, and commence the ascent by making a bee-line for the two gullies on the skyline. You will encounter bands of sandstone, most of which can be turned or easily climbed, and do not fail to note the immense Corrie Leith on your L which is almost symmetrically rimmed with sandstone. Select the gully that seems easiest and on attaining the ridge turn R for Stuc a'Choire Dhuibh Bhig. On a clear day the quartzite slopes of Beinn Eighe are most impressive and this coign of vantage discloses more clearly the true elevation of the ups and downs of its ridge. Then retrace your steps and be careful while passing along the narrowest sections of the ridge, with abysmal drops into the deep corries on your R. Proceed ahead by climbing Bidean Toll a'Mhuic and its satellite, beyond which you come to the large blocks of rough quartzite that deck the highest peak of Spidean a'Choire Leith. Rest awhile on this lofty perch to admire not only the entire summit ridge of your mountain which is five miles in length, but also its surrounding peaks. Strangely enough those to the north are not very beautiful, and Beinn Alligin in particular is most disappointing. But those to the south will hold your gaze by reason of their distinctive elevations, and especially that of Beinn na h'Eaglaise whose remarkable curving bands of sandstone will attract your eye. Now descend the western slopes of the reigning peak and make your way carefully over the sensational pinnacles of Am

Bruach Toll
a'Mhuic

Plate 108 **Route 45**—Looking west along the lofty ridge of Liathach

Fasarinen which fall vertically on your R into Coire na Caime. Hand- and foot-holds are ample and safe, but if you wish to avoid them follow the path below on their L. Continue up the gradually rising grassy ridge to Mullach an Rathain and then descend slightly L to reach the top of the grassy tongues that are the key to the descent beside the Allt an Thuill Bhain.

Benn Eighe

Plate 109 **Route 45**—Looking east from Spidean a'Choire Leith

Mullach an Rathain →

Meall Dearg ↓

Plate 110 **Route 45**—Looking west across Coire na Caime from Spidean a'Choire Leith

Corrie Below Mullach an Rathain

Plate 111 **Route 45**—A safe descent by Allt an Thuill Bhain

Mullach an Rathain Am Fasarinen Spidean a'Choire Leith

Plate 112 The mural precipices of Liathach seen late in the day from Beinn na h'Eaglaise

Beinn Alligin

Sgurr Mhor	3,232 feet	985 metres
Tom na Gruagach	3,024 feet	922 metres
Meall an Laoigh	2,904 feet	885 metres
Horns of Alligin	2,840 feet	864 metres

This is the most westerly of the Torridon Peaks, and rises immediately to the north of Torridon House and Inver Alligin. When seen from the new Shieldaig road its fine elevation commands attention by reason of two unusual topographical features: first, the great gash splitting the central and highest peak, Sgurr Mhor; and second, the three Horns of Alligin that extend eastwards, eventually to fall steeply to the moor. The same characteristics may also be observed from the private road that runs along the south shore of Upper Loch Torridon, and was formerly the connecting link between Ben Damh House, now the Loch Torridon Hotel, the River Balgy famous for its salmon and Loch Damh renowned for its trout. To photographers the viewpoints on this winding road, which is hemmed in by lofty rhododendrons, have much to commend them, due to several charming foregrounds where red sandstone cliffs enclose little bays that at low tide are rimmed with brilliant orange wrack.

The ascent and traverse of the summit ridge of Beinn Alligin is a sporting course much enjoyed by all keen climbers. There are no special problems to be encountered until the Horns are reached, where great care is needed in making the ascent by pressure holds of the first of them. Thereafter, the difficulties decrease and there is a final descent to the stalkers' path which leads back to the starting point of the climb—the fine old stone bridge spanning the deep gorge through which the turbulent waters of the Allt Coire Mhic Nobuil rush down to the sea.

The panorama from the summit is one of the finest hereabouts as it not only opens up an uninterrupted prospect of hill and sea round the western arc, but also unfolds a superb view of its eastern neighbours where the horizontal sandstone bedding is seen at its best.

Route 46. The Traverse of Beinn Alligin. Turn R at the foot of Glen Torridon, and after passing the cottages of Fasag continue along the shore of the loch. Turn R at the first fork and drive up the graceful sweeps of the single-track road, pass through a beautiful collection of trees and emerge at the stone bridge, immediately beyond which there is space to park several cars on the L. Thence the track begins and goes uphill through heather to the shoulder of the mountain, where turn L and walk up into the mouth of Coire an Laoigh. Follow the burn to its source on Meall an Laoigh which is the steepest section of the ascent; it ends on the skyline whence bear R for the cairn on Tom na Gruagach. On the north side this top is supported by vertical, terraced cliffs which are not completely disclosed until the next top is attained, but its chief merit is that of opening up a matchless prospect of Sgurr Mhor with its 1,800 feet gash, which plunges down with almost vertical sides into the depth of Toll a'Mhadaidh. Thence an easy walk will place you by the highest cairn from which the above mentioned features of the whole panorama are best observed. On a very clear day it is possible to pick out Cape Wrath in the far north and Ardnamurchan in the south. Now stroll downhill to the narrow neck of rock that joins the reigning peak to the first of the Horns. Climb it with care as the drops on the L into the depth of Toll na Beiste are sensational, then traverse the three tops and go down through boulders and heather to pick up the stalkers' path in Toll a'Mhadaidh, and so back by the Allt Coire Mhic Nobhuil to your car. It will be noted that locally this Route is recommended in reverse, as indicated on the cairn where the path to Coire Dubh branches R. This may be an easier ascent, but for keen photographers the other takes greater advantage of the lighting. Moreover,

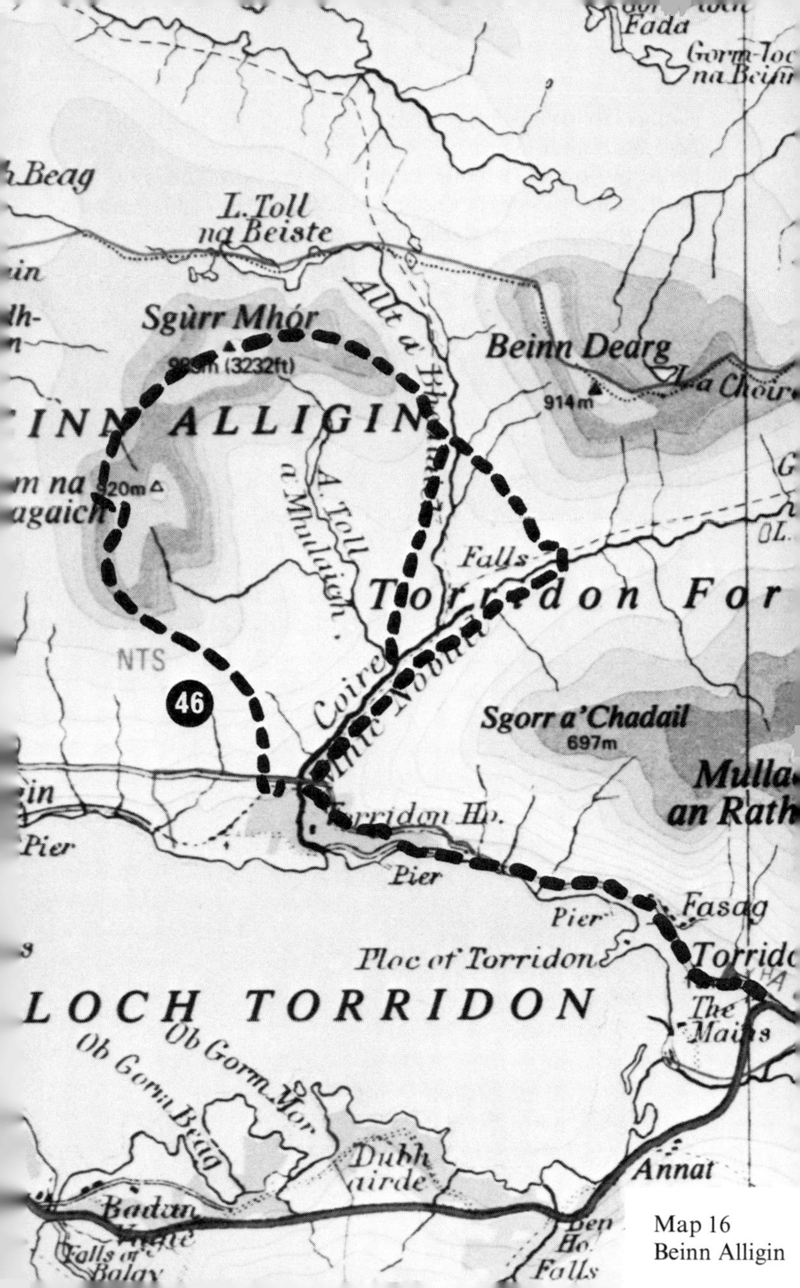

Map 16
Beinn Alligin

climbers following this path may have noticed a footbridge that was built in April 1972 across the upper extremity of the gorge, just over half a mile from the car park. It affords a shorter ascent to the Horns and in bad weather will be useful in the reverse descent to the stalkers' path.

Plate 113 **Route 46**—Beinn Alligin and Upper Loch Torridon from the New Road

Plate 114 **Route 46** — A close view of the peaks from the mouth of Coir an Laoigh

Sgurr Mhor →

Horns of Alligin →

Tom na Gruagagh

Plate 115 **Route 46**—Looking back on the first section from Sgurr Mhor

Plate 116 **Route 46**—The great gash in Sgurr Mhor seen from Tom na Gruagach

Plate 117 **Route 46** — Liathach from the gash on Sgurr Mhcr

Liathach →

Beinn Eighe →

Beinn Dearg →

Plate 110. The trickiest section of **Route 46** goes over the Horns of Alligin

The Beinn Eighe Range

Ruadh-stac Mor	3,309 feet	1,010 metres
Sail Mhor	2,990 feet	981 metres
Spidean Coire nan Clach	2,963 feet	972 metres
Sgurr Ban	2,960 feet	971 metres
Coinneach Mhor	2,944 feet	966 metres
Sgurr an Fhir Duibhe	2,935 feet	963 metres
Creag Dubh	2,835 feet	930 metres
Ruadh-stac Beag	2,731 feet	896 metres
Meall a'Ghiubhais	2,676 feet	878 metres

This great mountain, by far the largest of the Torridon Peaks,
is a complete range in itself and when seen from Kinlochewe
its north-eastern spur only is disclosed. If this were the whole
mountain it would be impressive enough to draw the climber,
as its crest is decked with a series of weird pinnacles, known
as the Black Carls of Beinn Eighe. During the drive down
Glen Torridon its southern front comes into view near Loch
Clair, but as the road runs along its lower slopes the view of it
is necessarily foreshortened. However, if the climber walks to
the adjacent Loch Coulin he will be rewarded by the best view
of the range, which not only reveals its stupendous
dimensions but also its tremendous covering of quartzite. The
ridge then swings round to the north-west behind Liathach,
and so the rest of it cannot be seen by the motorist. But if the
climber is prepared to walk from the adjoining car park
through the deep glen of the Allt a'Choire Dhuibh Mhoir that
separates the two peaks, he will be further rewarded by the
superb prospect of Coire Mhic Fhearchair which is hidden
away on its north-western slopes and considered the finest in
all Scotland.

The traverse of the ridge of Beinn Eighe is a considerable
undertaking for the average pedestrian and without transport

involves a walk of some twenty map miles, the last six of which can be saved by a ride back to Kinlochewe from Grudie Bridge, or from the ruined cottage in Glen Torridon. Moreover, the foreshortened view of the gaps between the several tops is misleading and on closer acquaintance will be found to involve much more collar-work than expected. However, such an expedition is free of all technical difficulties, other than a sudden deterioration in the weather, and on a long summer day will afford the tough climber an experience he will long remember. The usual starting point from Kinlochewe is just to the west of the hamlet and on attaining the first top of Creag Dubh much of the hard grind is over. On reaching a point opposite Liathach the ridge forks, with Sail Mhor on the L and Ruadh-stac Mor, the highest top, on the R. After visiting the latter peak there are two easy descents. 1, by way of the Scree Slopes to the north-west of the summit cairn, or 2, by returning to the junction whence a long stone shoot and easy rocks lead down to the floor of Coire Mhic Fhearchair with its lonely lochan. Thence, by following down the cascading burn the stalkers' path can be picked up on the R and easy progress made to Grudie Bridge, or by turning L past the lochans a cairned track leads to Coire Dubh and Glen Torridon. A conspicuous spur on the south side of the summit ridge, immediately above the ruined cottage in the glen, encloses Coire an Laoigh in which a stalkers' path can be used in bad weather for a rapid descent. It is also of great value to the climber who prefers to split up the long traverse into two less arduous days, as it affords easy access to the crest of the ridge with which it merges some 200 yards west of Spidean Coire nan Clach. This path as far as the 1,000 contour, is wet, uneven and rapidly disappearing. It is therefore better to start at spot height 343, near the Nature Conservancy plaque, where a drier path follows the R bank of the stream and joins the old one at the 1,000 feet contour.

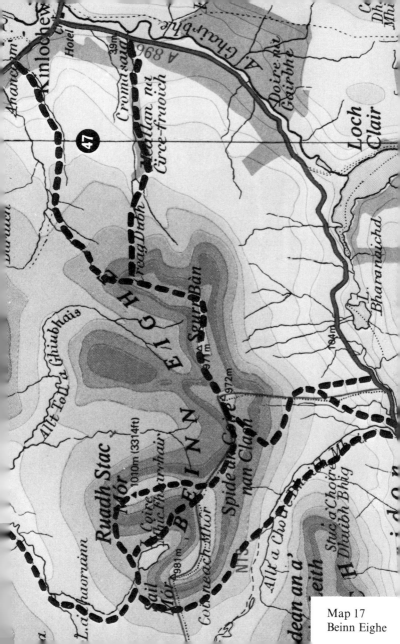

Map 17
Beinn Eighe

Route 47. The Traverse of Beinn Eighe. Leave Kinlochewe by
the path on the L to the west of the hamlet and climb steadily
to reach Creag Dubh, the first top on the ridge. An alternative
approach is to start from Cromasag and follow the south
bank of the Allt a'Chuirn for some distance, then cross the
burn to gain a steep grass slope that leads up to the ridge near
the first top. All the eastern peaks of the range consist of
Cambrian quartzite and on walking south along the ridge to
Sgurr an Fhir Duibhe the weird pinnacles or Black Carls are
soon encountered and will be noticed to be in an advanced
state of erosion. These are passed with care whence the ridge
narrows on the approach to this peak where the pinnacles
afford no difficulty save that of a 30-foot pitch near the top
which is more easily ascended than descended. On attaining
the cairn observe the views to the north in which Slioch is
prominent and with a distant prospect on its L of An
Teallach. To the south the peaks of the Coulin Forest are
clearly defined, but the gaze will be held by the ridge trailing
away to the west, to the L of which is a fine end-on view of
Laithach. Now descend R for some 400 feet to the first col,
with abysmal drops on the R, and climb the ridge to Sgurr
Ban, whence the going is easier all the way to Coinneach
Mhor. Continue the traverse, noting on the L the great rock
walls and corries of Laithach, and at the junction keep to the
R with an ascent of 450 feet to the reigning peak of Ruadh-
stac Mor, whose panorama is not dissimilar to that already
noted, save that of the view of Sail Mhor across the corrie on
the L where a deep gully cleaves its bold and steep face. Do
not attempt to descend on the north or east sides of Ruadh-
stac Mor as its slopes consist of steep, terraced sandstone, but
either retrace your steps to the junction on the ridge and go
down the long scree shoot to the floor of Coire Mhic
Fhearchair, or keep north-west from the summit cairn and go
down the scree to the lochan. Now walk round the lochan and
then view the rock wall opposite which is famous for its three
immense buttresses, the lower halves of which consist of red
sandstone and the upper halves of tapering quartzite.

Plate 119 **Route 47** — The first section of the traverse seen from Cromasag

Photographers should note that as this magnificent corrie faces the north-west, it is only illuminated satisfactorily on a summer evening; 8 p.m. is the ideal time of day which means a late return to your lodgings. Note also the flat floor of the corrie cradling the lochan at the base of the buttresses and then descend beside the cascading burn to the stalkers' path for Grudie Bridge (but NOT in the stalking season during September and October) or turn L for Glen Torridon.

Plate 120 Beinn Eighe from Loch Coulin

Plate 121. B.A. 17 ..... on the gabled crest of Sgurr an Fhir Duibhe

Plate 122 The white quartzite ridge of Creag Dubh seen from Sgurr an Fhir Duibhe

Liathach Spidean Coire nan Clach Sgurr Ban Sail Mhor Ruadh-stac Mor

Coire an Laoigh

Plate 123 Looking west along **Route 47** from the summit of Sgurr an Fhir Duibhe

Plate 124 Coire Mhic Fhearchair is the terminal point of **Route 47**

Slioch

Slioch	3,217 feet	981 metres
Sgurr an Tuill Bhain	3,058 feet	932 metres

This mountain stands in splendid isolation to the north of
Loch Maree and frowns upon the head waters of this
beautiful tree-fringed lake. It attracts attention not only by
reason of its unopposed superiority but also by its bold,
square, castellated summit. The ascent affords no difficulty,
save that of the long tramp to its base round the head of the
loch from Kinlochewe, a distance of some five miles to reach
Glen Bianasdail. This is the key to the climb, but it is
preferable to save the long approach slog by arranging for a
ghillie to row the climber across the loch from Rhu Noa, and
to pick him up in the late afternoon. The rather indistinct
track rises to the L of the glen and eventually enters a hidden
boulder-strewn corrie to the east of the peak. It is famous for
its spring Alpines. The summit cairn is some little distance
above and can be attained by an easy walk. If desired this
may be continued by traversing the almost level ridge to Sgurr
an Tuill Bhain.

NOTE. In summer, when the water in the Kinlochewe River
may be low, the approach to Glen Bianasdail can be
shortened by driving to Taagan and then fording the river to
the north-east of the farm.

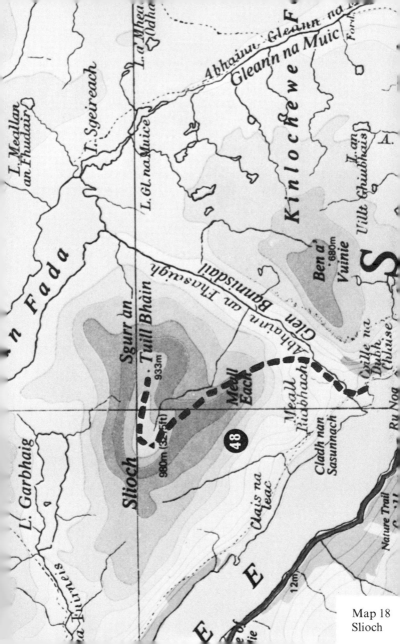

Map 18
Slioch

Route 48. Slioch from Rhu Noa. After being rowed across the loch, ascend the path that rises to the L of the glen. It passes through heather until the corrie is entered, whence a track leads to the summit cairn. The views of the loch below are enchanting and reveal the many islets at its foot. The Torridon Peaks to the south lack interest since their finest aspects are on the Glen Torridon side. But the panorama round the northern arc will hold the gaze by reason of the numerous blue lochans that stud the immense wilderness of peaks in which An Teallach and the Fannichs are prominent.

Glen Bianasdail

Plate 125 **Route 48**—Slioch from Loch Maree

An Teallach

Bidean a'Ghlas Thuill	3,483 feet	1,062 metres
Sgurr Fiona	3,474 feet	1,059 metres
Corrag Bhuidhe	3,425 feet	1,044 metres
Sgurr Creag an Eich	3,350 feet	1,021 metres
Lord Berkeley's Seat	3,325 feet	1,013 metres
Glas Mheall Mor	3,176 feet	968 metres
Glas Mheall Liath	3,150 feet	960 metres
Top above Cadha Gobhlach	3,150 feet	960 metres
Sail Liath	3,150 feet	960 metres
Corrag Bhuidhe Buttress	3,050 feet	930 metres

This range of hills is one of the most spectacular in Scotland and vies in grandeur with that of the Torridon Peaks and the Coolins of Skye. It rises due south of the head of Little Loch Broom and is usually climbed from Dundonnell where improved accommodation is now available. The three-mile-long main ridge is much indented and throws out three spurs which enclose two magnificent corries, one of which, Toll an Lochain, vies in splendour with Coire Mhic Fhearchair on the north-western flanks of Beinn Eighe. The best view of the range is obtained from the remote Road of Destitution, and when seen on a bright sunny morning its superb sandstone architecture is revealed, including detail of the cluster of peaks surrounding Toll an Lochain. To climb the reigning peak, traverse the ups and downs of the main ridge as far as Sail Liath, descend the stone shoot to Toll an Lochain and return to Dundonnell involves a long and strenuous day. Hence, unless the climber is experienced and in fit condition, An Teallach is best left alone.

Bidean a'Ghlas Thuill →

Plate 126 An Teallach from the Road of Destitution. —now much improved

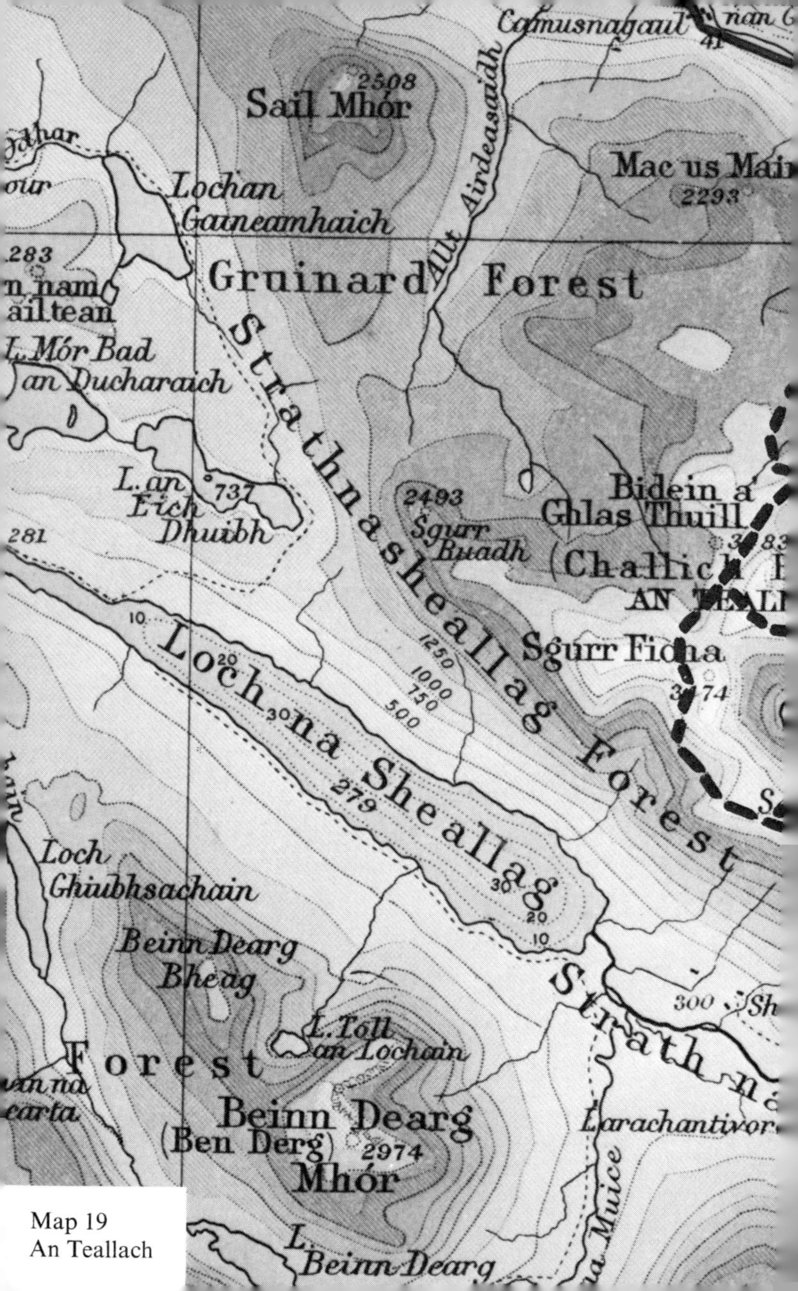

Map 19
An Teallach

500
1327
Ardin
L. na
Faoileige
Strath Beg
P.O.
Hotel
Dundonnell
Lo.
73
30
1193
Creag
Chorcurach
L. an
Duibha
49
Dundonnell Ho.
Mheall
Bruthach na
Garbh Choille
170
Corryhallie
Allt a' Chairn
1206
Fall
438
Coill a'
Bhun
Garbh Allt
Allt Gleann Chaorachain
Carn a'
Bhreabadair
1573
1665
Carn a'
639
L. Allt
Eigin
A 832
L. Coire
Chaorrachain
840
Fraoich
Meall
1503
a' Bhainne
Dundonnell Forest
1250
Lochain
Dubh
916
Allt Buidhe
Strathbeg R.
Lochan
Fada
Achneigie
Fain
1060
721
Carn
1820
nam Feithean
Lochain Coir
an Eich Ghlais
Ford

Route 49. The Traverse of An Teallach. Leave the road about
a quarter of a mile to the east of the hotel and walk up the
stalkers' path, whence follow the Allt a'Mhuilinn to its source.
Turn L and ascend Glas Mheall Mor without difficulty and
then wend your way round the rim of Coire a'Ghlas Thuill to
attain the dominating peak of Bidean a'Ghlas Thuill. From its
lofty cairn the whole of the ridge is disclosed twisting away to
the south and eventually to the south-east, in which the
graceful peak of Sgurr Fiona is prominent, followed by Lord
Berkeley's Seat which overhangs the corrie and is topped by
the four peaks of Corrag Bhuidhe. But before commencing
the traverse it is worth while to walk a short distance along
the adjoining spur in the direction of Glas Mheall Liath, if
only to gaze into the fantastic Hayfork Gully on the L whose
rectangular plan and perpendicular sandstone walls have a
most sensational aspect. Now begin the traverse by tramping
across the deep depression to Sgurr Fiona which unfolds a
closer prospect of the ridge ahead; it narrows considerably
and the pitches are longer and steeper, in which good and safe
foot-holds replace unsatisfactory hand-holds. Proceed
carefully and ascend the dizzy Lord Berkeley's Seat for the
striking view of the immense void below, and then climb the
Corrag Bhuidhe Pinnacles, the last of which opens up a grand
view of the remaining section of the ridge and also of Beinn
Dearg Mhor on the other side of the wide Strath na Sheallag.
Descend the last pinnacle with the utmost care and go down
the slabs that lead to the next col, whence scale Corrag
Bhuidhe Buttress and continue thence to the end of the ridge
at Sail Liath. Now retrace your steps to Cadha Gobhlach and
run down the stone shoot which gives the easiest and quickest
descent to Toll an Lochain. The simplest way back to
Dundonnell is to first make for a large boulder that is poised
conspicuously on a declining sandstone ridge, and then follow
it almost all the way down to the road near Dundonnell
House. The changing panorama of shapely hill, black lochan
and blue sea from the ridge of An Teallach is a great
attraction, but it is the ridge itself that will hold the gaze.

Sgurr Fiona →

L.B. Seat →

Corrag Bhuidhe →

Cadna Gobhlach →

Plate 127 **Route 49** – The ridge of An Teallach from Bidean a'Ghlas Thuill

Corrag Bhuidhe

Lord Berkeleys Seat

Plate 128 **Route 49**—The ridge from Sgurr Fiona

Plate 129 Beinn Dearg Mhor seen from Corrag Bhuidhe

C.B. Buttress →   Corrag Bhuidhe →   L.B. Seat →   Sgurr Fiona →

Plate 130 **Route 49**—Toll an Lochain is passed during the descent

The Coigach Peaks

Cul Mor	2,786 feet	849 metres
Cul Beag	2,523 feet	769 metres
Ben More Coigach	2,438 feet	743 metres
Sgurr an Fhidhleir	2,285 feet	696 metres
Stac Polly	2,009 feet	612 metres
Beinn an Eoin (Sgorr Deas)	1,973 feet	601 metres

Ben More Coigach

Climbers proceeding north from Ullapool get their first full view of this mountain from Ardmain Bay, whose graceful sweep of white shingle leads the eye across the water to its long summit ridge which is supported by a series of riven precipices. The peak comes into view again in the vicinity of Drumrunie Lodge when it is seen end-on, together with its spectacular satellite, Sgurr an Fhidhleir, which appears as a conspicuous sharp wedge on its R. While the ascent of the latter is a stiff rock climb that has not often been done, the ascent and traverse of the former affords no difficulties whatsoever and culminates in a magnificent bird's-eye view of Isle Martin and the Summer Isles, together with glorious vistas of hill and sea round the western arc. To reach the mountain involves a long tramp over boggy moorland, and since it is not so accessible as its more attractive neighbour, Stac Polly, it is seldom visited.

However, those wishing to reach the summit by a shorter route may do so by driving through Achiltibuie to Calnacraig where the resurfaced road terminates. Thence ascend the western shoulder of the mountain, cross the Allt nan Coisiche and go straight up the steep grassy slopes to the cairn.

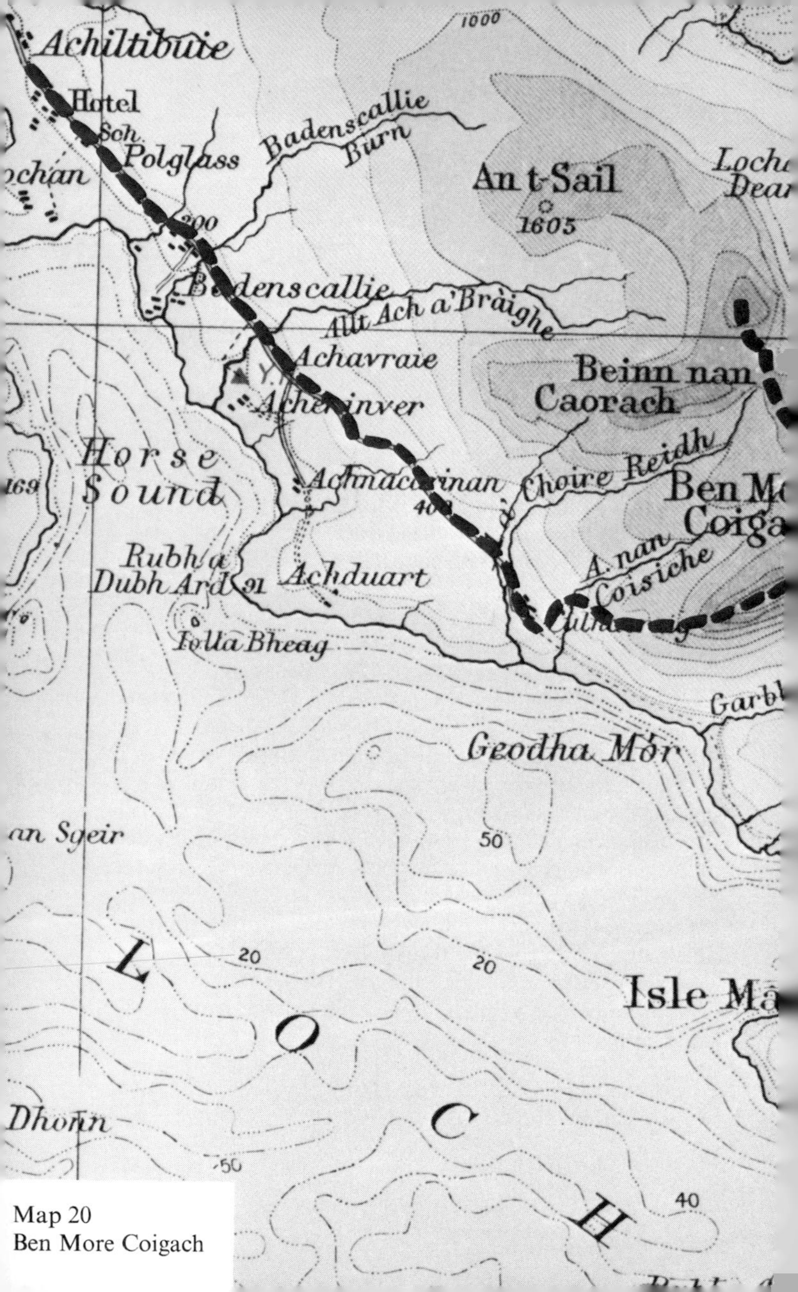

Map 20
Ben More Coigach

Beinn Eun
Feur-loch
173
A. Claonaidh
50
Lochan Tuath
Lochanan Dubha
Drumrunie Lodge
856
Allt a' Phollain Riabhaich
2000
1500
1000
500
A 835
408
L. a'Chlaiginn
L. Eadar dha Bheinn
Beanncan Beaga
254
Strathkanaird
Blughasary
Sch.
Polluchoire
Strath Kanaird
Power Sta.
177
Dun Canna
Meall Mór
Power Sta.
L. Beinn Deirg
Dam
N. Keanchulish
140
N. of Scot. Hydro-Elec. Board
S. Keanchulish
Loch Kanaird
L. Dubh
76
947 Creag na h-Iolaire
Ardmair
In Sgeireach
Cnoc

Route 50. From Drumrunie Old Lodge. Drive almost to the head of Loch Lurgain and park the car at a convenient place off the road. Set off across the moor and on reaching the Allt Claonaidh follow it to its source in Lochan Tuath. This lies at the foot of Sgurr an Fhidhleir, and after skirting its shore climb the deep corrie on the L of the peak. This steep route gives a close view of its sandstone cliffs and is not difficult, but on emerging on the skyline turn round to admire the fine retrospect which reveals the true elevation of Stac Polly to the L of the nearer Beinn Eun. Then turn R to visit this nearby summit and afterwards walk southwards to attain the lofty ridge of Ben More Coigach, which traverse to its terminus at Garbh Choireachan that overhangs the blue of Loch Broom. On a clear day all the above mentioned features are disclosed to advantage, together with Skye across the sea to the west, while far away in the south the great range of An Teallach tops the extensive skyline of mainland peaks. If a descent is not made to Achiltibuie, it is worth while to take in Beinn Tarsuinn on the return walk to the car.

Plate 131 Ben More Coigach—the summit ridge from Ardmair Bay

Plate 132 **Route 50**—Sgurr an Fhidhleir from Lochan Tuath

Plate 133 **Route 50**—Stac Polly from the lip of the Corrie

Plate 50. Ridges rising to the summit of Ben More Coigach

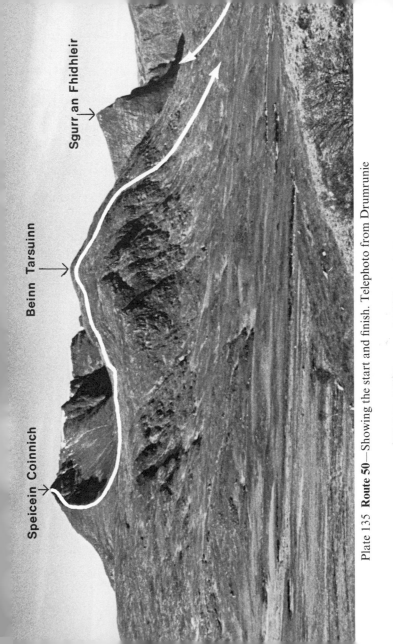

Speicein Coinnich

Beinn Tarsuinn

Sgurr an Fhidhleir

Plate 135   **Route 50**—Showing the start and finish. Telephoto from Drumrunie

Cul Beag

The south-eastern slopes of this mountain are grassy and rise gradually from Drumrunie Old Lodge to terminate precipitously on both north and west. In consequence the finest prospect of the peak is from Loch Lurgain, which reveals a gully slanting up to the R to split conspicuously its triangular elevation of sandstone. The easiest ascent is from the Old Lodge and the more difficult from Linneraineach. The panorama from the summit is disappointing, save that it opens up an end-on view of Stac Polly to the west; a close prospect of Cul Mor to the north; and a rather complicated vista of Beinn Eun and Ben More Coigach to the south.

Route 51. From Drumrunie Old Lodge. Leave the road about two miles to the west of the ruined Lodge and climb steadily over steepish grass, interspersed here and there with sandstone boulders, until the cairn is attained almost on the edge of the cliffs.

Route 52. From Linneraineach. This route is only for experienced climbers who should make a bee-line for the V-shaped gullies splitting the western face of the peak. The going is rough and steep in places, and a small cairn will be found at their conjunction. Scramble up the gully on the R with care and on emerging on the skyline bear L for the summit cairn.

Plate 136 Stac Polly and **Route 51** to the summit of Cul Beag seen from the moor

Plate 137 **Route 52** to Cul Beag seen across Loch Lurgain

Plate 138 **Routes 51** and **52** — A hazy view of Stac Polly from Cul Beag

Loch Sionascaig

L. Call
an Uigean

Eilean
Mor

L. Uidh
Tarruingeach

244

526

L. na
Dalach

Sch.

Inverpolly Forest

L. Doine
na h-Airbhe

222

L. Lon
nah-Uamha

d of Coigach

dagyle

2009

Stac Polly

54

Bad a'Ghaill
(Baddagyle)

20

500

1000

Car Park

Linneraineach

52

L. Bada
na h-Achlaise

Green
Loch

LOCH 173 LURGAIN

5

10

30

173

t Sail

1605

Lochan
Dearg

Sgorr
1973
Deas

Beinn Eun

Feur-loch

A. Claonaidh

Beinn nan
Caorach

2000

856

Lochan Tuath

Coig

choire Reidh

Ben More
Coigach

2438

2000

Pholl

Au

1500

Map 21
Coigach Peaks

L. a' Mhadail
787
Cam
Na Leitrichean
L. na Claise
CUL MÓR
2786
53
Drumrunie Forest
Elphin
P.O.
L. an Laoigh
Ln. Dearg
Ln. Fhionnlaich
Druim Pol Eoghainn
Ln. Dearg
353
A. an Loin Duibh
L. an Ais
Cnoc an t-Sasunnaich
L. nan Ealachan
Allt an Liath Dhoire
Lochan Fada
Car Loch Beag
771
51
575
Meall an Lo
Drumrunie Old Lodge
Feur-loch
Doire nan Se-sgillinne
Drumrunie Lo.
A. a' Chuaille
Meall na Sithinn
A 835
408
Féith

Cul Mor

This is the most northerly peak in Wester Ross and rises
steeply from the southern shore of Loch Veyatie. It looks its
best when seen from Stac Polly, but its twin summits, capped
with quartzite, are also conspicuous objects in the view from
Ledmore, which coign of vantage reveals the sharp rock
pinnacle, known as Bod a'Mhiotailt, decking its north-
western ridge. It may be climbed most easily from the county
boundary to the east, but is often scaled from Linneraineach,
on Loch Lurgain. But the great disadvantage of this approach
is the circuit of several lochans at its base, followed, however,
by the more interesting ascent of Longstaff's Gully. There is
an immense corrie, known as Coire Gorm, on its northern
precipitous front, which is encircled by fine mural cliffs of
sandstone and well worthy of appraisal.

Plate 139 The gullied western flanks of Cul Mor are well seen from Stac Polly

Route 53. From Ullapool. Drive along the road to Ledmore
and park your car near the Sutherland boundary. Pick up the
stalkers' path that winds its way westwards, and when it
peters out make for the col between the twin peaks. Descend
slightly to the west where a long line of sandstone crags rim
the precipices facing Stac Polly; note the wide gullies that split
them and also the curious formations of sandstone
hereabouts. Observe the strange elevation of the adjacent
peak of Cul Beag and then climb to the cairn on the reigning
peak. The panorama is extensive and noteworthy for the
innumerable lochs and lochans that deck the landscape of
both Wester Ross and Sutherland. The view to the north
encompasses the entire ridge of Suilven, together with Canisp
of its R, between which Quinag appears in the far distance. To
the north-east the great bulk of Ben More Assynt is
prominent and to the south-east appears the large group of
hills dominated by Beinn Dearg. But the moorland to the west
will hold your gaze, with the wedge of Stac Polly overlooking
the maze of lochans, of which the largest is Loch Sionascaig,
all of them backed by the blue of the Atlantic. Should you be
lucky enough to visit this peak in the early days of spring, you
may see a snow bunting which will hop around to pick up the
crumbs from your lunch.

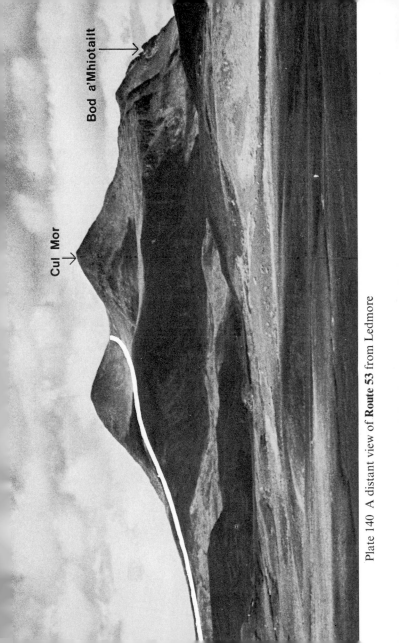

Cul Mor

Bod a'Mhiotailt

Plate 140 A distant view of **Route 53** from Ledmore

Plate 141 **Route 53**—The approach to the col between the twin peaks of Cul Mor

Plate 142 **Route 53** — The shattered western front of Cul Mor

Plate 143 **Route 53**—Suilven and Quinag from Cul Mor

Plate 144 **Route 53**—Coire Gorm

A great view from the summit cairn on Col Mor

Stac Polly

This little peak, with its bristling summit ridge of sandstone pinnacles, is the favourite of all mountaineers visiting Coigach. It is fourteen miles from Ullapool and rises above the narrow road skirting Loch Lurgain, from which it may be climbed in about one hour. Bold and steep buttresses rise at each end of the mountain, and that at the western extremity is the higher. There is a conspicuous saddle at the eastern end and this may be attained over steep talus slopes or by the zig-zags on its northern slopes, but almost any point on the ridge can be reached by a rough scramble over scree, followed by one or other of the several gullies that cleave the ridge. A little tower, with drops on either side, stands between the ridge proper and the highest top, but aside from the latter's more open prospect of the sea to the west, it has no other scenic attraction. The best vista of the ridge, with its numerous towers and supporting spurs, is obtained from the end of the broad spur near the summit. The weird formations of sandstone are a great attraction and those crowning the terminal points of some of the very narrow spurs can only be reached by a sensational scramble. They assume changing shapes as the climber moves along the ridge above them, and one of the most remarkable, but easily missed, is the Lobster's Claw which some years ago crowned a slender pinnacle in one of the gullies but has now disappeared owing to erosion. If the crest of the ridge is traversed faithfully it makes an entertaining rock climb, but a track below the pinnacles on the south side may be used to avoid the difficult bits. The whole of Stac Polly is the delight of the alert photographer and is the most rewarding and sensational subject in all Scotland.

Climbers have reported some disintegration of the little Tower below the western top and those who intend to ascend it should exercise every care.

Route 54. The Traverse of Stac Polly. Park your car in the new car park immediately below the peak, and then ascend the path above it to reach the level ground at the foot of the mountain. The topography of the peak will now be clear and you take a direct line uphill for the saddle, going R or L near the top of the long talus slope to allow easier progress or go round the eastern buttress and ascend the zig-zags on its northern slopes. On attaining the saddle, walk along to the cairn on the eastern buttress, which opens up fine prospects of both Cul Mor and Cul Beag. Then return to the saddle where you are confronted by a huge rock buttress which seems to bar your way. If you go to the L of it you will descend below the pinnacles, whereas by going down slightly to the R you will turn this obstacle and discover behind it a track that rises to the crest of the ridge. The going is now delightful, with spacious prospects on either hand; those on the L include Beinn Eun and Ben More Coigach beyond Loch Lurgain at your feet; those on the R reveal the innumerable blue lochans that characterise this part of Wester Ross and Sutherland, together with a wonderful view of the surprisingly long ridge of Suilven. On and on you go, enchanted by all you see both near and far, until you encounter the little tower which must be climbed if you wish to attain the summit cairn. Return the way you came, but walk out to the end of the first spur, now on your R, where in favourable conditions you will linger to enjoy the finest prospect of the unique sandstone pinnacles of Stac Polly, backed by Cul Beag, with a lovely vista of Loch Lurgain bounded by the white line of the road from Ullapool.

Plate 146 The bristling ridge of Stac Polly is best observed from the south

Plate 147 Route 54. The eastern prospect of the summit ridge of Stac Polly

Plate 148 **Route 54**—Cul Beag from the ridge

Plate 140 **Route 54**—Cul Mor from the ridge

Plate 150 **Route 54**—Suilven appears between the two western towers

Suilven **Canisp**

Plate 151 **Route 54**—Suilven, Canisp and Loch Sionascaig from the Northern Pinnacles

Plate 152 Weird pinnacles flank the south side of **Route 54**

Plate 153 **Route 54**—The elusive Lobster's Claw as it was in 1948

Suilven

Caisteal Liath	2,399 feet	731 metres
Meall Mheadhonach	2,300 feet	701 metres
Meall Bheag	2,000 feet	610 metres

This wedge-shaped peak, rising in splendid isolation from the lochan-strewn moors of Sutherland, is perhaps the most famous in Scotland and a well-known problem for the climber. Seen from the east in the vicinity of Elphin, it presents a sharp, tapering and inaccessible appearance, whereas when observed from the west in the neighbourhood of Lochinver its rounded summit cannot fail to catch the eye and has given rise to its popular pseudonym, The Sugar Loaf. Its summit ridge is one and a half miles in length, on which the most difficult peak to attain is the central one owing to the rim of guarding crags, below which the flanks of the hill fall so precipitously as to seem perpendicular. A strange feature that will surprise the climber is a stone wall spanning the ridge to the east of the Castle. Speculation suggests its erection to prevent deer from reaching the crowning peak and perhaps falling over its precipitous western front, but an opening has been left in its centre, possibly to allow access to sheep. Suilven rises some five miles to the south-east of Lochinver, of which two miles consist of a road to Glencanisp Lodge, whence a stalkers' path continues to a point north of the peak. Thence a string of lochans on a shelf at its base lead to a wide and rough gully that rises to the ridge. The same point of ascent can be reached by a path from Little Assynt, or a similar gully on its south side can be reached from Inverkirkaig by following the river to Fionn Loch, whose long circuit leads to the base of this gully. The complete traverse of the ridge and its three peaks is a tit-bit for the rock climber and should be commenced with the ascent of one of the gullies

Caisteal Liath

Meall Mheadhonach

Meall Bheag

Plate 154 Suilven from Elphin

Map 22
Suilven

or chimneys that split the western face of the Castle. The descent at the far end of the ridge presents no special difficulties.

Meall Mheadhonach

Caisteal Liath

Plate 155 Suilven and Lochinver

Route 55. From Lochinver. Turn east up the narrow road between the houses facing the loch and continue to Glencanisp Lodge. Pass behind it to pick up the strikers' path. Proceed ahead past Suileag where the path from Little Assynt comes in on the L, and later after passing Lochan Buidhe turn R and cross the moor to reach the attractive lochans on the shelf at the base of the peak. Then scale the wide gully opposite to attain the Bealach Mor at its centre. After a short rest turn L and traverse the airy crest of the ridge until you reach the gap beneath Meall Mheadhonach. Cross it and climb slightly to the R, taking every care on the steep sandstone slopes until you attain the rim of crags guarding its summit. Scramble up them without looking down and on reaching the cairn scan the splendid prospect to the east, noting the proximity of the adjacent Canisp. Continue along the ridge to Meall Bheag whose cairn is reached by a sensational ascent over a succession of sandstone terraces on the north side of this peak. Then retrace your steps to the Bealach Mor, whence climb the broader ridge to Caisteal Liath; its spacious grassy summit opens up a marvellous panorama of hill and sea, in which the Coigach Peaks are prominent to the south, and Quinag to the north. Note also the vista along the ridge to the east and the vast array of blue lochans that dapple the landscape in every direction. These routes are for experienced climbers only and should not be attempted by the ordinary pedestrian.

Route 56. From Inverkirkaig. Drive round the coast from Lochinver and park your car in the open space near the bridge over the River Kirkaig. Follow the path on the R bank of the stream through scenery that is softer than that of Route 55. Note the beautiful falls on the R and continue ahead to Fionn Loch. If you have not made arrangements to use the locked boat, you must bear L and walk round its shore. On reaching its western end cross the stream and turn R for the centre of Suilven. Then scale its long gully to join Route 55 at the Bealach Mor.

Plate 156 **Route 56**—Suilven from Fionn Loch

Plate 157 Suilven reflected in a wayside lochan on **Route 55**

Bealach Mor

Plate 158 **Route 55** ascends the gully to Bealach Mor

Plate 150 **Route 55** – Canisp from the lochan on Suilven

Plate 160 **Route 55** to Meall Mheadhonach

Plate 161 **Route 55** to Caisteal Liath

Plate 162 **Route 55**—A higher viewpoint reveals the wall on Caisteal Liath

Plate 163 **Route 55**—Meall Mheadhonach from Caisteal Liath

Quinag

Summit, on east ridge	2,653 feet	809 metres
Sail Ghorm	2,551 feet	778 metres
Spidean Coinich	2,508 feet	764 metres
Centre top	2,448 feet	746 metres
Sail Gharbh	2,414 feet	736 metres
Creag na h'Iolaire Ard	2,306 feet	703 metres

The three fronts of this striking Y-shaped peak present an entirely different aspect of the mountain, and the most picturesque view of it is that of Spidean Coinich and the summit ridge ending at Sail Gharbh. It is observed at its finest from the head of Loch Assynt and includes a glimpse of Ardvreck Castle in the middle distance. The long western ridge terminating at Sail Ghorm is well seen from the foot of Loch Assynt and also from the wild hill road to the east of Drumbeg, which reveals its facade of terraced sandstone seamed with deep gullies, some of which prove to be spectacular on closer acquaintance. The two bold and abrupt northern sentinels of the Y dominate the views from Kylesku and Loch Cairnbawn, and clearly disclose the immense Barrel Buttress between deep and nearly vertical gullies as the outstanding feature of Sail Gharbh; it is the main resort of the rock climber on this mountain, although ascents have been made by buttress and gully on the western face of Sail Ghorm.

The ideal centre for its exploration is Inchnadamph, but those climbers with transport may reach it from Lochinver or Drumbeg. The car should be parked in a large quarry on the right, almost opposite the starting point of the ascent, at spot-height 813 which is near the highest point of the new road between Skiag Bridge and Kylesku. The chief characteristic of the summit ridge is the broad flat pavement that terminates so

Picish

Allt na Claise

Ten Ardvar

L. Torr an Lochain

573

Nedd

Glenleraig

Glen Leirg

L. a' Bhràighe

Druim Dhonn

Falls

L. an Leothaid
(L. a' Leoid)

480

Gorm-Loch s Mòr

Bhaid

Gl. Salach

Gorm Chnoc

826

Glas Chnoc

Allt an Leothaid

1090

Creag na h'Iolaire

L. a' 295

Gleann Shalaich

L.Gleannan a' Choit

Allt Mòr

L. Letteressie

L. Lochassynt

275

Loch Beannach

260

L. na h-Innse Fraoich

221

L. Uidh na Geadaig

Little Assynt

224

L. Badnan Aigheano

208

215

L. na Garbh Uidhe

Inver

A. an Tiaghaich

Cnoc a' Ghlinnein

1091

L. a' Ghuil

ASSY

Inveruplan

Allt na

500

882

Cnoc an Leothaid

536

L. a' Ghlinnein

L. an Leothaid

L. Feith a Leotha

860

Fea Lec

Map 23
Quinag

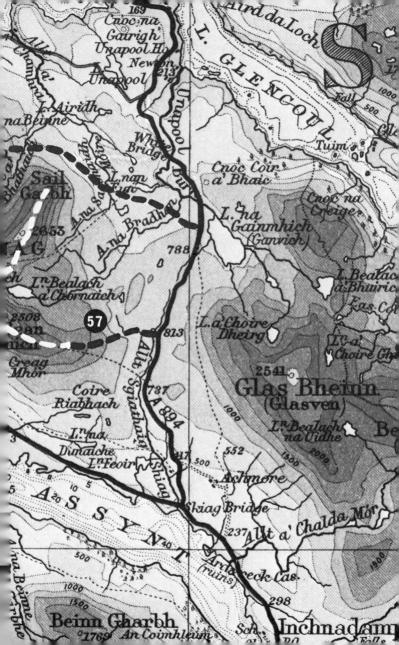

precipitously at Sail Gharbh, and the castellated eminences that crown the subsidiary ridge ending at Sail Ghorm.

Quinag consists mainly of purplish-red sandstone and is poised upon an uneven floor of Lewisan gneiss which is the chief geological feature of Sutherland; it rises to a height of some 2,000 feet on the north face of Sail Ghorm. White Cambrian quartzite caps the highest point of the eastern ridge, covers the summit of Spidean Coinich, and extends eastwards down its slopes to the Allt Skiathaig.

Plate 164 An islet in Loch Assynt

Spidean Coinich

Summit

Sail Charbh

Plate 165 Quinag and Ardvreck Castle from the head of Loch Assynt

Spidean Coinich

Sail Ghorm

Plate 166 The western ridge of Quinag from the foot of Loch Assynt

Route 57. Quinag from Inchnadamph. Drive to the above mentioned parking place and ascend the broad ridge to Spidean Coinich, with views of Lochan Bealach Cornaidh in the immense corrie on the R. This peak opens up a magnificent vista of Loch Assynt and a view of the full length of Suilven in the south. Traverse Creag na h'Iolaire Ard to reach the Bealach a'Chornaidh at the base of the Y and on attaining the Centre Top bear R for Sail Gharbh, noting the blue sea lochs ahead and the quartzite peak of Glasven on the R. Retrace your steps to the Centre Top and then traverse the eminences on the ridge to Sail Ghorm, which unfolds a fine panorama of the deeply indented coastline of Sutherland to the west. Now descend to the east of this peak, cross the Allt a'Bhaihaich and skirt the base of Sail Gharbh to reach the road, whence turn R to walk back to your car. Climbers should bear in mind that this route is a strenuous undertaking.

Those desiring to shorten the traverse by omitting Spidean Coinich may do so by following the Stalkers' Path which also leaves the road at spot-height 813 and gives direct and easy access to the Bealach a'Chornaidh.

Climbers who wish to attain Sail Ghorm by one of the deep gullies that split the western face of Quinag should leave the road at Tumore and follow the path through Gleann Leireag, leaving it on the R to reach the chosen route of ascent.

Plate 167 **Route 57**—Sail Gharbh and Sail Ghorm seen from a roadside lochan

Sail Ghorm →

Sail Gharbh →

Plate 169 **Route 57** to Spidean Coinich

Plate 170 Route 57 The head of Loch Assynt from Spidean Coinich

Plate 171 **Route 57**—Suilven from Spidean Coinich

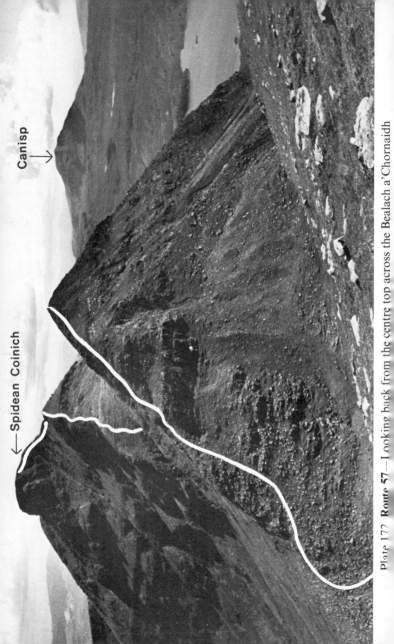

Plate 172 **Route 57**—Looking back from the centre top across the Bealach a'Chornaidh

Plate 173 **Route 57**—South western aspect of the summit ridge of Quinag

Spidean Coinich

Canisp

Plate 174 **Route 57**—Castellated eminences on the ridge to Sail Ghorm

Plate 175 **Route 57**—A spectacular gully on the ridge of Sail Ghorm

Foinaven

Ganu Mor	2,980 feet	908 metres
Ceann Garbh	2,952 feet	900 metres
A'Cheir Ghorm	2,839 feet	865 metres
Top South of Tower	2,646 feet	806 metres
Creag Dionard	2,554 feet	778 metres

The remote situation of this peak precludes the possibility of its ever becoming a popular resort of the climber, and like its near neighbour, Arkle, it consists of quartzite and its lofty undulating ridge is on this account worthy of a special visit. It straddles the vast moors, with their hundreds of blue lochans, to the east of Rhiconich and is separated from the more northerly peaks of Sutherland by the long, wild and forlorn stretches of Strath Dionard. It may be conveniently approached from the Durness Road some three miles to the north-east of Rhiconich, but can also be reached by an adventurous tramp through the bogs to the south of Loch Eriboll. To reach Foinaven, climb the mountain, traverse its long summit ridge, and visit its north-eastern spurs is a tough proposition for the fittest of mountaineers. But its bewildering state of erosion should be a sufficiently powerful magnet to attract those who wish to observe for themselves one of the most remarkable peaks in Scotland. For to sit alone on its crest and listen to the falling of its disintegrated quartzite blocks is one of the most eerie experiences in Britain.

Route 58. Foinaven from Rhiconich. Drive towards Durness and park your car at a convenient spot to the north of Lochan Cul na Creige. Make for the first top by crossing the gradually rising moor and avoid all boggy ground in the advance. Ascend the steep, grassy slopes of Ceann Garbh and follow the ridge to the highest peak of Ganu Mor. Continue along its

Plate 176 Foinaven dominates the wilds of Sutherland

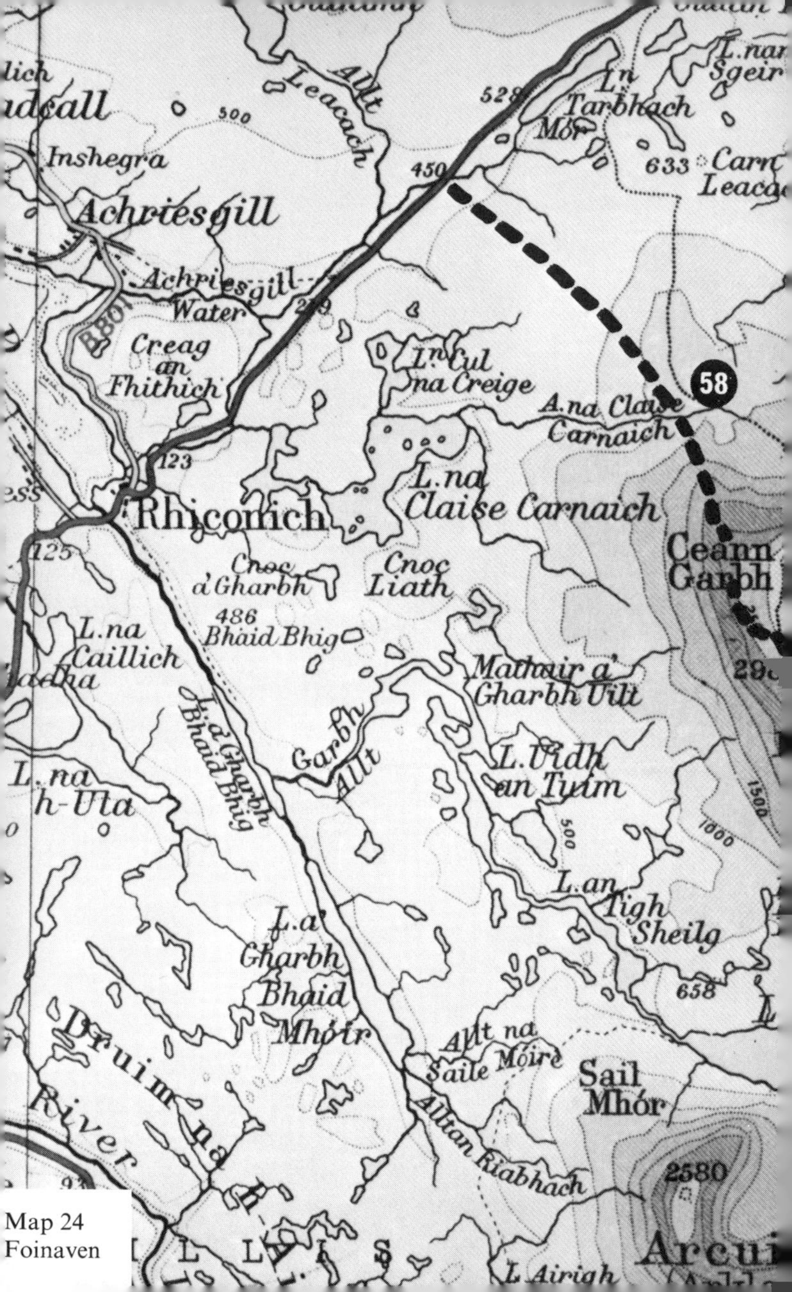

Map 24
Foinaven

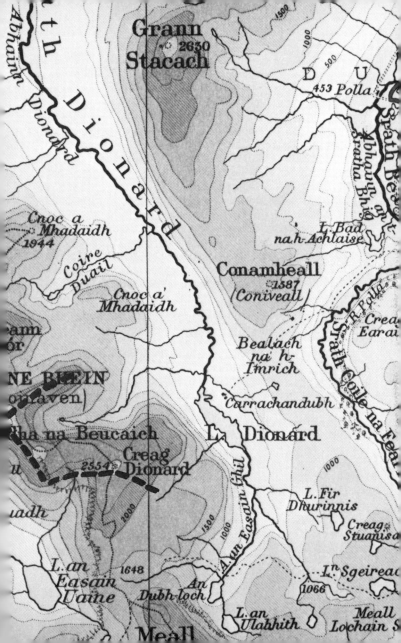

crest at least as far as the pass of Cadha na Beucaich, which is guarded by a Tower, and if time is not pressing and the weather favourable turn the latter on the R, cross the pass and bear L for Creag Dionard to examine its precipitous cliffs. On your return walk turn R to visit the central spur of A'Cheir Ghorm and just listen to the falling blocks of quartzite. Then regain the ridge and descend from Ceann Garbh to your car. The wide panorama is interesting because it includes a fine prospect of Ben Hope to the east and Arkle very near in the south, with Ben Stack peeping over its R shoulder. But it is the western vista that will hold your gaze, as the whole of the vast landscape is dappled with innumerable blue lochans which lead the eye to the illimitable stretches of the Atlantic.

Climbers who are staying at Kinlochbervie and have made the long traverse of Foinaven should take an off-day and visit SANDWOOD BAY. This is considered by many as the most beautiful in all Scotland and lies to the south of Cape Wrath; it is only accessible on foot. The bay is characterised by a vast sweep of golden sands, which are hemmed in on the south by lofty red cliffs, at the end of which stands a conspicuous stack known as Am Buachaille.

The best way to reach it is to drive for $3\frac{1}{2}$ miles along a well surfaced single-track road as far as some cottages and pass through a gate on the R beyond them which gives access to the moor. Two miles of very rough cart track must be negotiated slowly with care and the car parked on the R just short of the fourth lochan which is the limit for vehicular traffic. Thence about two miles of boggy track passes three more lochans to attain a broad ridge, beyond which Sandwood Bay comes into view below. The track runs down to the sands and it is perhaps half a mile across them to the succession of long rolling breakers. The bay is a lovely retreat, but to some conveys a sense of haunting. However, photographers who reach it on a sunny summer morning, when the light is on the curving cliffs, will be rewarded by a scene of exquisite beauty. The walk, there and back from the car, takes about two hours of easy going.

Plate 177 **Route 58**— View of the ridge of Foinaven from Ganu Mor

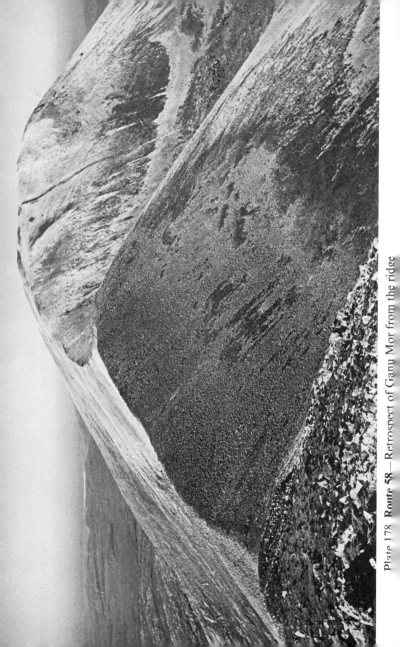

Plate 178 **Route 58**— Retrospect of Ganu Mor from the ridge

Plate 179 **Route 58**—Looking across a'Cheir Ghorm to Ben Hope

Plate 180 **Route 58**—Cadha na Beucaich is the last gap in the ridge

Plate 181 Sandwood Bay

Ben Hope

3,040 feet   927 metres

This mountain is the most northerly Munro in Scotland and
rises some one and a half miles to the south-east of the head
of Loch Hope. Its most imposing elevation is revealed from
the north in the vicinity of Hope Lodge, because its
precipitous, rocky north-western front is only seen to
advantage from this angle. To the south and east its slopes are
gentler and smoother, and cradle two large lochs and a
number of lochans. The latter are clearly disclosed from the
summit of Ben Loyal, while its western cliffs are well seen, and
are indeed conspicuous, in the spacious views from Foinaven.
They rise in two well defined terraces; the lower of about
1,000 feet is well shagged with trees, and the upper of about
2,000 feet is split up into numerous rocky buttresses.

Ben Hope may be reached by the wild moorland road that
runs from Altnaharra to Hope Lodge, and the first section of
about twelve miles affords an almost adventurous drive owing
to its uneven macadamised surface, now improved, flanked
with bog, and to the lack of ample passing places which are
few and far between. The second section begins at the
conspicuous Pictish tower of Dun Dornaigil, whence its
improved surface wends its way below the cliffs past the
keeper's house of Cashel Dhu, and thereafter through the
trees fringing Loch Hope.

Creag
Riabhach Bheag
1521

An Garbh allt

Beallach na
Creige Riabhaich

L. na
Seilg

Creag
Riabhach
Mhor

L. Bacach

Eilean
Mor

Me

Dubh-loch
na Beinne

Dubh
na Cre
Riabha

L.ª na Fearna

1040

BEN HOPE

L. a

2500

Ghabha Dhuibh

An Gorm L.

2000   2364

Muiseal

Creag
Riabhach

Creag
Chaol

1500

890

1303

59

A nan Eithreag

1000

Allt an A

34

Amhainn Srath Mor

Allt na Caillich

Falls
Allt na Caillich

Dun Dornadilla

1169

Cnoc
na Togaile

Allt Druim an Droinn

L.ⁿ Sgriodain

Strath More

172

345

94

1364

1000

Map 25
Ben Hope

Route 59. Ben Hope from Dun Dornaigil. This is a good starting point for the ascent because a car may be parked in the shadow of the tower. Just to the north of it the cascading Allt na Caillich descends from the moor and its L bank affords the easiest approach to the south ridge of the mountain. This is broad and relatively smooth, and rises at an easy gradient to the summit where the cairn is poised on its northern tip, surrounded on three sides by abysmal drops. The panorama on a clear day is extensive, in which the sea and sea lochs to the north, and the innumerable lochans in other directions, charm the eye. Ben Loyal is prominent to the east; Ben Klibreck in the south-east; Ben Hee in the south and the several peaks of Reay Forest in the west.

NOTE. If no parking space is available at Dun Dornaigil, leave the car near Cashel Dhu and follow the path on the north bank of the burn as far as the waterfall. Cross it and scale the ridge on the R, to join the above route.

Plate 182 Dun Dornaigil

Plate 183 Ben Hope and Loch Hope from near Hope Lodge

Ben Loyal

An Caisteal	2,504 feet	763 metres
Heddle's Top	2,465 feet	751 metres
Sgor Chaonasaid	2,320 feet	707 metres
Carn an Tionail		
Sgor a'Chleirich		
Sgor a'Bhatain		

This individual mountain rises from the swelling moorland some five miles to the south of Tongue and its western front, when seen from the vicinity of Lochan Hacoin, makes one of the most beautiful pictures in Britain. Known also as the "Queen of Scottish Peaks", it is admired alike by artists and photographers, and its particular splendour is due to the graceful pendent ridges that join its four western peaks of granite; they impart to the whole of it a grandeur that is altogether out of proportion to its height.

Climbers driving eastwards across the boggy uplands of A 'Mhoine catch glimpses of the peak, but it is only on coming down to sea level at the Kyle of Tongue that its real stature is evident. It dominates the landscape during the drive round the inlet,* but looks its best on attaining higher ground near Lochan Hacion whose blue suddenly appears below the road on the R, when the full elevation of the peak is revealed in all its glory. And strangely enough, when the mountain is seen from the Altnaharra–Tongue Road which skirts its eastern flanks, all its distinguishing features are hidden from view and completely belie its real charm.

*NOTE. A new bridge now spans the Kyle of Tongue to give direct access to the village, and this, the original road, branches off to the R before reaching it.

Sgor Chaonasaid

An Caisteal

Plate 184 Ben Loyal from Lochan Hacoin

Map 26
Ben Loyal

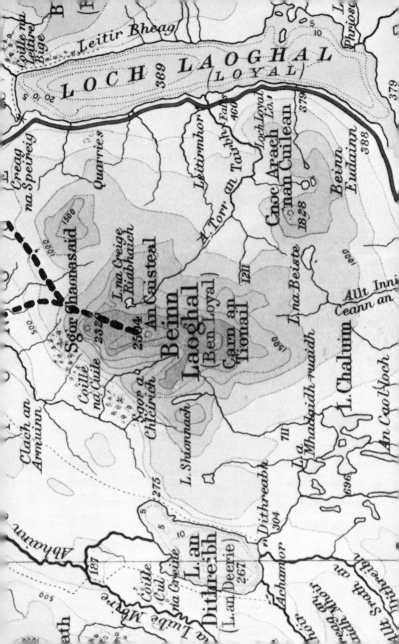

Route 60. Ben Loyal from Tongue. This peak can be climbed from almost any point on the engirdling moor, but is usually ascended from the Shepherd's Cottage of Cunside which is about one and a half miles to the south of the large farm of Ribigill: the latter is reached by a by-road that forks to the L from the Durness Road some two miles to the south of the village. Its prominent northern outpost of Sgor Chaonasaid is rocky and precipitous and should be avoided by all save the experienced rock climber. It is best to ascend the grassy slopes to the east of this sentinel and to then proceed due south along the gradually rising ridge to the commanding summit of An Caisteal. The same point of ascent may be reached with equal facility from the highway beside Loch Craggie, where a car may be parked in a convenient wide section of the single-track road. The summit plateau is disappointing and reminds of the Dartmoor Tors rather than of the typical Scottish Peak, and a good day is required to explore the whole of it and to visit all its tops. The panorama is stupendous and does not differ much from that of its near neighbour, Ben Hope, save that the eastern prospect comprises the wastes of Sutherland and Caithness, which are dappled with the gleaming blue of innumerable lochs and lochans.

Plate 185 **Route 60** — Ben Hope from the summit of Ben Loyal

The Lochnagar Range

Cac Carn Beag	3,789 feet	1,155 metres
Cac Carn Mor	3,768 feet	1,148 metres
The Stuic	3,571 feet	1,088 metres
Cuidhe Crom	3,552 feet	1,083 metres
Carn an t'Sagairt Mor	3,430 feet	1,045 metres
Carn an t'Sagairt Beag	3,424 feet	1,043 metres
Meikle Pap	3,211 feet	979 metres
Little Pap	3,125 feet	952 metres
Meall Coire na Saobhaidhe	3,191 feet	913 metres

On a clear spring day the climber travelling westwards from Aberdeen may catch a glimpse of the great snow-covered summit of Lochnagar before he reaches Ballater. But if he wishes to obtain a better view of it he should make for the bridge over the Dee where the vast plateau of the White Mounth will be seen rising above the nearer and more shapely Coyles of Muick. If he drives along Deeside he will notice the group from time to time, and not the least interesting of these prospects is obtained from the low hills to the north of Balmoral, whilst at Invercauld Bridge, further to the west, the mountain with its small conical summit is a conspicuous feature above the trees fringing the river.

Lochnagar dominates the Royal Forest of Balmoral and although its highest top is only the thirty-third in order of altitude in Scotland, the shapeliness of its foothills, combined with the superb crescent of cliffs forming its great eastern corrie, raise it to an important place in the fine mountain scenes in Britain. Its precipices consist of coarse red granite which weathers both horizontally and vertically, and these lines of weakness impart to the cliffs an illusion of gigantic masonry. In course of time the upper blocks become dangerously undercut and ultimately fall to the floor of the

Plate 186 Lochnagar from the Spittal of Glen Muick

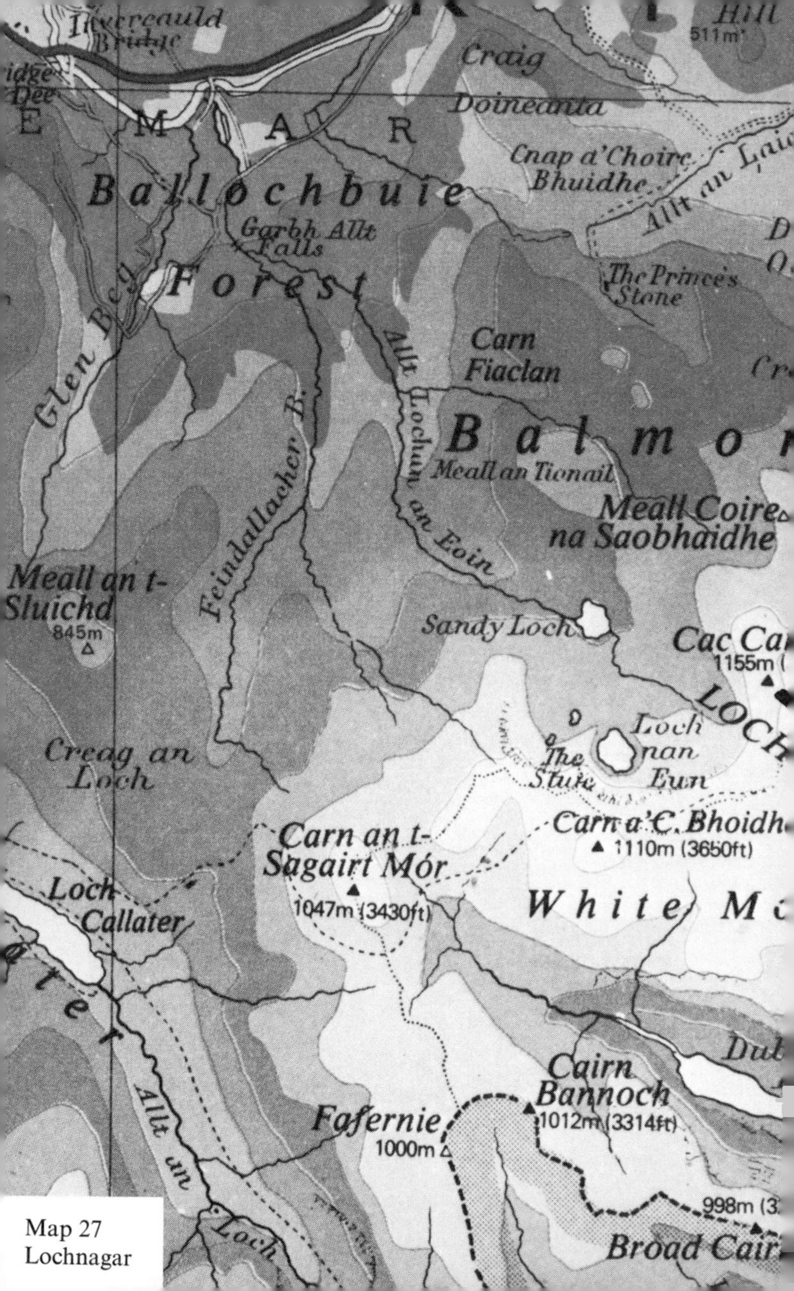

Map 27
Lochnagar

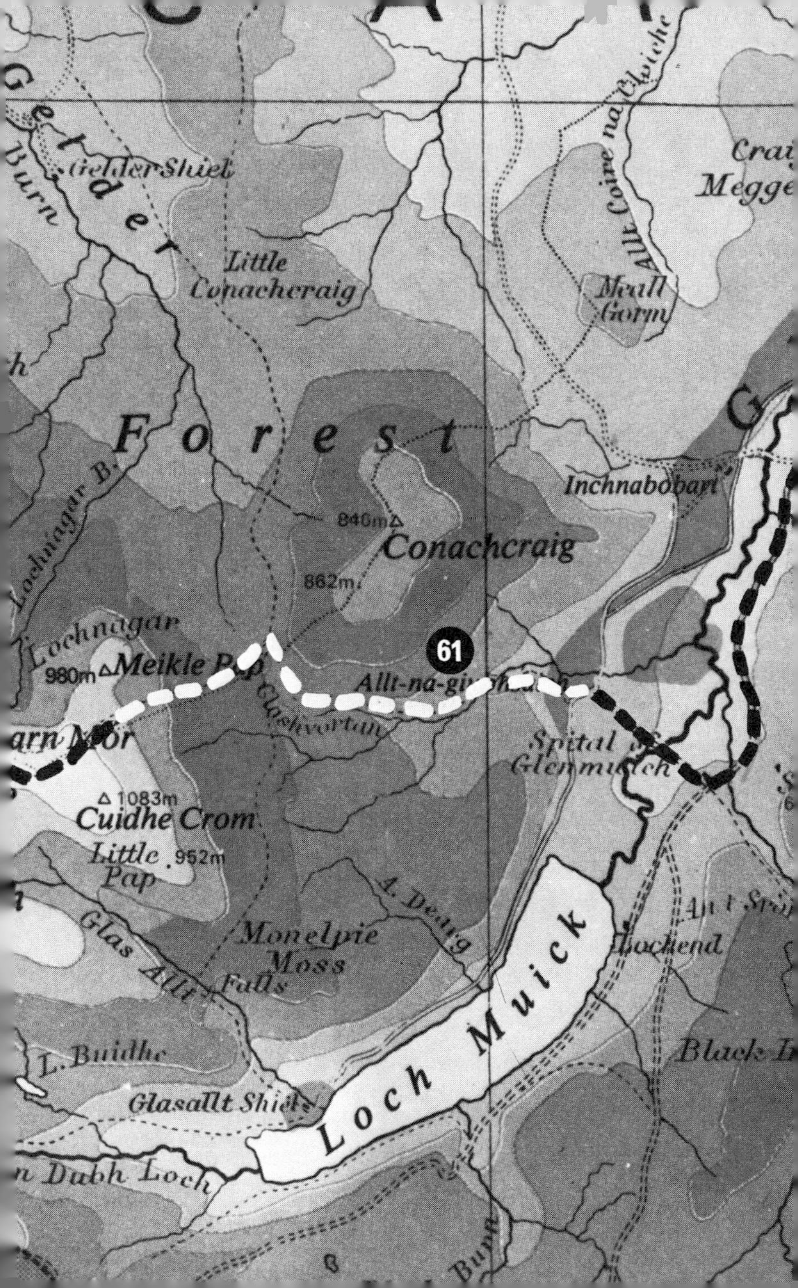

Gelder Shiel
Burn
Little
Conachcraig
Meall
Gorm
Forest
Inchnabobart
840m
Conachcraig
862m
Lochnagar B.
Lochnagar
Meikle Pap
980m
61
Spital of
Glenmuick
1083m
Cuidhe Crom
Little
Pap
952m
A. Dearg
Monelpie
Moss
Glas Allt
Falls
L. Buidhe
Glasallt Shiel
Loch Muick
Lochend
Dubh Loch

corrie some 1,200 feet below. They are thus a risky venue for the rock climber, but the mountaineer who revels in sensational snow ascents will find the prodigious gully known as the Black Spout an attractive and satisfying problem. The ascent of the mountain presents no difficulties or dangers if the eastern corrie is avoided, and climbers should keep well away from the snow cornices on the upper plateau owing to their unknown dimensions. The summit of Lochnagar is some fourteen miles from Ballater and about five miles from the Spittal of Glen Muick, so that even with transport to its base, the ascent requires a full day for the complete enjoyment of all its majestic scenes.

Route 61. Lochnagar from Ballater. Drive to the Spittal of Glen Muick and park your car. Then follow the path on the R where a bridge across the River Muick gives direct access to the Allt na-giubhsaich which is the starting point of the ascent. Take the path through the conifers and on emerging in the open moorland keep to it high above the L bank of the burn. Bear R to round the shoulder of Conachcraig, with views of the Meikle Pap overhead and on its R of the distant summits of Beinn a'Bhuird and Ben Avon. At this point the way can be confusing because the track falls on the far side of the ridge, whence, however, it branches to the L for the Meikle Pap. Thereafter the route is clear and at a height of 2,800 feet you encounter the Foxes Well, marked by a small cairn and affording the last drink of water on this ascent. On reaching the col the steep zig-zags of the Ladder rise to the L, but before tackling them turn R and climb to the summit of the Meikle Pap for the magnificent view of the long line of precipices engirdling the corrie, in which the Black Spout is prominent and also the dark lochan cradled at its base. Now retrace your steps to the col and climb the Ladder, eventually to pass the Red Spout on the R on your way to Cuidhe Crom which is an excellent viewpoint and worthy of a halt. Then continue your walk along the rim of the precipices and if they are snowbound make generous use of your ice axe. In due

Cac Carn Beag →

Plate 187 Lochnagar from the old Invercauld Bridge

course you will encounter the subsidiary peak of Cac Carn Mor, from which it is only a short step to the higher Cac Carn Beag.

Here you will find the excellent Indicator, erected by the Cairngorm Club in July 1924, with whose help you should have no difficulty in identifying many of the distant peaks, and on a clear day even the summit of Ben Nevis. Note also, but much nearer at hand to the south-west, the tremendous corrie dominated by the Stuic, a fine buttress above Loch nan Eun, and when retracing your steps look into the grim depths of the Black Spout before descending to your car.

At Cac Carn Mor climbers will notice a track coming up from the south-west, which is the usual route of ascent from Braemar by way of Loch Callater.

Black Spout

Cac Carn Beag

Plate 188 **Route 61** — The Corrie from Cuidhe Crom

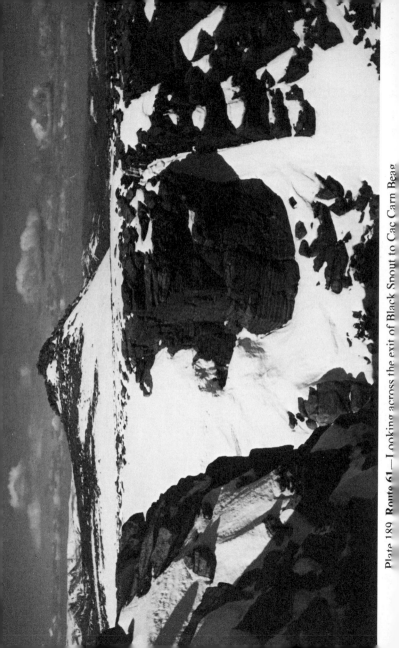

Plate 189 **Route 61**—Looking across the exit of Black Spout to Cac Carn Beag

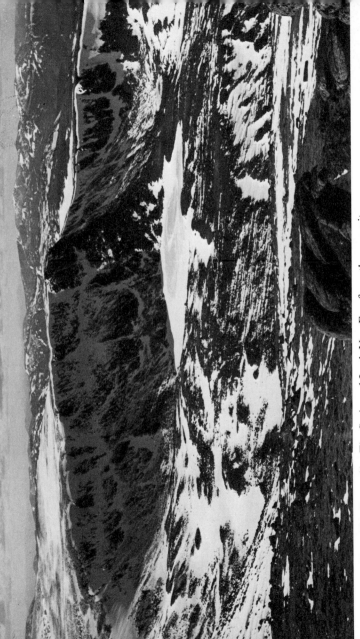

Plate 190 **Route 61** — The Stuic and Loch Nan Eun from the summit

Plate 191 **Route 61**—Cloud over Cac Carn Mor

Ben Macdhui Group

Ben Macdhui	4,300 feet	1,311 metres
Stob Coire Sputan Dearg	4,095 feet	1,248 metres
Beinn Mheadhoin	3,883 feet	1,184 metres
Derry Cairngorm	3,788 feet	1,155 metres
Lochan Buidhe	3,683 feet	1,123 metres
Cairn Etchachan	3,673 feet	1,120 metres
Sron Riach	3,534 feet	1,077 metres
Carn a'Mhaim	3,329 feet	1,015 metres
Lochan Uaine	3,142 feet	952 metres
Loch Etchachan	3,058 feet	932 metres
Carn Crom	2,847 feet	861 metres
Loch Avon	2,377 feet	724 metres

Ben Macdhui is the highest mountain in the Cairngorms and the second highest in Scotland. Together with its outlier Cairn Gorm, it forms the massive group of hills rising between the Lairig an Laoigh on the east and the Lairig Ghru on the west. The summit is scarcely well proportioned and consists of a flattish rounded top which perhaps presents its most graceful aspect when seen from Cairn Gorm to the north. The two peaks are connected by a broad high plateau which nowhere falls below the 3,600 feet contour. The supporting slopes of Ben Macdhui are set at a gentle angle, excepting on the west, where they fall steeply to the Lairig Ghru. The ascent of this mountain, therefore, presents no difficulties but vast distances have to be covered to attain its cairn.

Two famous lochs lie in the heart of the group: Loch Avon and Loch Etchachan; the former is set deep in the hills amid one of the most impressive and sombre amphitheatres in the Highlands and is so remote, that were it not for the Shelter Stone where a night may be spent, it is doubtful if many climbers would ever see it. The latter, lying in more open

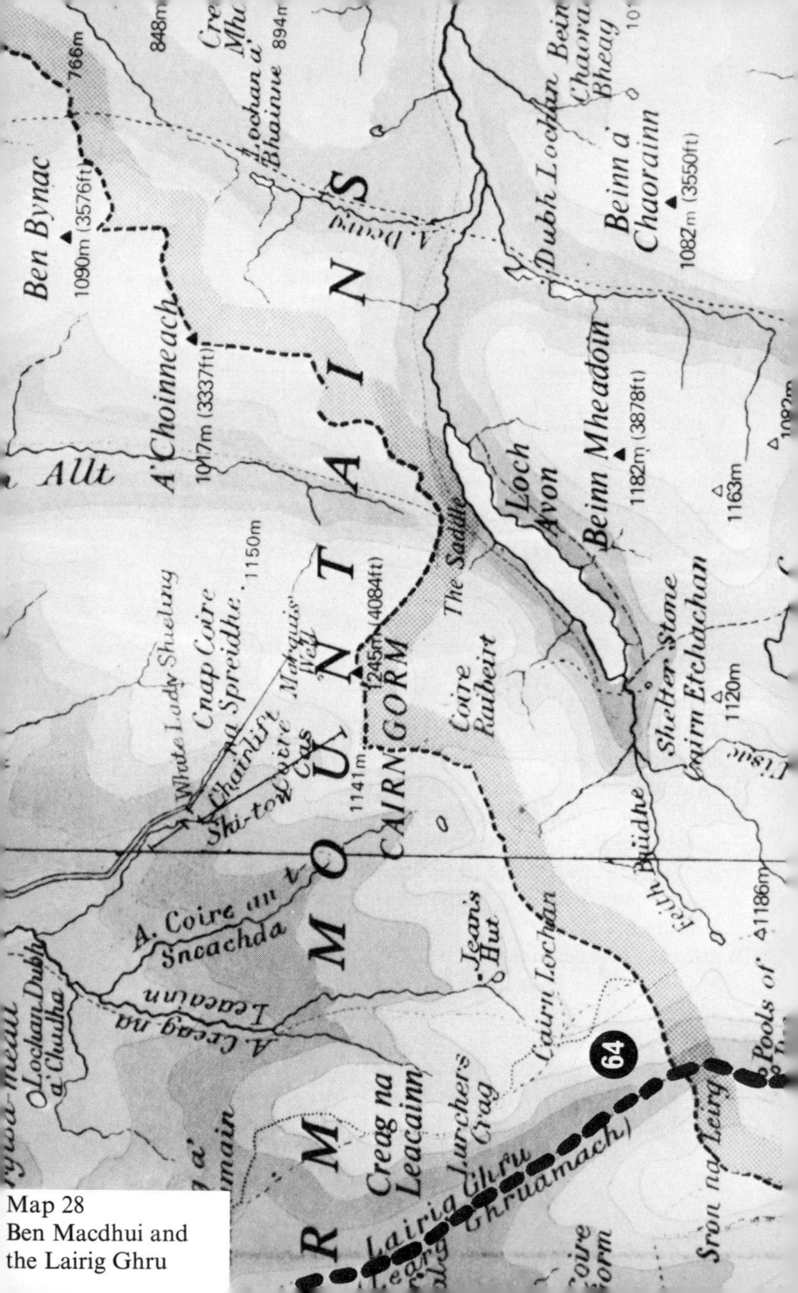

Map 28
Ben Macdhui and
the Lairig Ghru

ground, is of considerably less interest, and is passed in the Glen Derry ascent of Ben Macdhui.

As the crow flies the summit is actually nearer to Aviemore than Braemar, but unless its ascent is combined with that of Cairn Gorm, the expedition is lacking in interest. Those climbers wishing to undertake it should drive to Coire Cas, take the chair-lift to a point about 500 feet below its summit and walk across the plateau by way of Cairn Lochan to Ben Macdhui, descending by way of Creag an Leth-Choin and Rothiemurchus or as an alternative follow Route 66 which takes in the Shelter Stone. The mountain, however, is more usually ascended from Braemar by way of Derry Lodge, beyond which there is a choice of two routes. The more popular of these is through Glen Derry and Coire Etchachan, a total distance of seven and a half miles, but the more direct approach by Glen Luibeg and the fine ridge of Sron Riach is more interesting, revealing and two miles shorter.

Stob Coire Sputan Dearg

Derry Cairngorm

Plate 192 The satellites of Ben Macdhui from Black Bridge

Route 62. From Braemar by Glen Derry. Drive to the locked
gate beyond the Linn of Dee and park your car there unless
you have obtained permission to go as far as either Black
Bridge or Derry Lodge. Take the path going due north from
the Lodge, and after passing through the ancient forest of
gnarled pines cross the Derry Burn and keep to the R of the
gloomy glen until the cliffs of Beinn Mheadhoin appear
ahead, a distance of about four miles. Now follow the L fork
and climb the track that rises through the deep trough of
Coire Etchachan until you reach easier ground where Loch
Etchachan reposes amid a wilderness of rock and scree and
reveals to the north the rounded summit of Cairn Gorm. Turn
to the L and keep to the track that skirts the cliffs enclosing
Coire Sputan Dearg, whence bear R and walk up the easy
stony slopes to the cairn on the skyline. Ben Macdhui, like
Lochnagar, has an Indicator erected in 1925 by the
Cairngorm Club, from which you should be able to identify
many of the surrounding hills on a clear day. However, the
nearer tops that stretch from Cairn Toul to Braeriach on the
other side of the Lairig Ghru to the west will hold your gaze,
and the view of them is one of the grandest in the country.
You will be impressed by the vastness of An Garbh Coire,
with its sharp pointed summit of Sgor an Lochain Uaine,
known also as the Angel's Peak, rising steeply on the L and
just to the R of Cairn Toul. The skyline to the R encompasses
Braeriach, which is supported by Coire Bhrochain, and then
falls to Sron na Lairig and Rothiemurchus.

Beinn Mheadhoin

Plate 193 **Route 62**—Beinn Mheadhoin from the last trees in Glen Derry

Plate 194 **Route 62**—Looking down Coire Etchachan

Cairn Gorm

Plate 195 **Route 62**—The view from Loch Etchachan—Loch Avon lies in the dip in the middle distance

Plate 196 **Route 62**—A fine Whit-Monday on the summit of **Ben Macdhui**

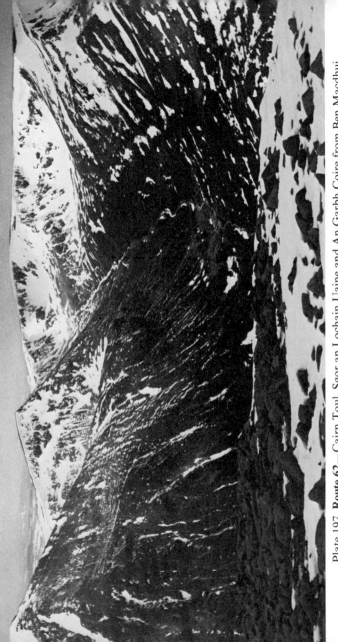

Plate 197 **Route 62**—Cairn Toul, Sgor an Lochain Uaine and An Garbh Coire from Ben Macdhui

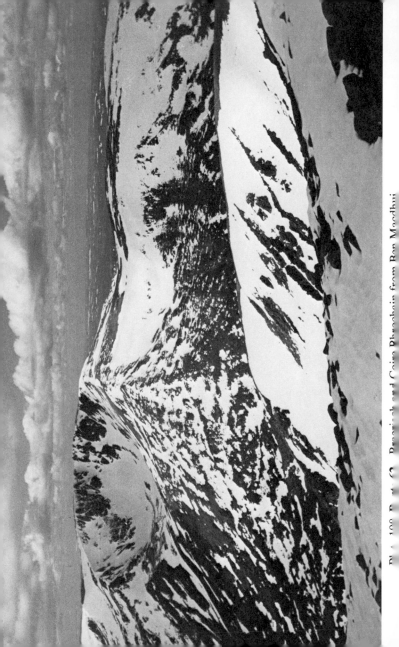

Plate 100 Braeriach and Coire Bhrochain from Ben Macdhui

Route 63. From Braemar by Sron Riach. Leave Derry Lodge and cross the bridge over the Derry Burn. After passing the nearby keeper's cottage at Luibeg, follow the Lairig Ghru path westwards through the trees with Carn a'Mhaim towering ahead on the R. In about two miles the path forks before reaching the Luibeg Burn and here you take the branch on the R and walk northwards through thick heather across the lower slopes of Carn Crom with a grand view ahead of Sron Riach. After crossing the Luibeg Burn the gradient increases and a stiff pull up the ridge will place you on its lofty crest where you will be rewarded by a magnificent prospect of Cairn Toul on the L beyond the long shoulder of Carn a'Mhaim. Bear R now for the cliffs of Stob Coire Sputan Dearg and if it is snowbound keep well away from the cornices overhanging the lip of the corrie, below which on the R you look down on the lonely Lochan Uaine, the second highest in the Cairngorms. On attaining the red granite blocks surmounting this top, turn L and walk up the easy stony slopes to Ben Macdhui.

Plate 109. **Braeriach, Figs. 63 and 64.** The path from Derry Lodge goes towards Carn a'Mhaim

Plate 200 **Route 63**—Stob Coire Sputan Dearg from Glen Luibeg

Plate 201 **Route 63** — Cairn Toul and Coire an t'Saighdeir from Sron Riach

Plate 202 **Route 63**— A near view of Stob Coire Sputan Dearg

Peaks enclosing the Lairig Ghru
from north to south

ROTHIEMURCHUS

	feet	metres		feet	metres
Carn Eilrig	2,435 feet	742 metres	Creag a'Chalamain	2,579 feet	786 metres
Carn Odhar	2,368 feet	722 metres	Creag an Leth-choin	3,448 feet	1,051 metres
Sron na Lairig	3,860 feet	1,177 metres	Ben Macdhui	4,300 feet	1,311 metres
Braeriach	4,248 feet	1,294 metres		3,534 feet	1,077 metres
Angel's Peak	4,116 feet	1,255 metres		3,329 feet	1,015 metres
Cairn Toul	4,241 feet	1,293 metres	Sron Riach	2,847 feet	861 metres
The Devil's Point	3,303 feet	1,009 metres	Carn a'Mhaim		
Creaghan nan Gabhar	2,368 feet	722 metres			
Sgor Mor	2,666 feet	813 metres	Carn Crom		
Sgor Dubh	2,432 feet	741 metres			
Castle Hill	2,366 feet	721 metres			

DERRY LODGE

The Lairig Ghru

This is the finest and most popular of the passes in the
Cairngorms and its traverse one of the most arduous in the
whole of Britain. The best long distance view of it is from
Speyside where it appears as a gigantic V-shaped opening
between Ben Macdhui and Braeriach. The approaches at
either end are full of variety and interest, but the pass itself is
the very epitome of austerity, barrenness and gloom. Its
passage is not the longest expedition in the district but is
enough to test the stamina of the fittest. The distance from
Braemar to Aviemore is 27 miles, but it is not everyone who
walks the whole way. A lift to Derry Lodge shortens it by 10
miles and another from Coylumbridge takes off a further two,
but the other 15 miles cannot be reduced by any form of
transport. A bicycle is a disadvantage rather than an asset. It
may even prove a nuisance, especially if you have a heavy
rucksack, for the going is of the roughest and the machine will
have to be carried, as it is quite impossible to wheel it along
the track for most of the way. A point not to be lost sight of
by those undertaking this walk is that no accommodation
exists between Mar Lodge and Coylumbridge, a distance of 22
miles. On a fine and warm summer night this is not a serious
matter, but in bad weather, not uncommon in the Lairig
Ghru, shelter may be urgently required. This may be obtained
at the Corrour Bothy below the Devil's Point and, in direst
need, a bed might be found at the keeper's cottage at Luibeg
or the Linn of Dee; but the risk remains and it should under
no circumstances be discounted.

It is a matter of opinion which direction affords the most
fascinating walk through the pass; but it is always an
advantage to go from south to north, because on a good day
the sunlight reveals the topography of the landscape more
clearly. In the reverse direction the sun is not only in one's
eyes, but its rays are refracted by the moisture and dust in the

atmosphere, when one's full appreciation of the scenery is undoubtedly marred.

Route 64. From Derry Lodge to Coylumbridge. Follow Route 63 to the fork in the Lairig Ghru path where the flat expanse of sand and boulders marks the cloudburst of 1829. Take the L branch and go ahead to cross the bridge over the Luibeg Burn and then ascend the rather steep spur of Carn a'Mhaim. From the brow of the hill you should turn round to admire the retrospect of the hills about Derry Lodge, to the R of which you will perceive the summit of Lochnagar rising above the vast expanse of moorland. The going is now easy but rather wet for more than a mile, and as you round the flanks of Carn a'Mhaim the prospect of Glen Dee and the green floor of Glen Geusachan, overshadowed by Beinn Bhrotain and the Devil's Point, increases in grandeur with every step. Threading the heather on your L runs the Allt Preas nam Meirleach, which rises in a small group of Lochans. If you can spare the time, it is worth while descending to see them because they make a charming foreground to the Devil's Point and Cairn Toul, the two superb peaks rising across the glen. During this part of the tramp you will have wondered how much further you have to go before sighting the pass itself, but before swinging round the bend which discloses it, your gaze will be riveted upon the magnificent symmetrical cone of the Devil's Point whose shapely top and rifted supporting crags make such a fine picture of mountain grandeur. Then, quite suddenly, it will be revealed stretching away to the north and you will doubtless pause to admire its stupendous proportions. On the L, and just beyond the Devil's Point, the skyline is crowned by Cairn Toul, its flanks sweeping down in one unbroken line past the overhanging corrie to the river, 2,400 feet below. Behind it there is a glimpse of Coire Bhrochain immediately beneath Braeriach, and this merges with Sron na Lairig whose slopes fall towards the pass. On the R the featureless flanks of Ben Macdhui are connected by a high rock ridge whose crest terminates with

Plate 203 **Routes 63** and **64**— Deer in the vicinity of Derry Lodge

Carn a'Mhaim. The rough track now drops slightly and then runs almost level for a mile and a half, passing the Corrour Bothy on the L between the Devil's Point and Cairn Toul. When you arrive opposite the latter you will realise the vastness of the distance which separates it from Braeriach, and a little further along the pass you will see the Angel's Peak high up on the L of the great amphitheatre of An Garbh Coire. If you scan the cliffs forming its crest you may be able to pick out the white line of the infant Dee descending from the Wells of Dee on the summit plateau of Braeriach. Thereafter the pass narrows and on approaching the summit it levels out, being almost choked in places by the large boulders that have fallen from the hill-sides. Here you will encounter the Pools of Dee, whose symmetry deceptively suggests the hand of man, and beyond them you will soon thankfully attain the highest point of the Lairig at an altitude of 2,733 feet. The descent is at an easy gradient for the first mile and a half and then its narrow confines end below the Lurcher's crag high up on the R. Looking back, the pass presents a picture of wild desolation, but this aspect is softened in the advance northwards by occasional glimpses of Speyside far below. The track drops rapidly but there are still two miles of wilderness before the first tree heralds the approach to Rothiemurchus. Passing through the thick heather you will shortly encounter a small clump of pines standing on top of a little hill. Here you will pause to gaze upon the vast expanse of forest stretching away for miles to the banks of the Spey and frowned upon on the L by the conical sentinel of Carn Eilrig. This coign of vantage is a good one for the appraisal of the gigantic proportions of the Lairig Ghru, now left behind, where the apparent overhang of the Lurcher is well seen high up on the L.

If you delight in the beauty of trees you will revel in the stately gathering which characterises Rothiemurchus, and if you are fortunate you may catch a glimpse of the tiny crested tit that lines its nest with deer's hair and makes its home hereabouts. Here and there you will notice a windswept birch,

Plate 204 **Route 64** – The Devil's Point and Carn Toul from a lochan beside the path

but it is the Scots Pines which are so magnificent. After two miles or so of the shady forest you will come to the cairn carrying the Braemar guidepost, whence the track forks. The R branch goes to Loch Morlich, the middle one to Luineag, some two miles below this loch, and the L branch, your direction, to Coylumbridge. It descends at first to join the R bank of the Allt Druidh, the burn which rises in the Lairig Ghru, and you advance past its junction with the larger stream of Am Beanaidh coming down from Gleann Einich. You will pass through a deserted clearing in the forest, carpeted with springy turf, and in a short distance reach the iron footbridge erected in 1912 by the Cairngorm Club, which spans the river below the ford. To give walkers an idea of the distances they still have to cover in either direction, the Cairngorm Club thoughtfully placed a tablet on the parapet of their bridge and it gives the following approximate distances and times.

To			
	Aviemore	1½ hours	4 miles
	Coylum bridge	¾ hours	2 miles
	Lairig Ghru summit	3 hours	5½ miles
	Derry Lodge	6½ hours	14 miles
	Linn of Dee	8 hours	18 miles
	Braemar	10 hours	24½ miles

To the north of the bridge the path is unmistakable and there are two signposts some little distance further on in an open expanse of heather. The L branch leads by Loch an Eilein to Inverdruie and thence to Aviemore, while the R fork, which is less circuitous, continues by the L bank of Am Beanaidh to Coylum-bridge. It passes a clearing covered with boulders and then picks up the rough road on the L coming from Gleann Einich. Thereafter it is only a short step to Coylum-bridge and civilisation.

Plate 205 **Route 64**—Looking north through the Lairig Ghru

Plate 206 **Route 64** — A wild retrospect near the summit of the pass

Plate 207 **Route 64**—An unsolved mystery in the Lairig Ghru

Plate 208. **Route 64.** The first tree in Rothiemurchus

Plate 209 **Route 64**—The last glimpse of the Lairig Ghru from Rothiemurchus

Cairn Gorm Group

Cairn Gorm	4,084 feet	1,245 metres
Cairn Lochan	3,983 feet	1,214 metres
Stob Coire an t'Sneachda	3,856 feet	1,175 metres
Lochan Buidhe	3,683 feet	1,123 metres
Fiacaill Arete	3,640 feet	1,109 metres
Creag an Leth-choin	3,448 feet	1,051 metres
Loch Avon	2,377 feet	724 metres

Cairn Gorm is the lowest of the 4,000 foot peaks bearing its name, but owing to its position almost at the northern end of the chain, it commands one of the finest prospects in the region. From Speyside it has some semblance of shapeliness, although it is rounded and far from striking except when seen from the vicinity of Grantown. If, however, its ascent on foot is combined with the high ridge walk to Cairn Lochan, the immense cliffs of the latter will make up for any tameness which may characterise its peer. Moreover, it is the most accessible of the great mountains; its ascent on foot is the shortest and easiest, and in consequence the most popular of them all, a fact borne out by the broad, well-cairned track rising in an almost direct line from Glenmore Lodge to its summit. But recent developments, mainly for the skier, have altered all this for the average pedestrian, who can drive up to Coire Cas at an altitude of 2,150 feet, take the chair-lift and be borne aloft to within a few hundred feet of the summit. In fact, the only footwork involved is from the upper station to the cairn on Cairn Gorm itself.

Taking account of this evolution, Route 65 is included on the assumption that climbers will scorn the ascent by the chair-lift and use their well-shod feet as the only means of progress from start to finish. However, since Route 66 is more strenuous the use of both car and lift should be condoned by

Map 29
Cairn Gorm

all, save of course by the toughest of mountaineers.

All climbers who traverse the Cairn Gorm–Ben Macdhui Plateau should remember that the three following bothies have been removed:

Curran situated beside Lochan Buidhe at MR 983010;
El Alamein on the north Ridge of Cairn Gorm at MR 016054;
St. Valery on the cliffs above the west end of Loch Avon at MR 002022.

Route 65. Cairn Gorm from Aviemore. Drive to the caravan park in front of the old Glenmore Lodge, stopping for a moment *en route* to admire the beauty of Loch Morlich, backed by the ridge you will eventually traverse. Park your car, put on your climbing boots, shoulder your rucksack and proceed on your way joyfully, ignoring completely all pressing offers of a lift up to Coire Cas! Walk up the new road through the remnants of the one-time fine forest of pines until you can pick out on the L skyline the perched block of Clach Bharraig. Scramble up to it and note the splendid retrospect of Loch Morlich, and then pick up the nearby track for the summit of your peak, passing in its higher reaches the upper station of the chair-lift with its nearby Ptarmigan Restaurant. The summit of Cairn Gorm is littered with great boulders and its cairn opens up a spacious prospect round the northern arc, in which Loch Morlich immediately catches the eye by reason of its intense blue set amid the green and brown trees of the engirdling forest. To the L the whole of Rothiemurchus is laid bare, backed by the winding Spey, Loch Alvie and the Monadh Liath. To the R the Moray Firth can be seen in the far distance, fringed with golden sands, and beyond it on the skyline rise the peaks of Sutherland and Caithness. To the south-west Braeriach tops the skyline above the summit of Cairn Lochan, and to the L its lofty ridge sweeps down to the Angel's Peak and Cairn Toul. Ben Macdhui is prominent in the south, with Derry Cairngorm on its L and the tors of Beinn Mheadhoin clearly disclosed on the skyline further to the L, while to the east a grand array of peaks, which include

Plate 210 Seen from Loch Morlich, **Route 65** follows the skyline to the right

Ben Avon and Lochnagar, close in the view.

Now walk due west off your peak and continue round the rim of Coire Cas, and then turn south along the lip of Coire an t'Sneachda whose shattered cliffs fall steeply on your R. Continue past the little col and climb steadily towards Cairn Lochan, passing the top of the Fiacaill Ridge on your R; its narrow escarpment forms the eastern wall of Coire an Lochain and is crowned by one of the few spectacular rock aretes in the Cairngorms. The cairn on the latter peak stands on the very edge of the cliffs, which you circle to reach their western side. From this coign of vantage you obtain the finest view of their peculiar architecture. They consist of granite, weathered both vertically and horizontally and are a splendid example of this type of Titanic masonry. Continue your walk by descending the ridge that falls to the north, and look back from time to time to get a comprehensive view of the precipitous cliffs, below which lies the famous Sloping Slab together with the two black lochans in the bottom of the corrie. At the base of the ridge you will encounter the rippling Allt Creag an Leth-choin, which you follow all the way back to the new road and your car.

Plate 211 **Route 65**—Upper station and Ptarmigan Igloo

Plate 212 **Route 65** seen from Cairn Gorm

Cairn Toul

Angel's Peak

Braeriach

Cairn Lochan

Faicaill Ridge

Plate 213 **Route 65**—The summit cairn is perched on the edge of the cliffs of Cairn Lochan

Plate 214 **Route 65**—Looking back into Coire an Lochain

Route 66. Cairn Gorm to Ben Macdhui by the Shelter Stone.
This route is for the experienced climber and should be
severely left alone by the ordinary pedestrian, who might find
himself in difficulties among the rocky escarpments
surrounding Loch Avon. Leave your car in the park and use
the chair-lift to reach Cairn Gorm quickly. Then descend due
south from the cairn into the grassy depression of Coire
Raibeirt which is hemmed in on the L by Stac an Pharaidh
and on the R by the Stag Rocks. Follow the burn down and
keep to the L of it to avoid the crags. On reaching Loch Avon
bear R round its shore, above which to the south you will
discover the cottage-sized block of rock known as the Shelter
Stone, which is situated amid some of the grandest rock
scenery in Scotland. Crawl into the space beneath it to sign
the visitors' book, and then walk across to the Garbh Uisge
which flows into the head of the loch. Scramble up beside the
stream for some 1,000 feet, taking a zig-zag course to ease the
angle of ascent, and on reaching more level ground, where
two tributaries of the burn merge, bear L for the top of the
cliff overhanging the Shelter Stone for the magnificent vista of
Loch Avon. Now return to the stream and follow it to its
source below Ben Macdhui. On leaving the cairn retrace your
steps for a short distance and then keep to the higher
contours, going north past Lochan Buidhe, until you
eventually reach Cairn Lochan. Finally walk round the edge
of the three corries back to Cairn Gorm and so to your car.

Plate 215 **Route 66**—The Cairn Gorm upper chair lift and White Lady Sheiling

Plate 216 Retrospect of Loch Avon from **Route 66**

The Storr

The Storr Rock	2,359 feet	719 metres
Old Man of Storr	160 feet	49 metres

Climbers proceeding from Kyleakin to Sligachan in the Isle of Skye will get their first glimpse of this remarkable peak as they skirt the peninsula between Loch Ainort and Loch Sligachan, and on a clear day will easily perceive its fantastic buttresses topping the Trotternish skyline. But since it rises from the ridge over six miles to the north of Portree, those who wish to explore it must drive to its base at Loch Leathan, whence the formidable cliffs are easily attained, the Sanctuary and the Old Man visited and the lofty summit ridge traversed in an easy day. However, the finest view of the Storr is revealed from the head of Loch Fada, a treasured resort of the trout fisherman, from which excellent coign of vantage its deeply cleaved buttresses and nearby Old Man stand up superbly on the skyline.

While the ordinary pedestrian can safely explore the bizarre rock scenery surrounding the Sanctuary and its many weird pinnacles, the traverse of the summit ridge should only be attempted by the experienced climber who will revel in the grandeur of the rock architecture and of the mainland peaks that rise across the Sound of Raasay, in which he should have no difficulty in identifying Slioch and the Torridon Peaks. However, although only 160 feet high the ascent of the Old Man of Storr is quite a different problem, and was only climbed for the first time in June 1955, by D. Whillans, J. Barber and G. J. Sutton.

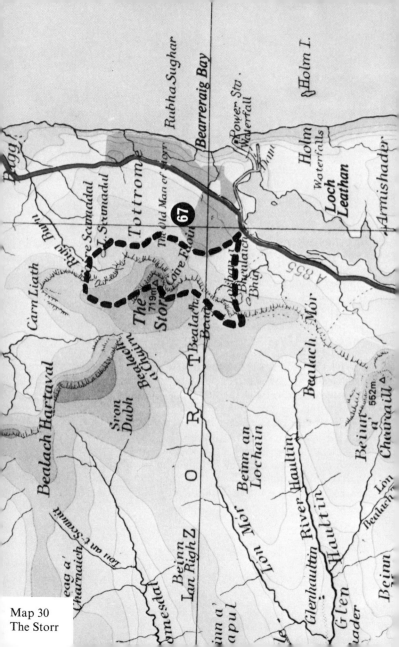

Map 30
The Storr

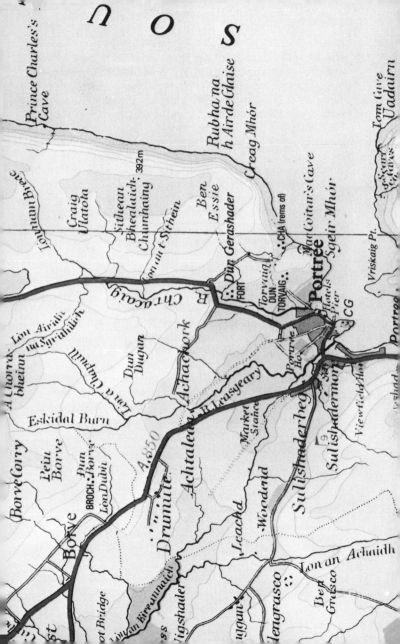

Route 67. The Traverse of the Storr. Drive north from Portree and park your car in a quarry at a point where the road round Loch Leathan turns east. Follow the rather indistinct path through the grass and heather which rises steeply in a north-westerly direction and leads up to the strange collection of rocks guarding the Sanctuary. Keep to the path which meanders away to the R and then goes straight to the Old Man, and climb up to it if only to examine closely its undercut structure of trap rock. Then pass round it to take a look at the nearby leaning Needle and make your way through the boulders at the base of the cliffs into Coire Scamadal, with its tiny lochan. Here you will find a break in the lower cliffs through which you can gain the ridge, whence proceed carefully to the L and climb along the crest of the buttresses and skirt the yawning gullies through which you will occasionally glimpse the Old Man of Storr far below. After passing the summit cairn the ridge bends to the L round the enclosing walls of Coire Faoin, and as you descend it you will obtain a splendid vista of the whole of the wild Sanctuary and its pinnacles, backed by the blue sea. The easiest descent is to follow the line of cliffs to the south, when you will eventually reach a trickling burn that has worn its way through them to the grassy plateau at their base, and beside which runs a sketchy track, whence a walk across the moor will lead back to your car. However, if you have a steady head you may prefer to descend the sensational track that winds its way down the north face of the last buttress and ends at the pinnacles guarding the Sanctuary.

Plate 217 The Storr from Loch Fada

Plate 218. Close-up of the Old Man of Storr

Plate 219 **Route 67** — Looking across the Sanctuary to the peaks on the mainland

Quiraing

Meall nan Suireamach	1,781 feet	543 metres
The Needle is over 100 feet high		30 metres

From afar this remote peak in the Isle of Skye looks quite uninteresting, as its eastern front appears as a broken wall of rock that frowns upon the lochan-strewn moorland sloping down to Staffin Bay. But on closer inspection it will be found not only to consist of the weirdest collection of perpendicular buttresses and pinnacles in Britain, but also to hide away in its uppermost recesses an oval Table covered with smooth, sheep-cropped grass of vivid hue, which might well make an excellent putting green situated in one of the most spectacular amphitheatres in the country. Moreover, its approach reveals on the R a detached and seemingly inaccessible pyramid of sheer rock known as the Prison, which when scaled at the back affords the finest prospect of the precipices and Needle opposite.

There are two ways of reaching Quiraing from the seven miles of twisting, resurfaced hill road between Staffin and Uig which passes over a low break in the Trotternish backbone at an altitude of 853 feet. Here you will find a car park which is less than 2½ miles from the Staffin fork and about a mile to the south of Quiraing. A sketchy track begins on the other side of the road, and after a few ups and downs it falls to the gently rising shelf to give easy and direct access to the Prison. A more revealing approach starts about a mile from the Staffin fork at a point opposite a conspicuous sheep-fold on the L, where two or three cars may be parked on a flat piece of ground beside a bridge. Thence the path rises gently across the moor to a grassy shelf that extends northwards to the base of the Prison, from which the steeper section of the ascent begins. Climbers staying at Flodigarry, to the north of Staffin,

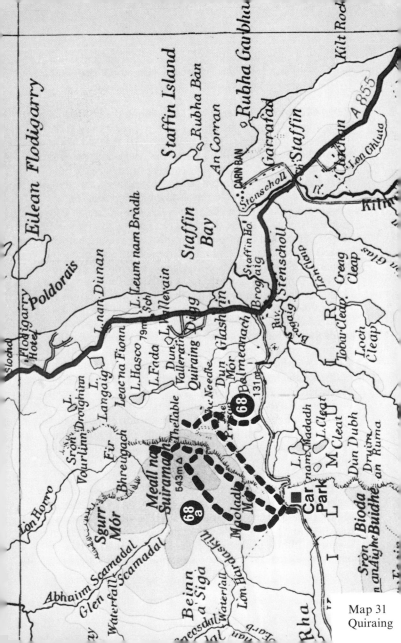

Map 31
Quiraing

may take a more or less direct line across the ups and downs of the moor and reach the Table by a stone shoot that issues from a narrow gully between its guarding pinnacles.

Route 68. Quiraing from Staffin. Drive along the Uig road and park your car about a mile from the above mentioned fork. Hereabouts you will discover the grassy path on the north side of the road, which follow on to the shelf and thence to its terminus below the Prison. Do not attempt to scale its precipitous western front, but instead ascend its grassy flanks to reach a rake that rises to the R, beyond which contour round to the L behind the first pinnacle until you attain the saddle that joins it to the second. The exceedingly steep and slippery grass here requires care in this short ascent, but the rewards are immense as the whole of the buttresses and pinnacles on the other side of the stony intervening gap are laid bare from this superlative coign of vantage. Now retrace your steps to the path and climb the steep track that rises to the L of the Needle, which is over 100 feet high. Keep to the track as it threads the gloomy recesses between the gaunt pinnacles and buttresses until the Table appears ahead. Go round it to the L where you will find a way winding aloft to its grassy top, which is one of the most amazing situations in all our homeland hills. Behind you rise the unscalable walls of Meall nan Suireamach, while in all other directions you look through the gaps between the pinnacles; to the L to the sea and its islands, and to the R to the Trotternish ridge trailing away to the south, both of which are enlivened by the glint of light on the many lochans strewn on the extensive moorland below.

At long last the Needle was climbed on August 19th, 1977, by a youth of $16\frac{1}{2}$ years. He is Kevin R. Bridges and began the very dangerous ascent by climbing a crack on its east face, above which he found the rock very fractured and loose. A traverse L and a grove led to a sound flake belay on the south-east arete, but his brother, Michael, who followed to this point considered it too risky to continue. Kevin climbed

Plate 220 The approach to the Prison by **Route 68**

Plate 221 The Needle from the Prison

Plate 222 **Route 68**—Looking down on the Needle and Prison from the Central Gully

directly above the belay for some 25 feet and then traversed R to the north-east arete and continued to a grassy ledge immediately below the summit. He placed four slings linked together round the top and abseiled down after leaving a small cairn there. Since the rock was so insecure he graded the climb as VS.

NOTE: Since a few of my readers report some difficulty in locating the car park, mainly I gather because they turn R at Brogaig instead of going straight on. Hence, QUIRAING FROM UIG might be a preferable approach. After passing through this village the road rises sharply eventually to emerge on the lofty open moor. Here a prominent guide post directs the motorist to turn sharp R and follow the single track road to its highest point at the car park. Some years ago this road was resurfaced and now has ample passing places, so there should be no problem if this alternative route is taken.

Plate 223 **Route 68** terminates on the flat grassy top of the Table

Plate 224 **Route 68** — One of the many views from the Table

Meall nan Suireamach

This grassy eminence is one of the more northerly tops of the Trotternish Backbone and from afar is seen to dominate the shattered cliffs of Quiraing. Those who have explored this bizarre collection of pinnacles and buttresses will have been impressed by the sheer rock walls enclosing the Table on the west. They are the only unscaleable guardians of the peak, as on all other sides grassy slopes, dappled with heather and bracken, lead up to the cairn. It is a rare experience to see a climber ascending the broad southern ridge which reveals a magnificent prospect of the sea far below and of the mainland peaks to the east, but culminates in a spectacular bird's eye view of Quiraing.

Route 68a. Meall nan Suireamach from Staffin. The most convenient starting point for this ascent is the car park on the col, already mentioned in the preceding monograph. As there is no track you just cross the road and go straight up the slopes opposite which involve a hard slog of some 600 feet. Thence you bear R and on reaching the crest of the broad ridge walk along to the cairn after a total ascent of less then 1,000 feet. Now turn R and carefully approach the edge of the vast sanctuary cradling the Table, a sensational prospect that may come as a surprise even to those who are familiar with this weird scene from below. Continue your exploration by strolling to the R along the edge of the precipices, noting Staffin Bay beyond the pinnacles and finally the upper section of the Needle from a dizzy point where the cliffs bend away to the south. Return along the declining grassy slopes and eventually down the steep ground to your car on the col.

Plate 225 The Table from the highest point of **Route 68a**

Plate 226 The rock pinnacles surrounding the sanctuary from **Route 68a**

Plate 227 Looking down on the Needle and Prison from **Route 68a**

The Peaks of the North Coolins

Sgurr nan Gillean	3,167 feet	965 metres
Bruach na Frithe	3,143 feet	952 metres
Am Basteir	3,069 feet	935 metres
Sgurr a'Fionn Choire	3,068 feet	935 metres
Bhasteir Tooth	3,005 feet	916 metres
Sgurr a'Bhasteir	2,951 feet	899 metres
Bidein Druim nan Ramh	2,850 feet	869 metres
Sgurr na Bhairnich	2,826 feet	867 metres
An Caisteal	2,730 feet	832 metres
Sgurr Beag	2,511 feet	765 metres
Sgurr na h'Uamha	2,416 feet	736 metres

Everyone who visits the Misty Isle of Skye to climb in the famous Coolins looks forward with great anticipation to catching the first glimpse of these peaks, which only come into view on the approach to Sligachan. And the excitement increases during the first ascent, which may well be that of Sgurr nan Gillean which acts as a powerful magnet to all who stay at the Sligachan Hotel. Climbed by one or other of the routes that lead to its shapely tapering summit, it is well known to mountaineers who have tasted its pleasures and also the safety of the black gabbro of which it is composed. But of all the peaks in Scotland, those which so liberally deck the Main Ridge usually involve more rock climbing, and other than Bruach na Frithe are not for the ordinary pedestrian. Nevertheless, if he does not suffer from vertigo and is invited to join an experienced party, he should have no great difficulty in following the so-called Tourist Route to the cairn on this superb mountain. And the rewards from its summit are immense; for much of the wild grandeur of the Main Ridge is revealed to his gaze as it swings round from R to L in a great bend to the south, with here and there a glimpse of the distant sea; as well as a spacious panorama of the Trotternish backbone to the north and of the softer lines of the Red Hills to the east, with on their R a magnificent prospect of the rock architecture of both Clach Glas and Blaven.

Sligachan is splendidly situated for the climber who desires to explore the northern peaks of the Coolins, and even those as far south as Bidein Druim nan Ramh may be reached and climbed in a day by a strong party. But as most of the southern peaks are so to speak on the doorstep of Glen Brittle, they are most conveniently ascended from this well-known centre. Moreover, easy as it looks from afar, no inexperienced climber should venture on the Main Ridge, save the above mentioned Bruach na Frithe on a clear day, as the peaks themselves are not only often difficult of access, but they are also subject to immersion by the mists which are not uncommonly encountered in this region. In such conditions, and without an intimate knowledge of the safe ways off this terrain, an adventure could easily result in accident or tragedy.

Map 32
The Coolins

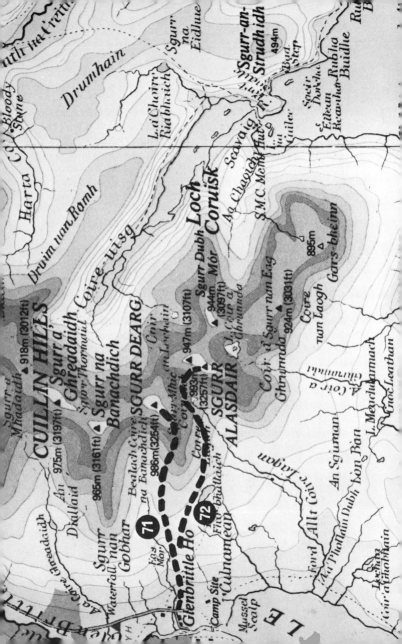

Sgurr nan Gillean

Route 69. The Tourist Route from Sligachan. Leave the hotel
by the Carbost road and take the path on the L which leads to
the power house. Cross the burn by a bridge and follow its
meanderings across the moor in a direct line with your peak.
Throughout this part of the walk the profile of Sgurr nan
Gillean does not change much except to become slightly
foreshortened, and since the Pinnacle Ridge rises on this side
of it you cannot see the deep clefts that make it so spectacular.
When you encounter the rippling Allt Dearg Beag, keep
beside it for some distance until you reach a cairn which
marks your way, and here turn L to cross it and make for the
dip on the R of Nead na h'Iolaire. This section of the track is
sketchy, but clearer on reaching the cairn overlooking Coire
Riabhaich, whence you bear to the R and climb steadily while
circling the corrie, with its gleaming lochan on your L, and the
striking view of Blaven which dominates Glen Sligachan. On
leaving the corrie the track steepens and the hard collar-work
begins. Cairns in plenty mark your course and you twist in
and out of the wilderness of boulders and scree lying at the
base on the Pinnacle Ridge, now on your R. Ahead towers the
shattered but almost horizontal skyline of the South-East
Ridge, up which you scramble over steep scree to reach the
cairn on its crest.

   While this is the shortest way to reach the ridge, it is more
interesting and revealing to bear to the L and take a diagonal
course for the diminutive peak of Sgurr Beag, because it
opens up a more comprehensive view of Sgurr nan Gillean
and its satellites. Its graceful pointed summit towers into the
sky overhead and is flanked on the R by the Pinnacle Ridge
whose deep rifts are now clearly visible, while on the L the
sharply indented Main Ridge trails away to the south on the
other side of the abysmal depths of Lota Corrie. If you have
time in hand it is worth while to walk to the end of the ridge

S. Nan Gillean

Am Basteir

S. a'Fionn Choire

S. a' Bhasteir

S. Beag

Plate 228   The northern peaks of the Coolins from the Sligachan Burn

where you will encounter the remarkable pyramid of Sgurr na h'Uamha, poised above Harta Corrie, but unless you are an experienced climber do not attempt to scale it. Now retrace your steps to the foot of your peak where the final ascent begins. At first the going is rough but easy and you keep to the L or Lota Corrie side of its crest. A few cairns indicate your way until the ridge steepens, whence you will appreciate the wonderful adhesive properties of gabbro. Up and up you go, making liberal use of your hands to ensure safe progress and bear to the R near the top where you will find a short hiatus over which you step boldly on to the summit platform with its small cairn. The last hundred feet or so have been an exciting scramble, with terrific drops on either side, and you will be glad to rest for a while by the summit cairn to admire the vast prospect of peak and sea that stretches all around you. Moreover, you will probably agree that this platform which is poised in the sky conveys the sense of isolation better than that of any other peak you have climbed, since no part of its supporting ridges can be seen as you sit by the cairn and you feel aloof from the turmoil of life far below.

The first thing to catch your eye may well be the Pinnacle Ridge to the north, of which you now have a bird's-eye view, and where you can easily pick out the fourth pinnacle, known as Knight's Peak, whose traverse is the key to the successful ascent of the whole ridge. Beyond it you will enjoy the vista of the coastline of Skye stretching from Loch Sligachan at your feet to the furthest tip of Trotternish, in which the Storr is the most conspicuous feature on a clear day. To the R you may speculate on the names of the various islands and the peaks on the mainland. To the south you look across Lota Corrie to the declining Druim nan Ramh, and beyond it to Sgurr Alasdair and its satellites, in which the lofty and difficult ridge of the Dubhs is prominent. To the east Marsco stands well in front of the Red Hills in which the graceful cone of Glamaig may charm your eye, and to the south-east Blaven rises finely above the remote stretches of Glen Sligachan. To the west and south the Main Ridge forms a semicircle to merge with Sgurr

Plate 229 **Route 69**—Clach Glas, Blaven and Glen Sligachan from Coire Riabhaich

Plate 230 The last section of **Route 69** to Sgurr nan Gillean, from the south-east ridge

Plate 231 Sgurr a'Bhasteir and Macleod's Tables from the summit

Alasdair, and you may find it of interest to name the many peaks that deck this famous playground of the rock climber.

Experienced mountaineers will probably descend the peak by its western ridge, where the passing of the detached and sensationally poised obelisk, known as the Policeman, is the crux of the descent to the Bealach a'Bhasteir below. Thence a return to Sligachan can be made down the stony corrie or by the more interesting alternative of taking in Sgurr a'Bhasteir, if only for its superlative prospect of the Pinnacle Ridge opposite.

Plate 232 The western ridge of Sgurr nan Gillean

Bruach na Frithe

This peak cannot be seen from Sligachan as it is hidden behind the nearer Sgurr a'Bhasteir and the best distant view of it is included in the due western prospect from Sgurr nan Gillean. From this lofty coign of vantage the Main Ridge slopes down to the Bealach a'Bhasteir, rises along the very thin crest of Am Basteir and then turns sharp L to take in the rocky bulge of Sgurr a'Fionn Choire, above which Bruach na Frithe dominates the skyline. It is, however, a prominent object in the view to the south from the path rising to the Bealach a'Mhaim, from which it is usually climbed. Its ascent is nothing more than a strenuous walk for the ordinary pedestrian, and may be combined to advantage with a visit to Sgurr a'Bhasteir. The easiest route is by way of Fionn Choire; first over grass which in the spring is dotted with Alpine flowers, then through a maze of boulders to the path ascending the scree which terminates on the Main Ridge at the Bealach nan Lice, whence the track on the R rises to the summit. But experienced climbers have two alternative approaches which are not difficult, include a good scramble and are thus of greater interest. One of them takes in Tobar nan Uaislean which is joined to the peak by a broken ridge that forms the southern wall of Fionn Choire; the other necessitates a visit to Coire na Creiche and its L branch Tarneilear, whence the gash to the L of An Caisteal is ascended and then to the L again over Sgurr na Bhairnich to Bruach na Frithe. The fine situation of this peak is such that it opens up one of the grandest vistas of the twisting ridge to the south, which is surmounted by many of the familiar peaks so readily reached from Glen Brittle.

Bruach na Frithe

Fionn Choire

Plate 233 **Route 70**—The entrance to Fionn Choire from Bealach a'Mhaim

Route 70. The Ascent from Sligachan. Leave the hotel by the Carbost road and turn L along the rough cart road leading to Alltdearg House. Before reaching it go to the R beside the wire fence and continue up the track that keeps to the L bank of the cascading Allt Dearg Mor. This rises to the Bealach a'Mhaim and reveals splendid views on the L of the northern peaks of the Coolins. A cairn marks the spot where you cross the burn, whence follow the rather sketchy track over grass, moss and stones into the mouth of Fionn Choire. This is bounded on the L by Meall Odhar and the ridge connecting it with Sgurr a'Bhasteir, and on the R by the ridge taking root at Tobar nan Uaislean already mentioned. For some distance the floor of the corrie is grassy and in great contrast to most of the other stony corries in the Coolins; it is famous for its spring Alpines. On attaining its upper reaches steep scree and boulders replace the gentler grass and the prospect on either hand is grim as you mount the zig-zags that terminate on the ridge at the Bealach nan Lice. At this point the gap between the cliffs is narrow and guarded by a small rock pinnacle on the L, beyond which to the south-east you may pick out on a clear day the strange pyramid of Sgurr na h'Uamha on the L and Sgurr na Stri on the R, backed by the glittering sea. Now turn sharp R and follow the well-trodden track to the summit of your peak. The splendour of the spacious panorama will attract your eye, but your gaze will be held by the twisting ridge to the south, which, however, is best photographed before attaining the cairn. You may be able to identify the peaks on the three great bends in the ridge, as follows: the first section on the L ends at Sgurr na Bhairnich; it then turns to the R over An Caisteal and Bidein Druim nan Ramh to Sgurr a'Mhadaidh; where it again bends to the L over Sgurr a'Ghreadaidh, Dearg and Alasdair to Gars-bheinn where the last section is partly hidden by the Dubhs ridge. This coign of vantage is a good one for the view of Blaven because the whole of its western front is seen above the gap between Sgurr Beag and Sgurr na h'Uamha.

Now retrace your steps to the bealach and bear R to view

Plate 234 **Route 70**—Bruach na Frithe from Sgurr na Bhairnich

the detached Bhasteir Tooth, known also as the Executioner, and its adjoining Am Basteir, both of which are the playground of the rock climber and conspicuous on the skyline when viewed from Sligachan. Immediately opposite, the ridge of Sgurr a'Bhasteir takes root and if care is taken no difficulty should be encountered in making its ascent. From its lofty summit you obtain the most spectacular prospect of the Pinnacle Ridge of Sgurr nan Gillean on the other side of Coire a'Bhasteir, and if you are a photographer the best time to make the exposure is between 3 and 4 p.m. in the spring. At this hour the westering sunlight skims across your subject to impart both contrast and detail.

The ordinary pedestrian should descend by way of Fionn Choire, but experienced climbers may prefer to scramble down the north-east ridge of the peak and pick up the moorland path beside the Allt Dearg Beag for Sligachan. But the best round trip is to ascend the ridge from Tobar nan Uaislean, visit Sgurr a'Bhasteir and return through Fionn Choire.

Gars Bheinn | Dubhs | Alasdair | Dearg | Ghreadaidh

Plate 235 **Route 70**—The twisting main ridge to the south of Bruach na Frithe

Blaven →

Plate 236 **Route 70** passes Am Bhasteir and the Bhasteir Tooth

Plate 237 **Route 70**—The pinnacle ridge of Sgurr nan Gillean from Sgurr a'Bhasteir

The Peaks of the South Coolins

Sgurr Alasdair	3,257 feet	993 metres
Inaccessible Pinnacle	3,234 feet	986 metres
Sgurr Dearg	3,209 feet	978 metres
Sgurr Thearlaich	3,208 feet	977 metres
Sgurr a'Ghreadaidh	3,192 feet	973 metres
Sgurr na Banachdich	3,166 feet	965 metres
Stone Shoot	3,135 feet	956 metres
An Stac	3,125 feet	952 metres
Sgurr Mhic Coinnich	3,111 feet	948 metres
Sgurr Sgumain	3,108 feet	947 metres
Sgurr Dubh Mor	3,096 feet	944 metres
Sgurr Dubh na Da Bheinn	3,078 feet	938 metres
Sgurr Thormaid	3,040 feet	927 metres
Sgurr nan Eag	3,031 feet	924 metres
Sgurr a'Mhadaidh	3,012 feet	918 metres
Gars-bheinn	2,935 feet	895 metres
Sgurr Thuilm	2,885 feet	819 metres
Sgurr a'Choire Bhig	2,872 feet	875 metres
Sron na Ciche	2,817 feet	858 metres
Thearlaich-dubh Gap	2,806 feet	855 metres
Sgurr Coire an Lochain	2,491 feet	759 metres
Sgurr Dubh Beag	2,403 feet	732 metres
Sgurr nan Gobhar	2,069 feet	631 metres

Walkers who wish to see more clearly the topography of this section of the Main Ridge could not do better than drive down to the Campsite at Glen Brittle. For the rising ground behind the Shop is crowned by the more distant ridge from Banachdich to Sron na Ciche, with the great mass of Dearg dominating the scene. Banachdich appears on the L and Mhic Coinnich, Alasdair, Sgumain and Sron na Ciche on the R. The next section from Dearg to Gobhar encloses Coire na

Banachdich and is well seen from the Memorial Hut on a sunny afternoon. However, the most spectacular section from Thuilm to Bruach na Frithe, which encloses Coire na Creiche, is revealed to perfection from the Picnic Site in Glen Brittle Forest. This is located on the R where the rising road emerges from the glen. The triangular peak in the centre is Sgurr an Fheadain, split in the middle by the famous Waterpipe Gully, and dominated by Bidein Druim nan Ramh on the skyline. The two inner corries are Tarneilear L and Mhadaidh R.

Sgurr Dearg

This peak rises immediately to the east of Glen Brittle and is bounded on the L by Coire na Banachdich and on the R by Coire Lagan. Seen from the doors of the Lodge on a sunny evening, it rises between Sgurr na Banachdich on the L and Sgurr Alasdair on the R, when the view of it is wholly magnetic and will be remembered with delight by all those climbers who have spent an invigorating day on the Main Ridge, of which these three peaks are a part. Its flat summit ridge is characterised by the narrow and slightly leaning obelisk known as the Inaccessible Pinnacle which affords the most attractive rock climbing problem on this mountain. Both ends of the adjacent ridge reveal the splendour of its neighbouring peaks, and include the narrow and sensational crest of Sgurr na Banachdich and the grandeur of the northern precipices of Sgurr Alasdair. But even on a calm day the ascent of Sgurr Dearg requires care though not difficult; nevertheless the ordinary pedestrian should not venture upon it unless in the company of an experienced climber, because the long precipitous shoulder connecting it with Sron Dearg is narrow in places when a steady head is essential.

Route 71. The Ascent from Glen Brittle. Leave the Lodge by the Coire Lagan path, and after passing Eas Mor on the L, advance straight towards the shoulder of the mountain. Here masses of scree make the ascent rather trying, but on reaching a conspicuous dyke below the first point on the ridge the going becomes easier. Beyond this small top the angle is reduced and you cross a vast expanse of scree while making direct for Sron Dearg, which looks like a titanic castle poised high on the ridge and extending right across it. The views on the L down into Coire na Banachdich are impressive, while those of Sron na Ciche on the R reveal its whole front clearly, especially the Terrace which rises diagonally from L to R. There is no easy way to the top of Sron Dearg, although you may be tempted to go over to the R, and when you attain its cairn the narrow shattered continuation of the ridge is seen ahead. On tackling this you will pass some sensational drops and one or two places which are rather slippery, but this long shoulder is soon traversed and you then walk forward to the summit ridge of your mountain.

The most magnificent prospect is on your R where you look across Coire Lagan to its engirdling ridge dominated by Sgurr Alasdair, the highest peak in the Coolins. This superb skyline from L to R includes Sgurr Mhic Coinnich and Sgurr Thearlaich. The whole of the great Stone Shoot is visible and, to the R of the reigning peak, Sgumain seems to be leaning over towards Sron na Ciche further to the R. Looking now to the L of this group you may be impressed by the bold outline of An Stac, but your gaze will rest upon the Inaccessible Pinnacle whose curving crest terminates abruptly upon the summit ridge. Continuing your stroll, now on the Main Ridge, you soon come to the northern tip of Sgurr Dearg which discloses the most striking prospect of Sgurr na Banachdich, right from the Bealach at your feet to its summit, with Thormaid, the Three Teeth and Sgurr a'Ghreadaidh on its R and above them a glimpse of Sgurr Thuilm.

If you are with a party of climbers, they may prefer to return to Glen Brittle by way of Coire na Banachdich where a knowledge of the intricacies of the route is necessary, otherwise it is safer to descend the way you came.

Plate 238 The main ridge from the campsite at Glen Brittle

Plate 239 Coire na Banachdich from the Memorial Hut, Glen Brittle

Plate 240 Coire na Creiche—consult p 485 for details

Plate 241 **Route 71**—Sgurr Dearg from Eas Mor

Plate 242 **Route 71**—The Inaccessible Pinnacle

Plate 243 **Route 71**—The ridge to Sgurr na Banachdich

Mhic Coinnich   Thearlaich   Alasdair   Sgumain

Plate 244 **Route 71**—Sgurr Alasdair and satellites from Sgurr Dearg

Sgurr Alasdair

This is the highest peak in the Coolins and when seen from
Glen Brittle its pointed summit is conspicuous on the skyline,
together with that of its satellite, Sgumain, below which the
ridge falls to the R to the almost level top of Sron na Ciche.
The finest view of it is obtained from Sgurr Dearg, but its
importance in the landscape is also disclosed from Sgurr nan
Eag, when it is seen beyond the shining surface of the lonely
loch on the floor of Coir' a'Ghrunnda. In this prospect,
however, its precipitous front is confused and much shattered,
whereas Sgurr Thearlaich on its R indicates the narrowness of
the cat-walk down to Sgurr Mhic Coinnich. The summit of
Sgurr Alasdair is the smallest in this range of hills and there is
barely room for the climber to sit down beside the cairn. It is
usually climbed from Coire Lagan by the great Stone Shoot,
whose ascent is extremely arduous, and on reaching the col a
short knife-edge of basalt connects it with the peak. It is taken
in during the complete traverse of the Main Ridge, when it is
reached from the col below the Dubhs by way of the
Thearlaich-Dubh Gap, but as this is a tricky problem it is
only tackled by experienced rock climbers. Another route
involving some scrambling is by the ascent of the South-West
Ridge, but since there is a very awkward *mauvais pas* at its
base, which must be climbed before the ridge proper can be
tackled, it should be severely left alone by the ordinary
pedestrian.

Route 72. The Ascent from Glen Brittle. Follow the well-
trodden path from the Lodge right into the gloomy recesses of
Coire Lagan and then walk over to the bottom of the Stone
Shoot. Go first close to the crags on the R, and when you
reach the band of rock near the middle of the shoot, go over
to the L close to the rock wall, at which point you enter the
grim portals of the shoot. This is the easiest course to take

Sgumain →   Alasdair →   Thearlaich →

Coir 'a 'Ghrunnda

Plate 245   **Route 72** — The dominating peak of the Coolins seen from Sgurr nan Eag

and the higher you get the smaller the stones, but by keeping close to one side or the other, where the stones do not roll so readily, progress is much facilitated. On emerging at the col there is a dramatic change of scene; for you are confronted by a splendid prospect of the Dubhs, with Gars-bheinn on their R, and if you go over to the far edge of the col you will get a glimpse of the Thearlaich-Dubh Gap below on the L. The backward vista down the Stone Shoot is impressive, as it conveys a matchless conception of the wild amphitheatre of mountains that enclose the corrie at your feet. Now tackle the narrow arete, using your hands to ensure safe progress, until you step finally on to the tiny summit of your dominating peak. Looking round the vast panorama, you will immediately note the narrow arm of rock that stretches westwards for a few feet, and then the side of the peak plunges down at a sensational angle in one seemingly unbroken precipice right to the floor of Coire Lagan. To the south-west the spectacular ridge falls to the col, and rises again to Sgumain with Loch Brittle and the illimitable sea in the background. To the north, and immediately overlooking the Stone Shoot, stands Thearlaich whose cairn is only 50 feet below and tops the cat-walk that falls steeply to the col below Sgurr Mhic Coinnich. Beyond this there is the finest view of Sgurr Dearg, whose seamed flanks drop sensationally into Coire Lagan and to the R of it the ridge trails away to the north to end with the shapely peak of Sgurr nan Gillean. The magic of this superb panorama is completed by the lovely lines of Blaven to the east and enhanced by the background in many directions of the blue sea, dappled with islands, and stretching to infinity.

If you have lingered on Sgurr Alasdair to revel in these scenes of mountain grandeur you will descend from the peak late in the day to Coire Lagan, accompanied by the clatter of rolling stones. And here, amid this desolation of rock and scree you may well linger again, standing beside the still lochan that is held in the grip of the hillside by a gigantic boilerplate, from which the seaward panorama stands out in

Plate 246 **Route 72**—Mist in the Great Stone Shoot

stark contrast to this mountain wilderness. Below you lies the long arm of Loch Brittle with Rhum and Canna floating serenely on the surface of the rippling ocean, relieved here and there by the white sail of a ship, or the smoke trail of a steamer. And if the evening is still with an unflecked sky stretching from the sunrise to the sunset, you will stand spellbound while you watch and wait. For the blue of the heavens will slowly change through every colour of the spectrum as the sun sinks towards the Atlantic away to the west, while the crags around you will be transmuted from pink to gold until day passes into night. Then the jagged skyline will be silhouetted against the twinkling stars and you will stumble down the rough track back to Glen Brittle, perhaps in the ghostly light of the silvery moon, but with your being saturated with the magic and mystery of the incomparable Coolins.

NOTE: Owing to limited space only four of the peaks of the Coolins have been included in this volume, but interested readers may consult the author's *Magic of Skye*, published in 1949, which contains a complete description of the Main Ridge, together with numerous photographs illustrating its fine topography and climbing problems from start to finish.

Plate 247 **Route 73**—Coolins panorama from the north

Two panoramas of the Coolins

Owing to the twisting elevations of the Main Ridge of the
Coolins it is impossible to see the whole of it from any one
viewpoint. The photograph below reveals only the most
northerly section, from Gillian to Banachdich and Gobhar,
and can be seen on a clear day, preferably by afternoon
lighting, from the Sligachan–Dunvegan road. After driving up
the two bends above the head of Loch Harport the new
highway straightens out and there is a car park on the
immediate L. Walk up to the nearby eminence and there it is!

The peaks from L to R are as follows:

Pinnacle Ridge of Sgurr nan Gillian
Ridge rising to Sgurr a'Bhastier
Am Bastier and Sgurr a'Fionn Choire above
Fionn Choire
Ridge of Tobar nan Uaislean rising to
Bruach na Frithe
An Caisteal
Bidein Druim nan Ramh above
Sgurr an Fheadain and the Waterpipe Gully
Four peaks of Sgurr a'Mhaidaidh
Sgurr a'Ghreadaidh
Sgurr Thuilm
Sgurr Dearg
Sgurr Banachdich falling to
Sgurr nan Gobhar

Route 74. However, the most spectacular view is from Elgol, but even here the southern section of the ridge is partially obscured by Gars-Bheinn. Seen under the most favourable conditions, occasionally with snow on the peaks, it is the most magnificent scene in Britain, enhanced by the blue of Loch Scavaig in the immense foreground. To reach Elgol involves a longish hilly drive, with the unveiling of many beautiful scenes on the way. The most arresting is that of Blaven from Loch Slapin and includes the adjacent Clach Glas whose traverse is beloved by the rock climber. After driving round the head of the loch there is a fine retrospect from the point where it narrows, and a few miles further along the road a gate and a stile appear on the R. Thence a path leads to Camasunary and Loch Coruisk for direct access to the Coolins. And finally there is the superb spectacle on reaching Elgol, considered by many as one of the finest in the world.

Plate 248 **Route 74**— Blaven, Clach Glas and Sgurr nan Each from Loch Slapin

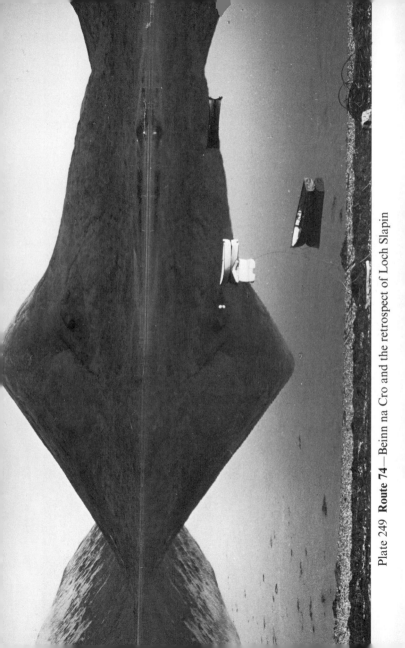

Plate 249 **Route 74**—Beinn na Cro and the retrospect of Loch Slapin

Plate 250 **Route 74**—A superb vista of the Coolins from Elgol

Sense on the Scottish Hills

"Look well to each step"

Climb if you will, but remember that courage and strength are nought without prudence, and that a momentary negligence may destroy the happiness of a lifetime. Do nothing in haste; look well to each step; and from the beginning think what may be the end.

Edward Whymper

1. Seek advice daily about local conditions and problems. Beware of avalanches and dangerous corniced ridges. Pay attention to weather forecasts. If bad stay in the valleys; conditions on Scottish tops can become Arctic.
2. Never go alone, but keep parties small, with an experienced leader. Don't separate. Leave a note of route planned and report forced changes at earliest opportunity.
3. Plan your expedition with a safety margin and turn back while there is yet time. Before starting note local rescue posts.
4. Wear tricouni nailed boots in winter or crampons: vibrams are dangerous on snow and ice.
5. Carry an ice-axe and practise braking. Also reserve food, torch, whistle and watch.
6. Wear warm and windproof clothes. Carry extra for tops, halts and cold.
7. Take a 1 inch map and know how to use it with a suitable compass (e.g. prismatic or "Silva").
8. If lost or caught in a blizzard, keep calm; seek or build temporary shelter. Vital energy can be lost fighting the wind—a dangerous foe.

9. If there is an accident send written message to nearest rescue post, giving accident position accurately. One member should stay with victim.

10. Learn life-saving first aid and carry simple first aid kit.

Copies of *Mountain Rescue & Cave Rescue* can be obtained from Mountain Rescue Committee, Hill House, Cheadle Hulme, Stockport, Cheshire.

Issued by the Mountain Rescue Committee of Scotland. Hamish MacInnes, Secretary, Glencoe.

This **Route Card** is reproduced with the permission of the Chief Constable of Inverness-shire and is similar to others in use elsewhere in Scotland. The idea is sound and if adopted and used consistently by all climbers and walkers throughout our mountainous country it could be the means of facilitating any call for Mountain Rescue. I hope the English and Welsh Police will favour its use and distribute the Route Card widely wherever climbers and mountain walkers are lodged. It is, of course, most important that NO DIGRESSION is made from the stated route, otherwise in the event of an accident searchers would be unable to locate the victim.

Let us know
when you go
on our hills

Names and Addresses: Home Address and Local Address	Route
Time and date of departure:	Bad Weather Alternative:
Place of Departure and Registered Number of Vehicle (if any)	
Estimated time of Return:	Walking/Climbing (delete as necessary)

GO UP WELL EQUIPPED · TO COME BACK SAFELY

Please tick items carried:

Emergency Food	Torch	Ice Axe
Waterproof Clothing (Colour ·	Whistle	Crampons
Winter Clothing	Map	Polybag
(Colour ·	Compass	First Aid

Please complete and leave with Police, landlady, warden etc.
Inform landlady or warden to contact Police if you are overdue.

PLEASE REPORT YOUR SAFE RETURN.

Index